I0018865

Cyber attack

© Copyright 2017 by William Edward Hunt
All rights reserved.

AK.1712.07

Library of Congress Control Number: 2017916649
CreateSpace Independent Publishing Platform,
North Charleston, SC

By this same author:
Amarna Decoded by Willian Albert – an in-depth look at the life and times of would-be Pharaoh Amenophis IV better known as Akhenaten.

Table of Contents

Contents

Chapter 1, help! The computer is...

...being held hostage by a handful of greedy corporations. Apple and Microsoft to name a couple. What we get is what they want us to get. Most of all they are blocking the gateway to the future. Only a small fraction, as little as 1% of all that is possible to do using computers has been done at this time. Given the proper environment you too could start a billion dollar company. As it now stands the most anyone can do is pick up a few crumbs that fall from the big computer corporations' banquet tables. Why settle for crumbs? A banquet awaits the ambitious.

The multibillion dollar corporations began in garages. Do you have a garage? Know where you can get a garage? You do. Excellent, you have the same facilities Steve Jobs and Bill Gates had available to them. All that's missing for you to compete with them is a little knowledge and a lot of ambition.

The first step for you is getting yourself computer educated. You cannot be a soldier in the army that attacks in cyber space as you are. You need a little basic training and after that a little advanced training. That's what we're about here, training an army to rescue the computer from its kidnappers. We must rescue the computer from the greedy corporations now holding the computer hostage, create the products of the future and get filthy rich like them.

I don't blame you for thinking you're not qualified. You're very likely the victim of corporate propaganda. Of course they don't want competition. Who does? They've decorated the computer in tinsel and cloaked it in mystery. And they control computer education too. They don't want you to know just how easy computer really is. Thumb through a book on C++ or one on JAVA for easy examples of controlling education. That sort of thing is what they're teaching at the university.

What's the main thing they don't want you to know? The digital computer is the simplest and easiest to understand device ever conceived. The power of the computer is in its simplicity. Computers are the simplest of all machines made of nothing but switches. They are no more high tech than ordinary light switches. That's all there be to computers. Anyone capable of understanding the ordinary light switch is also capable of knowing all there is to know about computers. Computers are just a bunch of switches no more difficult to understand than ordinary light switches.

You don't believe me do you? You think computers are the highest of high tech requiring brains to even understand much less design, implement, and use. Using computers requires a mysterious substance, some kind of royal jelly called software and firmware and God only knows what else. You have to be a brain and spend 4 full years in college with feet sticking out of books filled with stuff only geniuses can understand. And here I am telling you it's as simple as a light switch. Stick around and I'll make a believer out of you.

Flipping switches on and off is the only thing going on inside computers. There's nothing else to it. Even making objects using 3D printers is done by flipping switches. Computer programs are nothing but strings of switch settings that do nothing but cause switches to be turned on and off. The ordinary light switch is as high tech as computers get. Computing is nothing more than operating switches. You are smart enough to operate a light switch?

You can turn lights on? Great, that qualifies you to become computer literate and conduct your very own "Cyber Attack." Better said, you'll be qualified to create the computer products that eliminate the possibility of cyber attacking altogether. The world desperately needs cyber security.

Computer science is not the solution, it's the problem. English majors are supposed to know the meanings of words. Not necessary in the computer science department where they speak a language of their own with regular looking words having radically different meanings. Do you know what sugar is? How about syntax? OK, two easy words combined, syntax sugar means what? How about the word sketch? Know what a sketch is? Not in computer science.

Computer scientists use ordinary looking words with radically different meanings. Pure nonsense. That's not education. It's created ignorance.

We're going to take an in-depth look at the computer. Every word used to say what's going on will be defined in ordinary words any literate can read and understand. The only prerequisite is ordinary literacy. The ability to read this book is all that's required.

Computers are nothing more than collections of two positions switches that are identical in function to ordinary light switches. The only requirement to understand every word here is to know how ordinary light switches on the wall work and how to operate them.

You do know what's going on inside the light switch to make the light come on? Just in case you don't, inside light switches two wires are touched to each other allowing electrical current to flow through the light bulb. That's how high tech computers are. Make a note of it. And most of all notice that's so for absolutely all computers no exception for "Intel Inside" or any other no matter how clever the name.

The greedy multi-billion dollar corporations don't want you to know computers are nothing more than collections of switches. Chances are the billion dollar monopolies are manned by people who themselves don't know just how simple computers truly are. Anyone capable of operating a light switch and understanding the results has all the technical knowledge needed to invent competitive computer based products and compete with them. Those big corporations simply hate competition. Did you notice how quickly they cry patent infringement and sue?

Let me mention a couple of places computers belong that are wide open markets. Education itself desperately needs a minimal computer with a control panel. Control panels allow the student to see what's going on inside the computer. Computer based musical instruments, arrangements and performances are another market that's wide open. Want to make and edit movies and compete with Disney and Pixar? Did you notice how movies have degenerated into hardly anything more than special effects? That needs to be fixed. Yes you can do lots of things if you have the right computer. Why not make your own. You will never find a better one than the one you yourself make.

I'm left to wonder if those in control of the computer establishment themselves know computers are no more high tech than ordinary light switches. Allowing the computer to be invaded by crooks and bakers is a sign of gross incompetence so maybe incompetence is the problem. One look at the dollar figures going to the monopolies is a big clue. They're getting even more big bucks on an ongoing basis to detect and attempt to fight off viruses, malware, cyber attacks and the like. Looks like a case of create a problem and get rich trying to fix it. If cyber attacks were not possible there would be no need to fight them off or retaliate. To the big computer corporation's cyber attacks are not a problem they're the gold in the gold mine.

Those cyber warriors need competition and not from the computer science department. Computer science is where they get their training. I'm betting dollars to donuts no computer science professor has ever described the computer as a set of switches, knows software is nothing more than lists of switch settings or that computing is nothing more than flipping switches on and off.

Nothing is going on inside the computer other than turning switches on and off. This is not college level science it's kindergarten level gaming. Computers operate by flipping switches in sets. That all. Anyone can flip switches. Believe it or not nothing is ever done in the computer you cannot do by hand given a computer made of ordinary light switches.

Get this straight in your mind. Computers do nothing. People use computers to do things, steal your identity, or influence the outcome of an election and the like. Computers are made of switches. As we go along here we're going to realize we already know all about computers because we already know all about switches. I'm singing a one word song. "Switch" is the word. "Computers do nothing" is the refrain. The results I'm looking for is your education amounting to you realizing you're a lot smarter than you've given yourself credit for being.

Apple, Microsoft, Facebook, Twitter, you name them, one and all need competition from you. If you are smart enough to know all there is to know about ordinary light switches you're plenty smart enough to make and sell computer based products that are much better than theirs.

The first step is understanding computers are nothing but switches. Here's an easy to understand example of a one switch computer. The very first computer had but one switch. It was an amazing technological breakthrough. I'm talking about the telegraph. Telegraphs are one switch computers. You never thought of it like that did you?

Emailing is as old as the telegraph. Before the telegraph messages had to be carried by hand. It took days to get a message from New York to San Francisco. Then came the telegraph. Using the telegraph messages could be sent all the way across the continent as fast as the telegraph operator could flip the switch. Did you get that? Telegraph operators flip switches to email. The telegraph was the first messaging computer. Before it was replaced with multi switch computers pictures were sent over the telegraph.

The first electrically based computer was nothing but a single switch. The number of switches in modern computers is limited only by available resources thus it is fair to say there will never be an end to how many switches one can collect together to become a computer. Regardless it only takes one switch to compute. Cyber space is so modern it only dates back to the civil war era.

When a switch is a telegraph key or similar device the amount of information sent from one place to another many miles away is unlimited. And yes telegraph wires could be "tapped" allowing eavesdropping. Cyber security has been a problem ever since the beginning when cyber space came to be. Cyber space was born with the telegraph.

7

Before the telegraph wires were wires and nothing more. Telegraph wires need a better name to separate them from just plain wire. Cyber space is its new high-techy name. Wires connecting electric switches to each other is the proper definition of cyber space.

The one word lyric is "switch." The refrain is, "computers do nothing." There can be no better proof that's so than the one switch computer the telegraph. When a message comes in over the telegraph is that the telegraph speaking or a person? When a message comes in over the internet is that the computer speaking or a person? By comparison computers are no smarter than telegraph keys.

Telegraph keys sure are smart. They knew the Gettysburg Address almost as fast as Lincoln delivered it. OK, modern computers are smarter than telegraphs. They remember the Gettysburg Address while the telegraph only recited it. Computers know everything.

Nah, computers are no smarter than light switches. Hard drives and stick memories and the like are collections of switches. Information is written by turning those switches either on or off. Bulk memories begin as blank libraries fillable with all the accumulated knowledge of mankind. People use computers to accesses that knowledge the same way people go to the library and look something up. It's no more complex or complicated than looking something up at the library. It's a lot easier too. In defense of the library no one of record ever had their identity stolen at the library.

There's more than one kind of switch based upon the number of positions. Rotary switches like the ones used to pick the speed of multi-speed electric fans have more than 2 positions. Good news? All computer switches have but two positions, off and on. That makes computers several times easier to understand than multi-speed electric fans. Do you know how electric fan switches make them run at different speeds? How about a light switch? Know how light switches work? Computers are less complicated, easier to know all about than electric fans with more than one speed.

I see light bulbs going off in your head already. The notion computers are made of nothing but off-on switches is hard to swallow isn't it? Perhaps you find the fact that computers do nothing at all even more difficult. You don't know how the switch on electric fans make the fan run at different speeds do you? You do know how operating light switches turns lights on and off. Does either switch do anything or is it the switch operator doing it? Switches are tools used to operate electrical devices. Computers are electrical devices that are nothing more than sets of switches.

Switch is not a metaphor here. I haven't come up with a clever analogy for computers or computing. Switches and the operation of switches is the real McCoy. Computers are nothing but switches and computer programs are nothing but lists of switch settings.

I'm a member of the class of 1961. Let's see, this is 2017. If my calculator hasn't failed me I graduated college 56 years ago. There was no computer science college anywhere on earth at the time. All I know I learned from experience.

I saw my first digital computer within a month of graduation. I wrote my first "production" program the same day. Six years later I became a free-lance programmer.

In the year, 1971 I along with two others started manufacturing our own computers and dedicated computer systems in competition with IBM and others. When your groceries are rung up at the grocery store or you buy a burger at the fast food restaurant our hardware design and my software are being used or imitated. At the time we looked like geniuses. The genius was knowing computers are nothing more than sets of switches.

One other thing. Problems are solved by flipping switches, problems like taking the order, tallying the ticket, calculating the change, opening the cash drawer, printing the order on a printer in the kitchen, subtracting the items from the inventory, sending reports to headquarters over the phone and more. The list of all the problems solvable by flipping switches is for all practical purposes is endless.

The big computer monopolies have grown fat and lazy. They have the computer products market cornered. They control what we will get and how much we'll pay for it. In simple terms they have kidnapped the computer and hold it for ransom.

Let history be your guide. History has many words but only one sound, the clanging sound of hobnail boots ascending the marble staircase and the whispery soft sound of silver slippers sliding down the marble staircase. It always begins with revolution. Just a glance at history tells us revolution is the path to the future. Make that still another computer based revolution.

Do you have a product, see an open market? Maybe you're just curious. Read on and I will convince you computers are the simplest machines ever conceived. Most of all you'll realize you have all the talent necessary to write your own programs, create your own communications protocol and stop the nonsense going on over the internet. Above all else blind prying eyes totally eliminating the possibility of cyber attacks.

The word is computer literacy. When you finish this book you will be computer literate or well on the way there. Computer literacy involves knowing what computers are made of, how they work and how to program them. Open your mind and above all else try hard to discard all the false information that is now used to cloak the computer in a fog bank of ignorance.

Time's wasting. Let's get to work.

Chapter 2, it's all about switches

Computers are made of nothing but switches. Software is nothing but lists of switch settings. You may think arranging switches is a little above your pay grade at the moment. I suggest you wait until you've finished reading all I have to say here to make that decision. You should be able to makes lists of switch settings. Anyone can do that. That's called programming. You have every incentive to do that. Surely I don't need to tell you this. You already know your computer is filled with spies of one kind or the other. The only way to get rid of them is write your own operating system. Radical idea huh?

Operating systems are the simplest of programs for one with a minimum of writing skills. I've written dozens of them custom made for folks who don't want spies in their computers. We'll learn how to write programs later. For now we need to come to a complete understanding of what computers are before we start using them. Of course using computers is as simple as operating switches. Do you have the skills needed to turn on a light? You do? Great, you have all the skills needed to know all there is to know about computers and "work" them too.

We must crawl before we walk, walk before we run. We must understand a single switch computer before we can understand a many-switch one. So let's get clear in our minds what a single switch can and cannot do. A single switch can be off or on and must be one or the other at all times. That's either off or on at absolutely all times.

There are no keys on the keyboard for switch-off or switch-on. Therefore we must write switch-off or switch-on, or, we can assign two other keys that are on the keyboard to mean switch-off and switch-on. The number keys, 0, (zero) and 1 are normally used to indicate switch settings in the computer. We write 0 for switch-off and we can write 1 for switch-on. This fact has caused people to erroneously describe computers as having a bunch of zeroes and ones inside them. There are no numbers inside computers only ordinary switches that are at all times either off or on. Keep this in mind should I carelessly forget to remind you later on.

Remember, switch-off is <u>written</u> 0 and switch-on is <u>written</u> 1. That's how switch settings are written not what's inside computers. Computers are nothing but sets of simple two position switches functionally no more high tech than ordinary light switches. Saying things like computers are filled with zeroes and ones is expressing computer ignorance.

When one goes to the store to purchase a computer one is shown several. They differ from each other by the amount of memory and the speed of the processor. The rule seems to be the more memory and/or the faster the processor the higher the price. The clerk says, "This one has 4 gigs of RAM and a 16 gig hard drive" for example. Others have different size memories and hard drives. Most everyone know this from the experience of buying a computer.

The lay person has at best a foggy idea about what a gigabyte might be or what it looks like should one happen to see one up close. Of course a gigabyte is 1,000 megabytes. A megabyte is 1,000 kilobytes. A kilobyte is 1,000 bytes. But of course, a byte is a word you've often heard and wondered what it meant. Well, it's 8 light switches side by side. Sounds like some kind of 8 legged insect critter a spider even crawling around. It has 8 switches rather than 8 legs.

We're talking about computers and computers are all about switches. Memories are made of switches. Byte is a unit of measure of memory size in the same way a mile is a unit of measure of distance. A byte is 8 bits. A bit is another name for a switch. A little bit ot an 8 switch byte is a single switch, a bit, Nobody cares but 4 switches side by side is a nibble.

1 switch is a bit.

8 switches makes a byte, 8 bits.

4 switches, 4 bits are half bytes called nibbles.

Now you know. The least common denominator of computer memory is a switch called a bit. All that's left for total knowledge of memories is to come to an understanding of just what a bit might be. A bit is another name for a switch. Bits are switches, switches are bits. It's that simple. Know all there is to know about switches then you know all there is to know about bits and you know all there is to know about computer memories. And you thought they were made out of some kind of mysterious substance. Computer memories are just a bunch of switches no matter what they're made of.

A byte is 8 switches side by side. A kilobyte is 1,000 bytes amounting to 1,000 8 switch sets one after the other. Usually those sets are pictured with the next one below the previous like lines on a cash register tape. Of course a megabyte is 1,000, 1,000 byte ribbons laid end to end. And, a gigabyte is a million one kilobyte long ribbons laid end to end. A gigabyte is, 1,000,000,000,000 sets of 8 side by side switches. Every switch is always either off or on at all times with no other possibility. Think of a byte as a wall plate with 8 switches operating 8 lights that are always either off or on.

Memories can be made with as many switches as we like. The largest is no more complicated than a single light switch. There's just more of them. How many light switches do you have to have before you throw up your hands and declare, "This is way too complicated for me to ever understand?" To understand one switch is to understand all in the collection no matter the number of switches in the collection of switches.

You might want to pause for a moment and ponder just how much you can write on a gigabyte of memory. We're getting a little ahead of ourselves to talk about this but not too far. Individual letters of the alphabet, punctuation marks and spaces etc. need 8 bits/switches or one byte of memory each to be written. Thus a gigabyte of memory can hold 1,000,000,000,000 letters of the alphabet, and/or spaces and/or punctuation marks, and/or some other symbols. And, make a note of it, it's 100% switches. Most importantly it's no more complicated than a single light switch.

Guess what. A computer that changes just one little switch setting all by itself is broken. Only people have the authority to change switch settings in computer memory so when unexpectedly you see your memory seem to change all by itself you know there's either a people sneaking around in there or your computer is broken.

Computers cannot make mistakes. If you flip the light switch to its off position and the light doesn't go out did the light switch make a mistake and needs more training or is it broken? Does that logic fail when there's a lot of switches? That which is true for one switch is true for all switches.

Time out! I heard someone say I'm a clever fellow for using switch as a metaphor. Not so! I'm talking about the real McCoy. Switch is not an analogy or a metaphor as used here. I'm talking about everyday two position switches. The only difference functionally between ordinary light switches and the switches inside computers is how they are operated, turned on and off. Functionally they are identical to each other.

Ordinary light switches have mechanical levers while computer switches have electrical levers to operate them. A switch is a switch is a switch. Don't complicate it. Operating a light switch on the wall is simple. Operating an electrically operable switch in the computer takes less effort, is done with the mind rather than the finger. To turn the light on using a switch one must first think it and then do it. In the computer one thinks it and the computer does it. Programs are lists of thoughts. Programming is turning thoughts into actions by mentally flipping switches.

Not to leave you dangling wondering how one gets letters of the alphabet converted to switches let's briefly discuss it. Have you ever heard of Morse code? Morse code is how messages were sent through cyber space using the telegraph during and long after the very un-civil civil war. Letters of the alphabet are transmitted over the telegraph one bit at a time in longs and shorts usually referred to as dots and dashes. Think of the dots and dashes as switch settings. Dash is switch-on for a short time and dot is switch-on for a shorter time. Switch-off for a short time separates dots and dashes from each other. Switch-off for a longer time separates letters of the alphabet from one another. That's how telegraph operators communicate with each other. To make a byte represent letters of the alphabet etc. it's a matter of setting switches or if you like bits.

0's and 1's represent switches off and on that began as short switch-on and long switch-on called dot and dash.

Zero, 0 means switch off and 1 means switch on. There are no keys on the keyboard for switch off or on so symbols already on the keyboard are used. 0 and 1 have been chosen for writing switch settings. Here's a couple of 8 switch sets used to represent letters of the alphabet etc. Remember 0 means switch off and 1 means switch on.

Space bar	01000000
Letter A	01000001
Letter B	01000010
.	
.	
Letter Y	01011001
Letter Z	01011010

If you could see inside a memory the above is what you would see where you've typed text written on computer memory. There's sets of 8 switches with switch settings representing letters of the alphabet etc. and not drawn out actual letters the way it's done using pen on paper. This is called coding. Telegraphs used Morse coding done by toggling a single switch.

Ordinary light switches have off and on written on them. Computer memory switches have zero and one written on them. In the case of computers the writing is so small we can't see it. Computer scientists think the computer has zeroes and ones in its memory. Dumb!

Remember our definition of a digital computer. A digital computer is a set of light switches. We can drop light and simply say a set of switches. Guess what, a computer memory is a set of switches called bits. This forces us to refine our switch a little bit, pun intended. Switches are bits, bits are switches. The origin of using bit to describe a switch is unknown to me.

Keep in mind that memories are not computers. Computers have memory and just one other part called a central processing unit. It takes both a central processing unit and memory to make a computer.

Now you know memories are sets of switches with a single switch being the smallest possible memory. Central processing units are sets of switches too. Computers have two separate sets of switches one called the central processing unit and just one other called memory. That's all there be to computers. And you thought there was something exotic, mysterious, some kind of royal jelly needed to make computers. Believe it or not, you can make a computer with nothing more than light switches and do all computers do by operating those switches by hand.

I expect you are more than a little skeptical about computers having two parts only, a central processing unit and memory made of nothing more than switches. You've always described computer by what you see attached to computers, display screens, keyboards, printers etc. Computers are not seen just like your brain hidden inside your head is not visible to the outside world. Computers are electronic brains. All you see that you've always thought of as computers are actually the equal of skulls, arms and legs etc. that are independent of your brain. You must discard the notion computers have display screens, keyboards, blinking lights and so on. Knowing computers are not what you see but rather the brains part of what you see is a giant step towards complete understanding. It is perhaps the most difficult step for most all. Think brain and not whole body. Computer – brain. Computer system – whole body. Computers and not computer systems are the topic. We'll take computer systems apart at the seams later. Once you've come to a complete understanding of the computer, computer attachments will be a nothing to understand. Best of all you'll be qualified to invent your own attachments.

Computer system brains, the "thinking" part of computers are nothing more than collections of switches. They are no more complicated or difficult to understand than ordinary light switches. Think of it like this. Your brain is a computer. Your whole body is a computer system. Separate in your mind

16

brain and body. We're talking about the simple part of computer systems the brain. Displays, hard drives, stick memories, keyboards and the like are complicated, need a lot of explaining. Computers are simple. They're just collections of switches.

Let's examine the telegraph the one switch computer. To be a computer it must have both memory and a central processing unit. The memory is the telegraph key. The central processing unit of the telegraph is the telegraph operators' brains. It takes 2 keys and two operators separated by cyber space to compute on the telegraph. Did you notice the human brain and the central processing unit are equals in computing?

Computers have but two parts, a central processing unit and memory. We've seen what a memory looks like. Memories are as easy to understand as Paul Revere's famous ride and the signal used to inform the minute men. Central processing units are nothing more than collections of switches too.

Everyone knows what a light switch looks like and most even know about light switch guts. Most mechanical switches are spring loaded to quickly close and hold the position. Memory switches are a little simpler than ordinary switches having no moving parts at all to wear out or malfunction. In the end they are different embodiments of the same device serving the same purpose. Light switches "remember" whether the light is off or on. It's identically the same thing in computer memories. Memory switches remember if they are off or on. That's all they do. The thing to get straight in one's mind is the fact that switches are one bit memories. To know the light switch is to know all there is to know about computers.

We're going to use 0 and 1 to identify the states of memory and CPU, Central Processing Unit switches. 0 is switch-off and 1 is switch-on. If the computer system has a LED to show the state of a bit/switch the LED will be lit for a 1 and off for a 0. Early computers systems used tiny lights to show the states of memory switches. Now the state of individual memory switches is rarely if ever shown to the outside world.

The inability to look into computer memory needs to change. Designing a computer that can be stopped with the hardware to look inside its memory is a billion dollar market so wide open its hinges are sprung. There is no substitute as a learning tool. Lookout! "They" don't want you to have one of them. "They" got filthy, filthy rich and now thrive on your ignorance. Say goodbye to your ignorance as you read on.

You ignorance is assured by you not having a real computer you can program yourself. PC's of all kinds are not programmable by ordinary people. By definition computers are programmable. Thus PC's are not computers because they do not satisfy the programmable requirement.

I'm doing my best to educate you without training tools. Computers are so easy it's entirely possible for you to learn all about how they work without actually having one.

Charles Babbage invented a mechanical stored-program device that has come to be known as computer, 1833 before electricity had come into popular use anywhere. Thus it was a set of mechanical switches by necessity. And you thought IBM "created" the computer doing a similar thing as God supposedly did creating man. You don't suppose the human body is just a bunch of switches? Could be.

Computer memories are sets of switches. That's all they are. It's not unusual to find switches referred to in the literature as bits and cells. Thus bit and cell are synonymous meaning switch with all three meaning the same thing. It would not come as a surprise to find computer scientist experts have invented new words that mean the same thing. All literature generated by experts has to be read with care if it's at all readable. I'm not an expert I only know what I'm talking about.

Computers are collections of switches. Computers have two parts known as central processing units and memories sometimes called memory banks. Bank means bank where money/memories are stored. There, we have a new way of saying switches. Memory banks are collections of switches. Changes nothing. Central processing units are collections of switches. If you understand the light switch then you know all there is to know about the material required to make computers.

Making computers is a chore all by itself that is magnitudes greater than knowing all there is to know about their makeup and capabilities. That work, making computers by properly arranging switches has already been done. It's a once done and done for all times situation. Different makes of computers differ only in the number of switches and how they are arranged. Otherwise all are identical.

By now you should be getting the idea. The light switch is the most important invention of man right after the wheel and maybe even before the wheel. Most of all the light switch is the simplest and easiest to understand of all electrical devices. I'm sure you're still doubtful you know as much as I'm telling you know because the human mind thinks complex, complicated. Do you think the exotic high tech gadgets are beyond your meager mental capacity? Take the switches out of them and they're nothing but empty shells.

Let's get introduced to the programming, the art of operating switches through mental processes. Computer programs are documents written in computer languages. Therefore they involve both vocabulary and grammatical structure. Good news! The vocabularies of all computers is small in number of words and usually a dozen or less. Grammatical structure is identical for all with minor variations from one make/model computer to another.

Computer languages come in one of three varieties, machine language, assembly language and complier language. Machine language is the natural language of the particular make/model computer. It's the actual switch settings written using nothing but 0's and 1's indicating switch offs and on. Assembly language is identical to machine language with help from a program known as an assembler that converts somewhat people readable writing into switch offs and on. Both machine language and assembly language are natural.

The third variety of computer language is compiler language. Compiler languages are man-made thus they are unnatural. That means all is at the pleasure of a person or persons who are free to invent new words, create new grammatical structures, and make up other rules of the road.

Later we'll invent a computer language using regular words. The more closely computer languages are to the natural language of the computer the more powerful their vocabularies. The more closely their words are in meanings to their dictionary definitions the easier they are to learn and remember. In the meantime we need to come to a complete understanding of just what a computer is and unleash the computing brain power in the liberal arts college hidden behind "Computer is just simply too technical for the poor unfortunate's with peanut size brains." Prepare to be surprised.

Chapter 3, it takes many switches...

...to make a significant computer. With a single switch we can do a lot. We only need one switch, a telegraph key switch to do telegraph type communications. And, we can easily remember one thing that has but two possibilities, either off or on. To remember many things we need a lot of switches. You haven't forgotten, 0 means switch is off and 1 means switch is on?

Let's take a crack at learning to count using switches in sets. In the following the number on the left is the "count" value of switch settings in ordinary numbers.

One switch has but 2 possible settings/values:

```
0 = 0   off
1 = 1   on
```

Two switches side by side have 4 possible settings:

```
0 = 00   off off
1 = 01   off on
2 = 10   on off
3 = 11   on on
```

Three switches side by side have 8 possible settings:

```
0 = 000   off off off
1 = 001   off off on
2 = 010   off on off
3 = 011   off on on
4 = 100   on off off
5 = 101   on off on
6 = 110   on on off
7 = 111   on on on
```

Four switches side by side have 16 possible settings:

```
0 = 0000   off off off off
1 = 0001   off off off on
2 = 0010   off off on off
3 = 0011   off off on on
4 = 0100   off on off off
5 = 0101   off on off on
6 = 0110   off on on off
7 = 0111   off on on on
```

```
 8 = 1000   on off off off
 9 = 1001   on off off on
10 = 1010   on off on off
11 = 1011   on off on on
12 = 1100   on on off off
13 = 1101   on on off on
14 = 1110   on on on off
15 = 1111   on on on on
```

Did you notice that every time we add a switch to the set the number of possibilities doubles? One switch has but 2 possible settings. Two switches have 4 possible settings. Three switches have 8 and four switches have 16 possible settings. That's a trend. Every time we add a switch we double the number of possible settings. Logically, five switches have 32 possible settings, six have 64 and on and on to an unlimited number of switches side by side.

To get from one grouping of switches to the next we simply multiply by 2. That's easy enough to do isn't it? To go the other way, remove a switch from a set of switches side by side divide by 2 to get the number of possible settings. High powered math isn't required. Anyone can multiply and divide by 2. That's right, computers take the math out of math. That was the whole idea behind their invention, take the math out of math. Compute – to calculate. To calculate without having to calculate takes the math out of math.

Now it's time to notice something. First of all you've spent your entire life numbering things beginning with the number 1. That way you counted them at the same time you numbered them. Numbering things with the first one being number 1 is automatically counting whatever it is being numbered. In computer memory we start our numbering at 0, zero.

Numbering sets of switches making up a memory beginning with the number zero is automatically LOCATING them in the memory. Memories are made of sets of switches side by side and usually in 8 switch sets called bytes. Zero is the ADDRESS of the first set of switches. The word address means the same thing it has always meant, where the postman delivers the mail. Location also means what it has always meant, where a thing be. The first, 1st set of switches in computer memory is LOCATED at ADDRESS zero, 0.

We have two old words, locating and addressing with the same meanings and different applications. Locating data in memory is done by addressing the location desired.

New word, data. Data are switch settings. Computing is the changing of switch settings, data that are located in memory. Data is located in memory at memory addresses that begin at address zero. Zero is all-switches-off.

The address is how the postman knows who gets what mail. The address locates where the mail goes. Addressing sets of switches in memory is identical to addressing mail with the exception there's only one number for a memory address. Ordinary mail includes an addressee, a street, a house number, city, state and zip code. A computer address is a number beginning with the number zero that is the address of the first memory location, first house in the city.

Switch settings represent numerical values as witnessed by the above tables. By convention all switches off is zero. The rightmost switch on with all others off is one. The second from the right switch on with all other off is two. This goes on for every possible on-off combinations for a given side by side set of switches.

We use a particular set of switches called address switches to locate particular sets of switches in the computer's memory called data switches. All sets of memory switches have addresses that are numbers only. Think about memory as a city with but one street. The street is the memory. Any house can be identified by a number only leaving the street name out since there is but one street. Numbers are represented by switch settings. All address switches off is zero which is the address of the first set of memory switches, the fist house on the one and only street.

When we get to programming the power of addressing sets of switches within a group of switches will become obvious. In the meantime try hard to always begin numbering with the first number being zero, it's addressing rather than what you've done all your life, numbering and counting at the same time. Try to remember we're not counting but rather we're locating a single set of memory/data switches. And there's something else that beginning with zero allows us to do.

We can write actual numbers with sets of switches. I want to ease you into the notion of number systems. Most people think of number systems as being post graduate math material and not something ordinary people do. Number systems are a matter of nature. They're not man made stuff requiring a lot of fancy words with vague definitions to memorize. You were born with all the knowledge of number systems you'll need. It's just a matter of realizing what you already know.

My purpose here is to show you numbers can be and are written in switch settings. The largest possible number is relative to the number of switches side by side. Writing numbers in two position switches is writing them in binary, base 2 number system.

The base 10 number system is the standard for numbering. No doubt we do this because we have 10 fingers. If we only had stubs at the ends of our arms we'd use the base 2 system. With 10 fingers we can count to 10 and still keep our shoes on. With only 2 fingers we could only count to 2. Which is easier to do count to 10 or count to 2?

With the base 10, the decimal system we have 10 symbols representing base-values/count-values, 0, 1, 2, 3, 4, 5, 6, 7, 8, and 9. When we reach 9 we must add a digit to count farther, i.e. 10, 11, up to 100, where 3 digits are required and on and on indefinitely always adding another decimal place on the left as each set of base numbers is exceeded, when we've exhausted our set of symbols. With the base 2, binary system we only have 2 symbols representing base-values/count-values, specifically the digits 0 and 1. Think how much easier it would have been to learn your numbers in kindergarten if you only had 2 symbols to learn. You can count to 1 can you not?

In case you haven't figured it out the base of a number system is the number of symbols/digits needed to represent all single digit counts. In base 10 we need 10 symbols. In base 2 we only need 2 symbols. Base 2 is at least 5 times easier than base 10 and even then the CPU does all the arithmetic for us.

Every digit in a base 10 system has 10 possible values, 0 through 9. Every digit in the base 2 system has but 2 possible values, 0 and 1. Every light switch has 2 possible settings, off or on. That gives us an exact fit of 2 position switches to base 2 numbers. Thus light switches can be used to write numbers in the base 2, the binary number system.

We can also represent base 10 numbers using 10 position switches. Switches with 10 possible settings are a lot more than 5 times harder to manufacture and operate than switches with only 2 possible settings. We must have 10 contacts inside 10 position switches where we only need 2 inside two position ones.

We already know how to count in binary. Its 0, 1 and then we're out of symbols. In decimal we must count, 0, 1, 2, 3, 4, 5, 6, 7, 8, 9, before we're out of symbols. The next number after 9 in decimal is 10. Guess what, the next number after 1 in binary is also 10. When we exhaust our supply of symbols we begin again using 2 symbols. In base 10 we write 10 and in base 2 we also write 10. A count of 10 in decimal says there's 10 things. A count of 10 in binary says there's 2 things. Number and count-value are two radically different things that vary by number system base. Only in decimal are numbers and counts the same. In all other systems numbers must be converted to decimal to get their count values.

We'll take the binary number system apart at the seams later and understand its finest details. My purpose here is to introduce you to the fact that numbers are easily stored using two position switches but only in the binary number system. Numbers can be stored using multi-position switches with any number of positions. The complexity of both the switches and the number system relative to the number of positions doubles with the addition of a position to the switches. Two position switches that flip on and off are the simplest possible.

There isn't much to a number system once one comes to an understanding of one's own brain that came with all possible number systems built in, the simplest and easiest being the base 2, the binary system. All we need to remember when using switches to represent numbers is switch-off is a 0, (zero) and switch-on is a 1, (one).

Usually switches are grouped in side by side sets. Three switches as a set have 8 possible DIFFERENT settings. Therefore they have 8 possible numerical values ranging in value from 0 to 7. Computers are sets of switches. Information of all kinds are stored as switch settings with switches in groups of 8 as a general rule at this time.

Think about a wall plate with 8 switches side by side that turn on and off 8 light bulbs. This is the usual way of grouping switches in computers. 8 is the least common denominator. All groupings of switches are in multiples of 8 switches. In the early days most computers had switches grouped in sets that were multiples of 6 switches side by side.

Early computers had memory banks with many more switches per location than today's computers. Memories are arranged in sets of 8 today. When you go to the store to buy a computer its memory is stated in bytes. A byte is 8 switches side by side like an 8 switch wall plate. My first computer had 40 bits/switches per memory location. 40 is an even multiple of 8. The first maxi computer the IBM 709/7090 had 36 bits per location. 36 is a multiple of 6. As the computer has evolved 8 has settled in as the somewhat standard keeping in mind there is no standard. Information is "remembered" in off-on settings of switches by all computers.

Letters of the alphabet, punctuation marks and other symbols not on the typewriter keyboard such as arrows are represented with 0's and 1's in groups of 8 bits/switches. Since 8 is the more or less standard for the number of switches used to represent an individual letter or character there is a limit of 256 of them. Let's see why that's so.

1 switch has 2 possible settings
2 switches have 4 possible settings
3 switches have 8 possible settings
4 switches have 16 possible settings
5 switches have 32 possible settings
6 switches have 64 possible settings
7 switches have 128 possible settings
8 switches have 256 possible settings

A single switch has but 2 possible settings, off or on. An 8 switch memory location has 256 possible different settings and no more. 8 switches side by side is called a byte.

Switches must always be either off or on. Thus every switch in the computer is always off or on. Taken in sets of 8 they are always one of the 256 possible different settings with nothing or blank being erroneous descriptions. Generally speaking when one types a letter on the keyboard it goes into a memory location as a set of 8 bits representing the particular letter. For example, capital A is typed. Somewhere in memory it is stored in switches as 01000001. The 0's and 1's are off or on switch settings. This is how computers remember.

A very human mistake to make is to say a memory location has nothing in it. That's as ignorant as saying a switch's position is nothing. Switches are always off or on. Memory locations are made of switches thus they must always be either off or on.

Here we are learning how computers remember letters of the alphabet and other symbols. Imagine 8 ordinary light switches side by side. Every letter of the alphabet, punctuation marks etc. is represented by settings of 8 switches. Off, on, off, off, off, off, off, on represents the letter capital A. Off, on, off, off, off, off, on, off represents the letter capital B. We can save ourselves a lot of writing by saying 0 means off and 1 means on. That way 01000001 represents capital A and 01000010 represents capital B.

In this case, representing symbols on the keyboard 0 and 1 are not numbers. They represent switch off-on settings. A and B could have been used. Actually arrows, ↓ for switch-off and ↑ for switch-on are much closer than any other symbols but they are not on "regular" keyboard as symbols.

When the capital A is struck on the keyboard the keyboard translates it into switch settings specifically, 01000001, (↓↑↓↓↓↓↓↑). The programmer, a human being effectively inside the computer reads the key into the computer and stores it meaning causes a set of 8 memory switches to be set to, 01000001. When the contents of the memory location is displayed on a display screen, output to a printer etc. the display, printer or other device translates it back into capital A and displays or prints it. Keys are coded, stored, decoded and output. The keyboard does the coding and the display does the decoding.

Numbers in binary, base 2 system are stored in computer memory differently to letters of the alphabet etc. Above we listed all the possible switch settings for a 4 switch set and discovered there were 16 settings with numerical values of 0 through 15. Now we will see how switch settings are actually binary numbers. Characters such as letters of the alphabet are coded with different switch settings designated to mean different characters. The letter A has been assigned the settings 01000001. A could have been assigned any one of the 256 possible settings. The assignment was done by people and is arbitrary. Not so with binary numbers.

Groupings of switches in any number side by side inherently represent numbers in binary without any coding, (designating 01000001 to be the letter A is coding). A single switch is one of two possible numbers, 0 or 1 and is always one or the other. Two switches are one of 4 possible numbers, 0, 1, 2, or 3 and are always one of the four. Three switches are one of 8 possible numbers, 0, 1, 2, 3, 4, 5, 6, or 7 and are always one of the eight. With any number of switches as a set there is a limit to the size of the largest possible numbers.

A set of switches in the computer is identical to your auto's odometer. Both have a fixed number of digits. When all switches are on and one more is added the count rolls over just like your odometer rolls over 1 mile past 99999. You can think

28

of an 8 bit memory bank as being a string of odometers that roll over at 11111111. 11111111 has the numerical value 255. Add 1 and it overflows, rolls over to 00000000. When a number rolls over it "overflows" and the computer sets a flag bit called overflow/carry.

The largest number possible with a single switch is 1, with 2 switches its 3, with 3 switches 7. As the number of switches grows the size of the largest number grows as a multiple of 2 as well. For every switch added the largest possible number grows by the simple formula, 2 times the previous plus 1. From 2 switches with the max number 3 to 3 switches its, 2 X 3 + 1 = 7 to calculate the largest possible number that can be represented by 3 switches.

No. Switches/bits	Max Decimal Number
1	1
2	3
3	7
4	15
5	31
6	63
7	127
8	255
9	511
10	1,023
11	2,047
12	4,095
13	8,191
14	16,383
15	32,767
16	65,535
.	.
32	4,294,967,295

As the above table shows us the size of the largest number possible in 32 switches is still inadequate to hold the national debt but is plenty large enough for tallying tickets at the fast food restaurant.

You may have also noticed that 32 is an even multiple of 8. In an 8 bit memory that would be quadruple precision. In order to represent large numbers exactly in computer memory it's necessary to concatenate, lay side by side multiples of 8 bit memory cells to hold large numbers. You've probably noticed PC's advertised as being 64 bit. That means they use 8, 8 bit memory cells concatenated together per something. Since that something isn't stated we are left to assume 64 bit is just so much advertising froth.

Arithmetic is the next thing we're going to learn how to do. You may have failed arithmetic in every grade beginning with kindergarten. Most likely you had great difficulty memorizing the addition and multiplication tables. Now I'm going to scare the pants off you. You must memorize two switch, base 2 addition and multiplication tables, hold the multiplication table memorizing part. I don't want you to blow your brain gasket. The binary multiplication table requires you to memorize, "1 times 1 is 1." Outrageously difficult.

OK we won't do multiplication but we must do addition. And, killing two birds with one stone we'll firm up in our minds the relationship between actual numbers and switch settings. First we need to learn how to add sets of switch settings to each other.

Let's now memorize the addition table:

Adding numbers	Adding switches
0 + 0 is 0 carry set to 0	off + off is off carry off
0 + 1 is 1 carry set to 0	off + on is on carry off
1 + 0 is 1 carry set to 0	on + off is on carry off
1 + 1 is 0 carry set to 1	on + on is off carry on

Things were fine until we got to 1+1. Adding 1 to 1 is hard, as hard as it gets. You really don't have a problem adding 0 to 0 or 0 to 1 do you? 1 + 1 is a different game. Why? 1 + 1 is NOT 2 because we don't have a number 2 in switch settings. All we have for single digit numbers are 0 and 1. Enter carry/overflow bit.

Carry has another name, overflow. If we have a one switch odometer that is on and we add another switch that is

30

also on then the sum of the two overflows our one switch odometer. If we have additional switches it's called carry. If we do not have additional switches overflow is the name used. What do I mean by additional switches?

Suppose we are adding 2, 8 bit sets of switches putting the results into still another 8 bit set. And, the sum of the two is greater than 255, (max number in 8 bits is 255). The computer has a switch that will be turned on indicating the answer is erroneous because it cannot be contained in the space allotted.

<u>   Decimal   binary   .</u>
   130   10000010
+<u>126   01111110</u>
   256   00000000 overflow 1

255 is the largest number that can be held in 8 bits. Thus when we add two numbers with a sum greater than 255 our accumulator/odometer overflows.

When we do decimal addition we write the carry from the previous column above the next column and add it in. We do identically the same thing in binary. Addition is done right to left just like you were taught to do in grammar school.

Overflow →1,   11111100 ← carry bit/switch
   130   10000010
+<u>126   01111110</u>
   256   00000000 overflow 1

Above is a play by play of how the CPU adds for us. Before starting the addition it turns the carry bit off. One column at a time from right to left it adds 3 bits/switches at a time to get the answer for that column and the carry bit for the next column just like we were taught to do in decimal, i.e. 9 + 7 is 6 carry 1. Step one, add the right two bits of our two numbers plus the carry to get the right most answer bit and carry bit. The carry begins at zero and the two rightmost bits/switches are both 0/off thus the results are 0 with carry 0 as well. That's the very difficult, 0 + 0 + 0 is 0, carry 0. The second column is a little more difficult, carry 0 + 1 + 1 is 0, carry 1. The third column is carry 1 + 0 + 1 is 0, carry 1. Every column is the same to the last which is, carry 1 + 1 + 0 is 0, overflow 1. All we did differently in the last column is change the name of carry to overflow. Rarely if ever would a computer have two different switches for both carry and overflow. It's one switch with two tasks and two names.

overflow → 0,　00000000 ← carry bit/switch

```
 130   10000010
+125   01111101
 255   11111111 overflow 0
```

It's rather obvious 8 bits are totally inadequate to hold numbers of any size at all. To facilitate concatenating multiple sets of 8 bits to make larger numbers computers will usually have two add instructions, just plain add and add with carry/overflow. Just plain add clears, sets to zero the carry bit before doing the addition. Add with carry uses the carry bit from the previous add operation. The carry bit is set/cleared by the results of the operation and stays set/cleared until another arithmetic, logical or compare operation. Suppose one wanted to do 16 bit addition. That's two 8 bit bytes added to two other 8 bit bytes with the results saved in still a third pair of 8 bit bytes.

(a,b) + (j,k) → (x,y) where, a, b, j, k, x, and y are all 8 bits wide. First one adds, k to b, results to y. This sets the carry bit for the next operation. Then one adds with carry, j to a, results to x. This is how large number arithmetic is done. Remember, the CPU does all the work. The program tells it what to do. The carry/overflow bit allows any size numbers regardless of how narrow memories are in switches.

The carry/overflow bit forces us to update our addition table. As you recall we only had 1 significant thing to memorize, 1 + 1 Is 0 carry 1. The carry must be added to our table:

```
0 + 0 + carry 0 is 0 carry 0
0 + 0 + carry 1 is 1 carry 0
0 + 1 + carry 0 is 1 carry 0
0 + 1 + carry 1 is 0 carry 1
1 + 0 + carry 0 is 1 carry 0
1 + 0 + carry 1 is 0 carry 1
1 + 1 + carry 0 is 0 carry 1
1 + 1 + carry 1 is 1 carry 1
```

That's not too difficult is it? 1 + 1 + 1 is 3. 3 is written in light switches as on, on, 11 binary. One can be a good

32

programmer without knowing how to do arithmetic at all. During my 45 year career in computers both hardware and software I never needed to know the details of how the computer actually adds switch settings to each other. I wrote a dozen or more math packages with multi precision addition, subtraction, multiplication and division sub programs. Didn't need to know the details of how the computer did it just the instructions, the words I needed to say to cause the computer do it for me.

Our purpose here is for you to come to a complete understanding of how letters of the alphabet and other symbols and numbers are stored in memory made of off-on switches. Symbols such as letters of the alphabet are coded using codes invented by people. You now have enough knowledge to Google ASCII codes, go to a web site such as Wikipedia.org and be able to understand the actual switch settings for individual symbols. ASCII is the most widely used coding at this time. Binary numbers on the other hand are not coded as such being stored in natural state with the maximum size being determined by the number of memory cells/locations employed.

The above being said I'm herein suggesting the ideal computer does arithmetic in decimal. The actual arithmetic must be done in binary. However, there is the possibility of creating a pseudo computer that does arithmetic in decimal via a process known as simulation. We'll discuss that in detail later and outline a pseudo computer that operates in directly readable ASCII. Until the human body evolves to having more or less than 10 fingers decimal will be the number system of choice. There is no reason not to make theoretical computers that are base 10. I did it for junior high kids, 1968. They caught on to how computers work right away without ever so much as hearing the word binary.

Letters of the alphabet, punctuation marks etc. are usually coded in ASCII. Decimal, base 10 symbols 0, (zero) through 9 are also coded in ASCII. When 0 through 9 are hit in the keyboard they are coded, stored in memory and sent over the telegraph just like the letters of the alphabet. 0, (zero) is 00110000, 1 is 00110001 etc. We do not do arithmetic using

ASCII codes. That can be done behind the curtain with all being in decimal otherwise.

Knowing how ball point pens work is not necessary to fruitfully use them. Knowing all about ball point pens will never turn one into a writer. Knowing how to do arithmetic is not necessary to write programs especially operating systems and even ones to make animated motion pictures. Those who know how to use a calculator already know plenty enough to add up numbers using the computer, figure sales tax, total the ticket, get the money and calculate the change due.

Chapter 4, central processing...

...units are known as CPU's. Clever way of naming them don't you think? Surely you've heard the term, "electronic brain." CPU's are the thinking parts of electronic brains. Memories are made of thoughts and of course thoughts are stored in memories. We will now come to a complete understanding of the part of the computer that is the brains part, the computer's thinker. Never forget, computers don't think. All the thinking that seems to be going on is actually a human being known as a programmer doing the thinking.

Computers have two parts, a central processing unit known as the CPU and a memory. We've taken a glimpse at memory and seen that information is written in switch settings no more technical from the computer user's viewpoint than an ordinary light switch. Guess what, CPU's are nothing more than a bunch of switches too. Switches making up CPU's just like those making up the memories are known as bits and cells.

Bits/switches in both CPU's and memories are organized in sets identical in structure to your auto's odometer. If you understand your auto's odometer then you understand both memory and CPU structure. Both are nothing more than sets of two position off-on switches. Auto odometers are sets of 10 position switches making them 5 time more difficult to use than computer odometers with only two position switches.

Sets of CPU switches have descriptive names relative to how they are used. All have the common name of REGISTER. Think of CPU's as the Register family with every member of the family having a differed first name. I wrote REGISTER in all caps to emphasize its significance. Registers are special one-word, odometer-memories physically contained inside the central processing unit independent of the computer's regular memory. Register on CPU's are little memories.

Both computer CPU's and computer memories are composed of nothing but switches organized in sets. A near perfect example of a CPU register or a memory location either one is the auto's odometer. Odometers have a fixed number of digits. Computer registers have a fixed number of bits/switches. Auto odometers are sets of 10 position switches. CPU registers are sets of 2 position switches.

We need to learn a new word, WORD. Everyone knows what a word is. Well, there's words and then there's computer words. Computer words are sets of bits just like bytes are sets of bits. Computer words are fixed in width just like the odometer in one's auto.

Bit – one switch

Byte – 8 switches side by side

Word – 1 or more bytes side by side

CPU words are even multiples of bytes. Thus the smallest possible word is one byte wide. Some computer memories are arranged in bytes. In that case their memory words are one byte wide. Words in most CPU's today are 2 or more bytes wide. CPU words vary in width according to the particular CPU. All are multiples of bytes. 16 bit CPU's have 2 bytes per CPU word. 32 bit CPU's have 4 bytes per CPU word.

It can be a little confusing since word has two different definitions relative to which part of the computer we're discussing. CPU words and memory words may be different widths. Another possible confusion factor - bytes are different widths from one make of computer to another.

In the early days many computers had 6 bits wide bytes. The first minicomputer, the PDP-8 had 2 byte words. Since byte is indeterminate saying it had 2 byte words is not definitive. It turns out the PDP-8's bytes were 6 bits wide and not 8 bits wide. The PDP-8 had 2, 6 bit bytes per word for both CPU and memory thus the PDP-8 had 12 bit wide words. There were 36 bit word computers. The IBM-7090 had 36 bit words. Each of IBM-7090's words had 6, 6 bit bytes. 8 will not divide evenly into 36 while 6 will, 36/6 = 6. Computer words are almost always multiples of bytes no matter the width of the byte employed. Keep in mind the word byte changes meaning from one make and model computer to another and from CPU to memory.

We'll use the simplest computer ever commercially produced, the PDP-8 as an example of the basic CPU. Both the PDP-8's memory words and CPU register words are 12 bits wide. In computer lingo words are units of measure that divide evenly into bytes.

All CPU's have small on-board memories called register banks. The PDP-8 CPU memory was 4 words long. Think of them as a family with each having a different first name with a common last name of registers. They're also identical in size having the same widths in number of switches. This is so for all makes and models of computers. All have registers. Different makes/models have different numbers of registers.

We usually distinguish between the CPU's on-board memory and regular computer memory by using the word memory to identify regular memory and register when referring to the CPU's on-board memory. Thus when I say memory I mean the computer's regular memory. When I mean CPU memory I use the word register. Memory – memory-memory. Register – CPU-memory.

CPU's and regular memory are separated. They are physically connected to each other with sets of wires called busses. Busses connect CPU registers and memory words. There are single chip computers called microcontrollers with CPU and memory in a single package. This does not change the separation of CPU and memory. It means the wires connecting the CPU and memory are a part of the integrated circuit.

We must memorize the names of the CPU's registers. In order to qualify as a CPU a minimum set of 4 registers is required. 4 isn't that many to remember is it? There must be an instruction pointer register, an instruction register, a memory address register and an accumulator register. CPU's usually have three single bit registers called flags as well.

The absolute minimum CPU in my opinion is that of the PDP-8. It has a 12 bit instruction pointer register, a 12 bit instruction register, a 12 bit memory address register and a 12 bit accumulator register. The PDP-8 also has a single overflow/carry bit. That's all we need to remember to program the PDP-8. Anything less and it wouldn't qualify as a computer. It would also be useless as well - too large for a paperweight or door stop either one. Maybe a boat anchor?

Let's list those registers and take a crack at memorizing them.

Instruction pointer register
Instruction register
Memory address register
Accumulator register

Three flag bits – carry/overflow, zero and minus

Two sets of 12 wires each called the memory address buss and the memory data buss connect memory to the CPU's registers. Sets of wires connecting memory and CPU registers are called busses. The PDP-8 design has two busses that are 12 wires wide each. They are the memory address buss and the memory data buss. Just about all if not all microprocessors have the same two busses differing only in widths, (number of wires). For example the very popular Z-80 has a 16 wire memory address buss and an 8 wire data buss.

This is a little mind twister, maybe. I have zero difficulty visualizing it. In a box we have the CPU and its several registers. In another box we have memory and its many words. The two are joined together with two sets of wires, busses.

Central Processing Unit
Register
Register
.
Register

Memory address buss   Memory data buss
↓↓↓↓ . . . . ↓   ↓↑↓↑↓↑ . . . . ↓↑

Memory
1st Word, address 0
2nd Word, address 1

. . . . .

Last Word, address is length of memory - 1

Above we have the basic schematic of all computers, no exception. To know one is to know them all. CPU's are made of nothing but switches arranged in sets called registers. Memories are made of nothing but switches arranged in sets. Sets of CPU switches are connected to sets of memory switches by sets of wires called busses. Notice that addressing is always from CPU to memory while data goes both ways.

On board the CPU there are minibuses that connect CPU registers to the memory access data busses. At no time is more than one CPU register or more than one memory location

38

connected to the memory address buss and the memory data buss. When the computer computes one register and one memory location are connected together via the memory address and memory data busses. Computing is duplicating switch settings in the selected CPU register in the selected memory word OR duplicating the switch setting in the selected memory word in the selected CPU register. This isn't all there is to computing but it is most of what is going on.

Computing involves two other steps. Switch settings in the selected CPU register are "worked on." What do I mean by worked on? The switch settings in a CPU register can be altered by the switch settings of one other CPU or memory word. Altering amounts to duplicating switch settings and doing arithmetic both ordinary and Boolean. That's all.

If you never head of Boolean arithmetic don't worry about it. We'll take the 10 seconds needed to learn it later. Best description of Boolean arithmetic is arithmetic easy enough for people who flunked arithmetic to learn so they wouldn't feel too bad about flunking.

The third possible computing step is the alteration of computing flow. CPU's do one thing at a time one after the other until they find the thing to do next is somewhere other than next thing on the list. This is called jumping and branching as well as other things like skip, call and branch-and-link and perhaps others I can't think of at the moment. All change the flow of computing. The CPU does instruction, 0, 1, 2, 3, and then there's a jump to 15 instruction. It then does, 15, 16, 17, and on and on until another jump instruction.

We've reached the deciding moment for you. Either you can think simple or you can give up. All that's going on in computers is the flipping of switches. That's all. Let's add the word orderly to that mind boggling activity, turning light switches on and off. Computing is the orderly operation of switches. Switch settings determine what switches will be turned on and off. Thus computing can alter itself. A set of switches can cause itself to be altered. It's rarely intentionally done but it is entirely possible for an instruction to address itself.

Instruction? There's a word that's usually thrown in the stew without any explanation of what it might mean.

Instructions instruct. Hopefully you already knew that. In computer, instructions are switch settings in memory that instruct the CPU. Now we know where to find instructions, memory and that instructions instruct the CPU. Instructions instruct the CPU to do some rather trivial things, arithmetic and logical operations and jumping and nothing more. Prepare to be amazed at how little instructions do.

Instructions instruct the CPU to do arithmetic and logical operations and to alter the flow of getting instructed. This is called program execution. Programs are lists of switch settings amounting to one instruction per CPU word. The CPU does what instructions tell it to do one after the other until it finds a program flow altering instruction. Then it picks up execution at the location indicated by the instruction.

Computer literacy begins with knowing, having on quick recall the basic computing cycle. I like helpers, little expressions or acronyms to remember things like, Most Vegetables Eaten Make Joe Sick Until Noon Passes – Mercury, Venus, Earth, Mars, Jupiter, Saturn Uranus, Neptune, Pluto. This is how I remember the planets and their relative distances from the sun. FIRE – Fetch present instruction, Increment instruction pointer so it points to the next instruction, Resolve address, Execute the present instruction. FIRE is how I remember the basic computing cycle.

FETCH INSTRUCTION

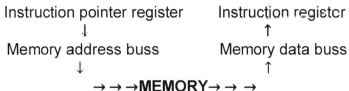

CENTRAL PROCESSING UNIT	
Instruction pointer register	Instruction register
↓	↑
Memory address buss	Memory data buss
↓	↑

→ → →MEMORY→ → →

Above we have a diagram showing the settings on the memory address and memory data busses during the "fetch" portion of the instruction execution cycle. The instruction pointer register is gated onto the memory address buss and the instruction register receives data from the memory data buss. The contents of, switch settings of the data location addressed by the instruction pointer register are duplicated in the instruction register. That's all.

After the CPU has "fetched" the <u>present</u> instruction it adds one to the contents of the instruction pointer register so it points to the <u>next</u> instruction in memory thus getting ready to access the next instruction. This step is called instruction pointer updating.

Instructions have two parts, an operation code and, optionally according to which particular operation a memory address. If a memory address is required the address portion of the instruction is copied into the memory address register.

Memory addresses within instructions may be simple or complex. Simple addresses are copied directly into the memory address register. If complex the address is "resolved" to a simple address and then copied into the memory address register. Simple – a single number. Complex – requires the contents of other memory or CPU word(s) to get a single number. At this point the CPU has all the information needed to "execute" the instruction. The instruction is executed meaning what it requests/instructs/commands/operates is done by the CPU ending the "present" CPU cycle.

Execute Load and Store Instruction
CENTRAL PROCESSING UNIT

Memory address register   Accumulator register

↓   ⇅

Memory address buss   Memory data buss

↓   ⇅

→ → →**MEMORY** ⇆ ⇆ ⇆

Above we have a schematic showing the settings on the memory address and memory data busses during the "execution" portion of the instruction execution cycle. This applies to all load/read-from memory and all store/write-to memory instructions. Some instructions do not access memory. Memory access instructions are the most complex yet all they do is nothing more than changing switch settings in either memory or CPU registers.

Think simple. Nothing going on but duplicating switch settings.

FIRE - Fetch, Increment, Resolve and Execute. All CPU's no matter the make model or design of the computer do nothing but FIRE. You can think of CPU's as machine guns with instructions being the equal of bullets. Programming is loading bullets into CPU ammunition belts called memories.

The CPU first uses the instruction pointer register's contents to find the present instruction in memory. If the instruction being executed requires a memory access the memory address register is used to point to it.

Example: A PDP-8 unique instruction, DCA address. DCA is a PDP-8 unique instruction. DCA reads "deposit, duplicate the contents of the accumulator switch settings in memory at the specified address, and then clear the accumulator. Clear - turn all switches off." Suppose the address was 27. The CPU copies the address, the number 27 into the memory address register. 27 points to memory location 27. 27 is a simple address. At this point the CPU has all the information needed to "execute" the instruction.

When executing a DCA instruction the CPU does the follows: The contents of, switch settings of the memory address register are gated onto the memory address buss. At the same time it gates the accumulator register onto the memory data buss. Then it sets the memory read/write control line to write and sets the memory enable control line to enable. This causes the switch settings in the accumulator to be copied into memory at the location pointed to by the memory address register, (memory location 27). Afterwards the accumulator's switches are all turned off.

DCA, deposit and clear is unique to the PDP-8 as no other of the multitude of computers have such an instruction. All others only copy the contents of the accumulator register or other register into the memory location with the contents of the accumulator register or other register not being changed. Only the PDP-8 changes the accumulator register's contents. This brings us to a computer scientist expert stupid-jerky.

A point of amusement to me is the fact that the PDP-8 actually "moves" the contents of its accumulator register to memory and the only computer ever that does so. All other computers "copy" the contents of registers to/into memory locations leaving the contents of the register as is. In spite of nothing actually moving an official computer scientist committee has decreed the "move" instruction written, MOV to be the **standard** assembly language mnemonic. Computer scientists have strict standards. Their universal MOV decree officially makes "move" and "copy" the same thing. Oh yeah, moving and copying are the same thing. This is the work of mental giants. When computer scientists make copies using the computer science copy machines the original goes to the duplicate and the copier bed is emptied. The original packs its bags and moves to the duplicate. This explains why computers are so hard to understand in computer science class. They're learning to do things that can't be done.

I used two, maybe even three new words in the above description of an instruction's execution. They are execute, gate and buss. A buss as used in computer lingo is a set of wires. Registers and signals are carried on computer busses just like people are carried on people busses.

We will be using the original standard for duplicating switch settings, L and ST. L mean load – the switch settings in a memory location are duplicated in a register. ST means store – the switch settings is a CPU register are duplicated in a memory location. At the end of either the two words will be identical to each other.

All busses in the PDP-8 are 12 wires wide. There's an individual wire per register and memory bit/switch connecting them to each other. Computer busses qualify as cyber spaces.

In case you haven't guessed it data means switch settings. That's all. Of course switch settings represent all sorts of things when taken as sets from simple numbers to images of people and things in photographs.

Now about computer gates. More than one CPU register can be connected to the memory thus gates are used to pick one out of many. In the case of the PDP-8 two registers are connected through gates onto busses to memory. In the first part of the instruction cycle the instruction pointer register is "gated" onto the memory address buss AND at the same time the instruction register is gated onto the memory data buss. In the last step of the basic execution cycle the "resolved" address portion of the instruction is gated onto the memory address buss and the accumulator register is gated onto the memory data buss. In both cases we have two possible CPU registers each that are gated onto the two busses, memory address and memory data. All computers have two busses, one for memory address and one for memory data.

Memory – a lot of off-on switches in sets. Memory address – a particular sets of memory switches. Memory data – the off-on settings of an individual set of switches.

As used in computers, gates are no different in function than ordinary gates. With two corrals the cows will go in the corral with its gate open. Cows are the data. The field is the memory and the corrals are the CPU's registers. The buss is the path from field to barn.

In summary, knowing the basic computing cycle is a critical step along the road to total computer knowledge. Computers do nothing but flip switches. They operate in cycle orchestrated by a special switch called an oscillator. Oscillators switch from off to on and back to off.

Each step in the FIRE cycle is initiated by the oscillator switch via a device called a sequencer. Things happen in sequence meaning one after the other. The sequencer is, you guessed it a set of switches that are caused to go on and off by the oscillator switch. The sequencer is the equal of a symphony orchestra conductor. Different events, steps in the FIRE cycle happen as directed by the sequencer/director.

Chapter 5, all digital computers...

...are collections of switches grouped as follows:

Central Processing Unit
Oscillator
Sequencer
Registers, Flag Bits, Gates

Data-Buss Address-Buss M-Access-Controls

Memory

Above we have a schematic block diagram of ALL digital computers. All of the above pieces and parts are made out of nothing but switches with an oscillator switch being the only switch with any degree of complication. Busses are wires connecting the Central Processing Unit to the Memory. The data bus connecting CPU registers to memory has one wire per switch in memory words. The memory address buss has as many wires as required to address the last memory location. A gigabyte memory would have a lot of address buss wires, so many I'm declining to count them. The settings on the memory address buss wires points to one and only one memory word at a time and always points to one at all times. Access control switches control memory access. They consists of two switches, one that selects either read or write, and a do-it switch that is toggled one time from off to on and back to off to access a particular memory location, cause its switch setting to appear on the data buss. The memory address is put on the bus selecting a particular word of memory, the read-or-write switch is set and then the do-it switch is toggled, goes from off to on and back to off completing a memory access cycle. If the read-or-write line says read the contents of the memory will appear on the data bus. If it is write then the settings on the data bus are stored, will be remembered in/on/at the selected memory word.

All of the above is orchestrated by a sequencer that goes from step/state to step/state. The sequencer is controlled by the oscillator switch being turned off to on and back to off.

State/step 1, fetch the present instruction from memory.
Step/state 2, add 1 to the number in the instruction pointer
register thus pointing to the next instruction.
State/step 3.1, reconcile the address if an address is required
by the present instruction.
State/step 3.2, do the operation, execute the instruction.

It's that simple. That's all that's happening inside the
computer no matter the computer. It's all happening according
to instructions written in a document called a program that is in
memory. Programming is the art of writing instructions that are
stored in memory and executed by computer's CPU.

CPU's are now manufactured using integrated circuit
technology. Most if not all are single units, just one piece of
material. The name for single chip CPU's is microprocessors. If
it hasn't happened already sooner or later entire computers,
both CPU's and memory will be single pieces of material with
connections to attachments and power only. That's how animal
brains and bodies are made.

Single "chip" computers are now available. These chips
are called microcontrollers. They can be found at Amazon.com
even. Unfortunately their documentation is often so poor they're
not generally usable without a lot of unnecessary custom
training. When enough people demand it, offer to pay for it, it
will happen. There will be basic computers available to the
general public that are readily programmable by anyone. All
issues are economic. It's an untapped many billions of dollars
market. Billion air anyone?

Apple, Microsoft and all other billlon dollar corporations
that now control the world of computers were started in garages
by ordinary people. They had the advantage of readily available
parts and fabrication equipment that has now vanished from
even the hobby marketplace. Fabricating your own computer is
now a monumental task where it was once done with the
greatest of ease. I went from an idea to a working prototype in
less than a day more than once. I had all the equipment and
materials needed bought from a multitude of possible suppliers
at hobby shop prices.

You don't suppose there's a conspiracy among those
who now control the computer world to prevent new upstart
competitors? They have a patent by difficulty to compete. I

believe good old fashioned Yankee ingenuity will win out in the end with Microsoft and Apple being the most vulnerable. The first step is education. Desire is the prime mover. Desire without knowledge is desire unfulfilled. You too can be a billion air. All it takes is an easy to make computer anyone can program. Would you pay $50 for one so you could follow along here and do a little experimenting? A billion or more people on earth would jump at the chance.

With that being said, PC manufacturers in particular advertise their wares based upon the latest and greatest microprocessors used. You've probably noticed the microprocessor is the first thing on the list of features of a particular PC on sale at Walmart. CPU chips are also classified by how fast their basic oscillators switch from off to on and back to off.

Here's an example of a PC being sold at Amazon and other places as well; [Brand name] with Intel i5 3.2GHz Processor, 8GB Memory. This says the CPU chip in this particular PC is called i5 by its manufacturer, Intel Corp. i5 is a name and nothing more. Fred by any other name would still be the same person. Same is true for i5. The i5's clock-switch runs at 3.2 gigahertz. A gigahertz cycle is 1 divided by 1,000,000,000 seconds long in time. Another way of looking at it is the i5's CPU clock-switch goes from off to on and back to off 3,200,000,000 times every second.

The i5 has cores and cash memories. Cash memories are extremely fast memories on board the CPU chip. They are intended to speed up execution. It's been my experience they slow things down. Never the less cash memories are advertised as extremely desirable features of modern microprocessors. Arithmetic intensive programs are speeded up, maybe. The fact a CPU has high speed memory available can be ignored for the most part. You will have to pay extra to get it and it's the only game in town for the most part so break out the check book. Go deeper in debt?

Computer literacy requires getting clear in one's mind what's going on inside the computer. The computer has an oscillator commonly known as a clock. Clocks go tic toc. That's switching from one state or condition, on or off to another. There's that word switch again. Things that switch from one state to another must be switches. The computer's oscillator is a switch that is continuously toggled from off to on back to off and on at some speed. That speed is stated in hertz, one hertz being one off to on back to off cycle per second. Hertz and cycle are synonyms. The speed at which the computer executes instructions is at some factor of its clock speed.

It takes a minimum of three clock cycles to execute any instruction. Most instructions require more than three clock cycles. The slowest element also determines instruction execution speed. A computer with a slow memory may require a dozen or more clock cycles to read or write a single byte of memory.

Basically, the CPU instruction cycle begins with a cycle counter register at zero. The instruction cycle counter is a hidden counter in that it is rarely if ever available to the outside world. Every clock tic-toc the instruction cycle counter is incremented by one. Thus it counts from zero to some number. Each number represents a state of execution for the presently executing instruction. This is the CPU's sequencer.

There are three basic states of execution of any given instruction done in sequence:

State 1, fetch the present instruction from memory. The contents of the memory location pointed to, addressed by the contents of the instruction pointer register are read into, duplicated in the instruction register.

State 2, one is added to the contents of the instruction pointer register. At the end of this step the instruction pointer register points to the next memory location after the location of the present instruction.

State 3, the instruction is examined by the CPU. If it requires another word of memory to be complete states 1 and state 2 are repeated. This continues until a full instruction has been read into the instruction register, (64 bit CPU's with 8 bit memories must do steps 1 and 2 eight times to fetch a complete instruction). When a full instruction is in the instruction register the CPU executes it.

Instruction execution is itself a multi-state affair.
State 3.1, if the instruction requires a memory address the CPU resolves the address. A memory or a CPU register access is

required to resolve indirect addresses to simple addresses. Addressing modes will be covered in detail later.

State 3.2, do the actual instruction. Instructions alter the contents of memory and/or CPU registers. That's all instructions do. Instructions cause the contents of a memory location or/and the contents of a CPU register to change. Change – turning switches on and off. Think simple.

There are several ways to implement the basic cycle. A state counter that is cleared and incremented to go from state to state is one way. No matter how it's done all digital computers operate in this three/four step cycle. The cycle's controller is the CPU's clock. The clock is a switch that goes on and off. Everything happens in time thus this switch is called a clock. The clock-switch is the computer's drum beat.

Now we'll address the notion of a computer's INSTRUCTIONs. Instructions are like words in a language and they are verbs for the most part. The more words one knows the easier it is to say something. The more instructions one knows the easier it is to say something in computer language.

This brings us to a computer epiphany. Computers are brains that think the thoughts of people thus they are extensions of the human mind. As systems, computers with attachments turn human thoughts into actions. To operate a monkey wrench one needs to hold it in ones hands. When the monkey wrench is an attachment to the computer it is operated with ones thoughts. Instructions are thoughts thought by the programmer while programming that are thought over and over again by the CPU. Photos capture one's image to be looked at over and over again. Programs capture one's thoughts to be thought over and over again.

Now I'm going to ask you to do something that will either be extremely easy or impossible. You must give up, totally rid your mind of something you've heard your entire life. Repeat after me, "Computers do absolutely nothing." You don't believe that do you? All your life you've heard of all the marvelous things computers do. Computers drive cars for example. Odds are you've gotten this far in this book hoping to gain enough knowledge to train computers the way animal trainers train animals. Computers are machines. Machines do nothing.

Above all else machines may not be autonomous. They may not make decisions else they must be arrested.

All decision that seem to be made by computers are actually decisions being made by programmers. People do things using machines. Computers are machines. People use computers to do things. What is done using computers is always determined by people. People who decide what computers will be used to do are called analysts. The people who use computers to implement things analyzed are called programmers. Analysts and programmers are often one and the same person.

Programmers cause computers to "appear" to do things by writing programs that are stored in the computer's memory and executed one instruction/word at a time. You only think you see the computer doing something. It's not the computer doing that. It's a human being known as a programmer doing whatever it is using the computer to do it. The thoughts of the programmer are thought over and over again by the CPU. Thoughts thought by programmers can do whatever is possible given the attachments to the computer. 3D printers print thoughts. They turn thoughts into physical objects. This is the power of God.

You can correctly think of the programmer as being inside the computer looking out at you. It's not the person but the person's mind in the computer. Programming is literally giving the computer a piece of your mind.

If you are going to be a good programmer, create objects, write sensible letters to strangers in computer language, whatever, you must think in terms of mentally getting inside the computer. You can't physically get inside a computer but you can and must mentally get inside to program. When you write a letter it is you speaking to the reader not the paper. Computers are the equal of papers with the added ability to dynamically change what the reader will read next. Everything the reader reads must have been written beforehand by a writer known as a programmer.

Let's try that again, "Computers do absolutely nothing." I agree, computers surely put up the appearance of doing all sorts of things. It's not the computer doing that. It's a programmer using the computer to do that the same way a mechanic uses a wrench to turn a nut and musicians use violins to make music. Computers are used by people to do all sorts of things and never do things all by themselves else they are broken.

With the right attitude and education programming is as easy as writing letters. It's a matter of where one be relative to the task at hand. Those who learn their vocabulary and grammatical structure can operate a pen and write with the greatest of ease. Those who learn computer vocabulary and grammatical structure can write computer programs with the greatest of ease. Just what words are in computer vocabulary?

A little good news. Most computer vocabularies are fewer than 2 dozen words long. The PDP-8 computer's vocabulary is a measly 8 words long. I claim to have learned to program in seconds after reading the first page of an old fashioned, really describe the computer manual that was likely written by an ED, Doctor of Education and an English major. That manual was well written. It described a now extinct computer named Recomp manufactured by also now extinct North American Aviation best known for the P-51 Mustang fighter plane of World War 2. In terms of instruction set the Recomp is head and shoulders above anything on the market today. Computers have gotten less powerful and especially so with microprocessors replacing discrete processors.

One and all computer words are tiny little things called instructions and sometimes called commands. Instruction and command are synonyms in computer lingo. They instruct or if you please command the CPU, tell it what you want it to do. The very polite will neither command nor instruct but make requests instead. Keep in mind it's a set of switches you're talking to so be careful what you say. Switches are highly emotional with tender feelings that are easily hurt.

Just like words in any language a single computer word says very little while a small set can say it all. Very little can be done with a single request/instruction/command. You may encounter the word operation used as well as request, instruction and command.

Think of a computer program as a felt hat. Each instruction is but one hair in the hat. It takes a lot of hairs a felt hat to make. It takes a lot of instructions to do much of anything. Yes, it is possible for a single instruction to throw the switch that launches the missiles that destroys the world. Let us hope that instruction is never executed.

Step 1, FETCH the present instruction from memory. Step 2, INCREMENT, add one to the instruction pointer getting ready to fetch the next instruction but before we fetch the next instruction, step 3, EXECUTE, do what this instruction says. Then go to step 1 and do it again just as fast as possible because any single instruction does next to nothing.

It is critically important for you to get the basic computer cycle down pat. FIRE is a good way to remember it. FIRE – Fetch, Increment, Resolve and Execute.

Computer literacy is our goal here. Knowing the basic computer cycle is the first step to becoming computer literate. All that's left is learning how to "pull the trigger" and FIRE away at ignorance. Who knows, maybe you'll hit something you can take to the bank.

Chapter 6, a long time ago…

…vocalist Dean Martin sang, "Mem - o - ries are made of this" caucusing young girls to swoon and old girls to outright cry. At the time Dean recorded that song computer memories were made of cores. Core memories have now gone the way of the dinosaur becoming objects of curiosity at the museum. Today memories are made of MOS. Not just any MOS but CMOS. We've gone from memories made of this through memories made of cores to memories made of MOS and now we have memories made of CMOS yet functionally memories have not changed.

MOS – metal oxide on silicone. Metal oxides – rust. Silicone – glass. Computer memories – dabs of rust on glass.

Memories are one of the two computer parts. You should now have a good idea what memories are and how they fit into the scheme of things. We will now look at some of the memory types and take a look at a little computer history at the same time.

Functionally memories are the same. All memories are sets of switches no matter what they're made of. The human brain where memories are made of "this" store "this" in switches called neurons. Try as hard as one may there's no getting around memories being nothing more than a pile of switches, light switches being perhaps the most common switch there is.

But first we need to address an issue that's sure to leave you emotionally disturbed. It certainly disturbs me. Question, do we write in or do we write on memory? Do we read from or do we read out of memory? When stuff is fed to computers do computers eat it or do they smear that stuff in or on their memories? When you get fed stuff to remember do you write in or on paper? Get the idea yet? See the semantics problem? I find myself switching back and forth from in and on. Writing in computer memory and writing on paper are the same things, different writing instruments and media. Do we write in or on paper? Is stuff in or on the computer?

Now that you have a little more than a hint at what computers really are do you see the ignorance in the statement, "fed to a computer?" We're forever hearing some great scientists fed facts of one kind or the other to a computer for computer analysis. Computers being thinkers they must analyze stuff the way psychiatrists analyze fruitcakes. Scientist feeding facts to computers implies scientists have bowls full of facts with spoons in hand shoving spoonful's at a time into the computer's mouth. What's the point of this you ask? You cannot trust anything you've ever heard on television, over the radio or even from the Internet about computers. Sad but true, all too often the same applies to the computer science college.

You may have noticed I'm questioning what's being taught in computer science class. The whole world reeks of ignorance on the simplest machine ever conceived. It's just a bunch of switches. What sort of idiot would try to feed anything to a set of switches or expect a switch to do something or insist a switch made a mistake?

No matter what material computer memories are made of they are no more complicated functionally than light switches and therefore they can do no more than light switches. That alone tells us there's unrealized power in switches. We've only scratched the surface of doing all that can be done using computers. Notice it's us doing the doing not the computer. It's also obvious one never feeds anything to a single switch or piles of switches either one. Switches are always turned either on or off. So tell me how anyone can feed something into or onto switches.

Now we're going to learn something we already know but have been afraid to even think about. Memory is anything that remembers. One of the more common memories in use today is paper. If you're reading this from a paperback book you're looking at one of the most common memories there be. The paper you're looking at remembers what I wrote ON it. If you're reading using a Kindle or other e-book you're looking at switch settings, zeroes and ones, dots and dashes arranged in the shapes of letters of the alphabet on a display screen that I wrote IN it.

The earth itself is a memory. Cave men wrote on cave walls. Those cave walls are memories because they remember what cave men wrote on them. It's not uncommon to see someone using a stick to write on the ground. Memories are everywhere. We just haven't realized the true meaning of the word memory. Memory is any media used to remember information. Information – anything that informs.

Computer memories are just a bunch of switches with the clever name, bit. Bits are switches, switches are bits. Writing on computer memory is done by turning those bit-switches on and off just like turning light switches on and off. We're done. That's all there is to computer memory. Well, not exactly but all one needs to know to program, preset switches in banks of switches.

There's several kinds of memories people commonly use that are far from switches. Paper is likely the most popular memory. There's also things like chalk boards called blackboards and erasable ink boards called white boards. There's also writing devices, pens, pencils and even computers. An easy program to write is one that reads from the keyboard and writes to a printer. That's a lot clumsier to do than simply taking pen in hand and writing whatever it is directly on the paper.

Anything that has two possible states and is always in one or the other of those two states is a switch. Remember, switches of all kinds are always, must always be in one state or the other either off or on. Computer memory switches are no exception. Paper can have nothing written on it but there's no such thing as nothing in/on a computer's memory. There's always something. Switches are always either off or on from the time they are made until they fall apart.

It's my understanding the first digital computer used relays for memory bits. A relay is an electrically operable switch. I'm reasonably sure the computer used by British intelligence at Blexly Park to decipher German enigma coded messages during WW2 had a relay based CPU and a relay based memory as well. I could be wrong. I'm basing that on a friend of mine who as a hobby recreated what he claimed to be the enigma decoding computer. He made a small memory using relays. The clock was purposely made to run so slowly we could see individual steps in the basic cycle as the instruction pointer was gated onto the memory address lines, the memory responding and the relay settings of the memory location indicated copied into the instruction register. All are nothing more than sets of relays. The relay was the most common electrically operable switch available at the time. Notice they're switches and not some variety of mysterious life form, royal jelly or any other mysterious exotic thing.

There's a short list of memory types in use today you've probably heard about with ROM, RAM and DRAM being perhaps the most common. What do we already know about all three? But of course they're nothing more than a bunch of switches. They're just made out of different "stuff" and they're electrically operable.

ROM is an acronym meaning, Read Only Memory. Right away you should have a problem. What possibly could a read only memory have written on it if it is truly read only? The answer is itself erroneous. The answer is, nothing can be written on or in a read only memory. You didn't forget there's no such thing as computer memory containing nothing. All computer memories have something at all times. If a memory is read only no room is left for it to have anything "meaningful" written on it. Right away we know there's a problem. Thankfully it's a naming things problem and not a real one.

Let's try WOM instead of ROM. WOM, write once memory. We can expand that to WORM, Write Once Read as often as we like Memory. Thus the notion of a book WORM. Books are written once and read over and over again by book worms. ROMs are written once and read over and over again by computer CPU's.

We don't want to speak badly of the dead. The individual who coined ROM is probably dead by now. Most likely it was decided by committee. It dates the 1960's or even earlier. I'd be surprised if someone hadn't suggested WORM instead of ROM at the time but was overruled. A rose by any other name…

ROMs are memories that are written but one time, manufacturing time. The final step in the manufacturing process can be and is most likely done outside the actual chip foundry. One time programming is done by "blowing fuses" inside the chip. All the bits in the memory are manufactured either on or off. By selectively applying a high current individual bits are permanently turned to the other state. In the end ROMs are programed meaning fed data once only. No! They're not fed. Their switches are either turned on or turned off.

To appreciate the value of ROMs let's briefly revisit the raw computer. It consists of a CPU and memory. When the computer is turned on it immediately starts executing the program in memory beginning at memory location zero. If all the memory is both write and read type its contents at power on time are unknown and often referred to as garbage. Thus the first memory locations are made of ROM chip(s) containing a program named the bootstrap loader and perhaps other programs as well. ROM's have had complete operating systems written "once" in them. Bootstrap is a term that comes from a mythical person who could levitate, lift himself into the air by pulling on his bootstraps. The bootstrap loader loads the first program to be run into the computer's memory from some device such as a hard drive and then turns control over to that program. From that time forward it's like monkeys in a barrel with every program giving way to the next based upon operator commands. Operator, that's you via an input device such as a keyboard or mouse.

ROMs are write once memories, sets of switches that are used to store fixed information. An often application of ROM memories are tables of data such as trigonometric and logarithmic tables as well as dictionaries. Technically DVDs are ROMs. Thus we know DVD's have pictures and words written on them in the form of switch settings.

It doesn't have to be a mechanical switch to be a switch. Any device that has two states, can be changed as least one time from one state to the other and must always be in one or the other of two possible states is a switch. Switches inside computer memories are electrically operable at least one time. ROMs, Read Only Memories are written once and usually at the time of manufacture.

We're suddenly using two words, read and write while discussing sets of switches called memories. Reading is making a copy of memory switch settings while writing is duplicating a set of switch settings in/on memory. It's the same thing we do when reading and writing using paper. Read – see what's written on the paper. Write – copy thoughts in one's mind onto paper. Thoughts – neuron switch settings.

ROMs come in several flavors with different names. EPROM, EEPROM and Flash Memory are three common ones. All have to do with the initial settings of their switches. EPROMS are erasable, can be set back to the initial unwritten state using ultraviolet light. They are very useful for program development. The program is "chiseled" into the EPROM. Then the EPROM, a chip in computer lingo is physically installed in the computer. If it is necessary to change its contents then it can be erased by taking it out of the computer and putting in under an ultraviolet light. After a few minutes its switches will be restored to the ready to be programmed state.

EEPROMs are identical to EPROMs except they are electrically erased rather than needing ultraviolet light. That makes it possible to "field" alter information in EEPROMs. Being electrically erasable also eliminates the need to either remove them from the machine or use special equipment to program them. EPROMs require ultraviolet lights and special equipment to program. EPROMs must also be removed from the computer where EEPROMs can be reprogram in place. EEPROMS are field reprogrammable meaning can be changed, erased and written to without taking them out of the computer and using special equipment.

There's still another variety of field programmable ROM called Flash memory. Flash memory is like ordinary read/write memory. It can be written to as though it was read/write type memory. Its limitations are two. First it usually takes a little longer to write Flash memory thus the program doing the writing must delay after every write to flash memory instruction. Secondly, Flash memories have a limit on how many times they can be rewritten before they permanently malfunction. It's usually a large number but still small enough that care must be taken using Flash memory for high volume data. You'll be amazed at how fast writing a million times to memory can be done with a CPU executing 50,000,000 instructions per second. At a gigahertz rate it only takes .001 seconds for a million operations. Rewriting Flash memories at that speed would make them like old fashioned flash bulbs, one flash followed by a pop and dead.

The other kind of memory is known as RAM. RAM is an acronym most likely decided by committee that means Read And write Memory. Again we have a problem. It should be write and then read memory. We cannot read something that has yet to be written. With people it's learn to read first and then write. With computers it's write first and then read. Why the difference? Computer memories begin, are powered on with unknown writing in/on them. Read first and read garbage. Again we have a naming problem that can confuse the beginner. Try to not be confused. After all is said and done it's just a bunch of switches.

RAMs come in two types, DRAMs and SRAMs. Putting a D or an S in front of RAM is done to indicate the variety of technology used to make its switches. DRAM is "dynamic" while the SRAM is "static." Dynamic – a flurry of motion. Static – lazy, listless.

You may think of yourself as a dynamic person full of energy up at the crack of dawn, a rolling ball of fire. Or maybe you're static, low energy like me. I have an excuse. I'm 82 years old. In this upside down world of computer names dynamic rams are grossly inferior to static rams. Both can be written and rewritten an unlimited number of times. Dynamic rams are generally slower than static ones in most instances but have another handicap. DRAMS must be refreshed. New word - refreshed.

Do you know what a capacitor is? Capacitors store electricity. Anything that traps electrons is a capacitor. In junior high you at least saw the jar with strips of aluminum inside it that stood out making an upside down Y shape when the nail head on top of the jar was touched by a charged object. A comb run through ones hair will become charged and hold that charge for a while thus combs are capacitors.

Tiny little capacitors are used to make the switch parts of dynamic rams. Switches in dynamic rams are capacitors that are either charged or not charged. Charged means having electrons trapped on them. In switching terminology not charged is switch off while charged is switch on. We're still talking switches. So what's dynamic about DRAM's?

Capacitors will lose their charge relatively fast. Electrons captured on/in capacitors "leak" off/out into the environment rather quickly. Memories made of capacitors will forget what they know if they aren't reminded frequently. You could safely say DRAMs are born with Alzheimer's. Reminding a DRAM what you want it to remember is necessary else it forgets.

Reminding DRAM's what one wants them to remember is called refreshing as in refreshing ones memory. Lawyers often help witnesses who conveniently forget refresh their memories. Take President Trump and his forgetful about Russia and WikiLeaks family and appointees for easy to understand example of can't recall. Those tiny little capacitors/computer-neurons lose their charge rather quickly and must be recharged to max charge before they forget they were charged. If there's still enough charge left at recharge time to recognize it was charged then it's recharged.

Refreshing requires both circuitry and time. Thus DRAMS are usually the slowest links in computing. The computer can run no faster than its memory. Memory is accessed/read every cycle. Remember - fetch, increment, resolve address, execute and do it over and over again. Fetching is reading the contents of a memory location. Every capacitor of a DRAM must be refreshed as many as a thousand times a second else it forgets and the computer appears to go crazy for a moment and hopefully it will stop altogether before a lot of damage has been done.

SRAM switches are latched either off or on and stay that way until changed by the program or power is turned off. New word, latched. Latched means what it says, held in one positions. A latched closed door stays closed. SRAM have latched switches that can be written and read as often as desired. Once set or reset, on or off they stay that way until changed by the program or power is turned off.

Latches are electrical devices with two states. They stay in the state they are in at any moment until changed by the program or power is removed. Ordinary light switches are latches. They are held either off or on by a spring inside them. Latched means locked in place.

One last memory type. From the golden days of yesteryear comes the thundering hoof beats of core memories. The very first memories were made using latching relays. Relays used to make single bits of memory no matter how small occupy more space than a many gigabyte RAM occupies today. Thus primitive computers occupied a lot of space. A single relay might use more electrical power to be set and reset and remain latched than an entire multi gigabyte CMOS memory computer. In spite of the difficulty of making any size relay memory primitive computers were constructed and programmed to do extremely sophisticated tasks. Messages sent using the enigma code believed to be unbreakable were decoded by British Intelligence with a blink of the eye using a relay memory and a relay register computer while the Germans themselves painstakingly entered each coded letter one at a time into a machine and hand recorded its translation. The computer was instrumental in the defeat of Nazism. It's my understanding the Browning light machine gun, the Browning automatic rifle and me trusty M1-gun-bullet-launcher helped out a little in defeating the Nazis.

The first truly dramatic breakthrough in computer memories came with the invention of core memory. Core is a foreign word that translates into English as donut. I believe core means heart in French. Computer cores are tiny donuts made of iron alloy. Computer core memories are sets of cores knitted together by women working in places that soon became known as core houses. All kidding aside core memories were sewn together using needles and thread-size copper wires.

It taxes my literary capabilities to describe core memories. I'll try. Individual cores are one-switch memories. A core is either magnetized or not magnetized that translates into off or on. Notice we always have one of two possibilities and must have one or the other at all times. So the fundamental element of the core memory is an iron alloy metal object in the shape of a donut that is either magnetized or not magnetized.

Cores were arranged in highly elongated matrices. The width of the memory usually had the same number of cores/switches as a given computer's words were wide for one dimension, (in case you forgot a word is the width in number of switches of the CPU's registers and memory locations). The other dimension is the number of words in the total memory. Back then memories were usually the same width in bits as the CPU's registers that are always one word wide, i.e. 8 bit machines had 8 core wide memory banks, 12 bit machines 12 core wide memories, etc. The other dimension of the matrix was the length of the memory in words. 4096 or 2 to the 12th power was the usual length of the matrix although they may well have been constructed using 4, 1024 word long patches laid end to end or even 16, 256 word long strings. I'm not sure but 256 words may have been the more or less standard "patch" of core knitting's.

One wire per column was strung the length of the memory with one loop through the center of every core in that column. This wire was called the sensor or detector wire. It detected the state of magnetization of cores in its column. The first step in constructing a core is the stringing of each column with a single wire looped one time through each core and around its outside. This is a painstakingly tedious process that had to be done by hand. Many tried with all failing to automate it. The end product is a necklace-like string of cores usually 1024 cores or factor of, 256 or a multiple of 1024 long.

Next a second wire was strung straight through the centers of each core creating a sting of cores like a string of beads with two wires, one straight through the center and the other wound once through the center and around the outside of every core. The sensor wire was looped one time around each core in the string and the other was simply strung through the center of each core. The end product was a string of cores with as many cores as the target memory was bits/switches long.

Next, as many strings of cores as the computer's memory words were bits wide were laid side by side. 8 bit machines had 8 strings of cores, 12, 12 strings and so on. Wires were then run crosswise straight through the centers of the cores one wire per row of cores, a row of cores being one memory word. Thus there were as many cross wires as there were words in the memory.

A core memory looked like a narrow belt when laid out on a table. It was a small number of cores wide and many times that number long, i.e. 8, 12 or 16 wide and 4096 long.

Every core had three wires associated with it. First was a sensor wire looped one time through its center and around its outside. Two other wires passed through its center one vertically and the other horizontally in a plus sign configuration.

Those little cores could be either magnetized or not magnetized. Magnetized was usually read as switch-on while not magnetized was usually switch-off but that was arbitrary and surely varied from one make of computer to another.

Writing on a core memory amounted to supplying enough current to magnetize cores. Notice that each column has an individual wire and every row also has an individual wire. Those two wires were used to select individual cores within the matrix of cores.

Writing was done one bit/core at a time. First the core was demagnetized by passing an alternating current through its center in both straight through wires. If the desired setting was off then demagnetizing was all that was done. If the desired setting was magnetized then half enough current was passed through each of the two straight through wires through the center of the core to magnetize it. By only half enough current to magnetize passing through each of the two wires only the single core selected by its two wires was magnetized with all others only getting half enough current to magnetize them.

To read a bit half enough current each to magnetize the selected core was passed through each of the two wires. If the core was magnetized already there will be no signal on the sensor wire. If the core was not magnetized it will be magnetized causing a pulse, short lived voltage to appear on the sensor wire. This is the destructive reading of a memory.

In the reading process non magnetized cores were magnetized thus at the end of reading all cores read were magnetized. In order to maintain the original settings cores read had to be rewritten. Reading was immediately followed by writing back the original settings thus it took twice as long to read as to write.

Destructive reading means the contents of the memory location are destroyed when read. At the end of the read portion of the memory access cycle all cores of the selected word will be magnetized. Thus it is necessary to rewrite the original contents. Writing is done by demagnetizing the cores that were demagnetized before being magnetized during the reading process. Demagnetizing was done by passing only half enough alternating current through the two wires passing through the centers of the selected cores.

Core memories were a breakthrough that was readily accepted. They had the problems of being labor intensive and therefore expensive to manufacture, used a lot of electricity and they were relatively slow but lightning fast compared to relays.

Compared to all other memory technology at the time, relays etc. core memories were a dramatic breakthrough. And they had another highly desirable feature.

Core memories never forget even when the lights go out. Magnets stay magnetized. MOS memories forget the instant power is off. That made the giving up of core memories in favor of MOS painful to the extreme for many. Computers with core memories were not susceptible to power outages that are sure to happen at the most inopportune times. MOS memory has won the argument big time with battery operation and battery backup solving the flaky wall power problem.

I hope I managed to describe core memory well enough you at least have a feel for how it works and can appreciate how dramatic a breakthrough it truly was at the time. I'm not aware of a single core memory based computer still running. There surely is one somewhere in a museum if nowhere else. Forgetting the history of core memories is like forgetting about the minute men who fought and won the battle of Bunker Hill. Without core memory to bring computing to its feet we'd still be adding up the ticket on our fingers.

Chapter 7, most people think…

...peripheral devices are computers. Once upon a time in the movies computers were depicted as banks of blinking lights and spinning tapes on large-reel tape recorders. That gave way to television screens with keyboards. Now Hershey chocolate bar size boxes with flat LCD touch screens are thought to be computers. Of course none of these are computers. We can have any and all of that with no computer at all.

Let's take a moment and consolidate the position. We've had more than a glimpse at the CPU, central processing unit and memory. It's only human to wonder when we'll be getting to the parts of computers you're familiar with. I wouldn't be surprised to find out you've been wondering where the LCD display and the keyboard and all the other obvious parts of computers as you think them to be are going to be covered. In simple terms when are we going to cover the confusion factors? Confusion factors because they confuse the ignorant.

LCD displays, touch screens and the like are NOT parts of computers. Computers have but two parts, central processing units and memories. Make a note of that. Blinking lights and spinning tapes were Hollywood's version of computers in years past. Couldn't be farther from the truth if they'd used animated talking squirrels and called them computers. If this was 1970 you'd be asking where's the spinning tapes and blinking lights? Repeat after me, "Computers have but two parts, central processing units and memories." Why make it hard on yourself? It's only 2 things to remember, CPU and memory. Above all else don't forget all we're talking about is switches. Blinking lights, spinning tapes, LCD displays, touch screens, you name it have no more to do with computing than your toes have to do with the operation of your brain. They got this much straight, computers are electronic brains. Let's drop the electronic part.

Computers have been made using pneumatics. Slide rules are analog computers. Abacuses' are probably the first digital computers. Fingers are used to compute. Electronic brains are but one variety within a family of artificial brains called computer.

Let's separate in our minds **computers** and **computer systems**. Your brain is a computer while your whole body with brain is a computer system. All the things your body dose are controlled by your brain. Everything a computer system does is controlled by the computer. The computer be it a human brain or a device bought at the store is controlled by a human being. Thus everything a computer does is actually done by a person. Did I mention "Computers do nothing?" Did you believe me? Still don't believe me then burn this book and go turn yourself in. I don't know where but surely there's a place for people that thick headed walking around in a daze mumbling words like cyber to themselves.

OK, so you're not ready to give up your prejudice but you'll hang around anyhow. Maybe this will ease your troubled mind a little. Computer systems have an unlimited set of PERIPHERAL devices suitable for every task the human mind can conceive of and embody. You got to first think it and then you must embody it. Maybe you'll invent the computerized scoop shovel or computerized can opener. You can't invent anything computerized unless you know what a computer is.

New word, PERIPHERAL. Peripheral means on the periphery, at the edge of. LCD displays are peripheral devices. They are not a part of the computer but they are a part of the computer system should the computer system have one. Computer, brain. Computer system, whole body brain included. If the LCD display was a part of the computer itself then not having it or taking it away would eliminate the computer. If your finger was a part of your brain then cutting your finger off would cut your brain off as well. Good fences make good neighbors. Put a fence between computer and computer system.

Bottom line, we must separate the computer from all the things we see connected to computers. Things connected to computers are peripheral to the computer itself and not an integral part of the computer. Peripherals are integral parts of computer systems. The things you've been calling computers are actually computer systems including the most misidentified thing since dolphins were thought to be mermaids, I-phones. I-phones are computer system with a telephone peripheral and a troop of Russians spies inside them hunting for Hillary Clinton's missing emails.

Time out. Think about it. Can you see your own brain? Of course not. You know it's there inside your head but you cannot see it or above all see it work. The same is true for computer systems. We're limited to knowing there is a computer and at best we can only see the container holding it. Computers are effectively invisible the same way the human brain is invisible.

Now you should know the computer is an extension of your own brain and the computer system is an extension of your whole body your brain included. What YOU and not IT can do with computer systems is limited only by your imagination and abilities. That includes inventing new computer peripherals.

The computer, the brain part of the computer system has but two parts, a CPU and a memory. The CPU controls all that happens within the computer system via programs in memory created by human beings. Thus human beings control everything that happens in computer systems.

By now you should know we're talking about switches. Programming is setting switches in the computer's memory. Doing whatever is "written" in those switches is done by other switches inside the CPU, central processing unit. What can be done by flipping switches has no limit. What you can do is limited by your ability to turn switches on and off.

Computers, computer systems are no different than monkey wrenches. Monkey wrenches don't do things. People do things using monkey wrenches. What would you think if someone told you his monkey wrench made a mistake and removed the wrong nut? To err is human and only human. Monkey wrenches, automobiles, you name it and especially computers never make mistakes. People are forever doing the wrong thing using many tools and blaming the tools for their shortcomings. When a baseball player makes a fielding error he always looks at his glove as if it was to blame. Computers are tools. People making mistakes using computers blame the computer. "The computer made a mistake" is the same as saying, "I made a mistake" with the added ability to fool the computer ignorant.

You should already know something about HOW the CPU controls attachments to the computer called peripherals. But of course it does it by setting and resetting switches, turning switches on and off. There's nothing going on in a computer or computer system other than switching, turning switches on and off. That's all. To know how switches work is to know all there is to know about how computers work and how peripheral devices are controlled by the computer programmer.

The wheel may well be the most important invention of mankind but the switch is the most powerful. All computing power is in the orderly operation of switches done by an author called programmer. Programs are written. Writing requires knowing how to write. That includes vocabulary, grammatical structure and, critically important having something to say.

In the vocabulary of the computer there are words categorized as input/output instructions. The traditional shorthand way of saying input/output is IO. Peripherals are usually referred to as IO devices. Often those devices are categorized as input only, output only or both input and output types. A keyboard is an IO input only device. One never writes to or outputs to a keyboard. Printers are IO output only devices. One never reads from or inputs from a printer. Touch screen devices, LCD displays that respond when touched are bidirectional, both input and output devices. Keys are read based upon where touch screen displays are touched just like keys are read when keys are struck on a computer system's keyboard. What one sees on a touch screen has been output from the computer.

One need not be real bright to notice a computer with no IO devices at all is the equal of a brain in a jar. Brains in a jars and computers with no IO devices can think as hard as they please but we have on way of knowing what they are thinking. No cheating! Having a voice come out of the jar with a brain in it and nothing more cannot happen. To make sound there must be a sound making device attached to the brain. Any attachment of any kind and it's not just a brain in a jar it's an animal in a jar. The same is true with computers that are often and correctly referred to as electronic brains.

CPU's MUST have IO instructions else it's impossible to input data or output any information. It's not necessary to have independent IO instructions. There are CPUs that access IO devices through ordinary memory locations/addresses. The Motorola 68000 series microprocessors does it through regular memory addresses. In the main computer's memory addresses are set aside by and at the pleasure of the computer system designer for accessing IO devices. Those CPU's don't have separate IO instructions.

Computers that use regular memory locations for IO addresses don't need separate IO instructions. This tells us that IO instructions are identical in function to some of the other instructions. L, load and ST, store instructions are usually all that's necessary to access IO devices that share addresses with memory. IN and OUT are the equals of L and ST in systems with separate memory and IO addresses.

There's a subtle bit of information here. Whether or not a peripheral device shares its address with memory it's still a memory. When we write to a printer for example the printer "remembers" what we wrote by printing it on paper for us thus it's a memory and a familiar type as well. When we input from a keyboard or any other device the data is nothing but switch settings in memories on the device's interface.

Interface – hardware that connects the particular IO device and the CPU. CPU's with separate IO addresses must have a second set of address and data busses. They are identical to and are accessed identically the same way as memory address and data busses. IO FIRE – Fetch the IO instruction from computer memory, Increment the instruction pointer, resolve the peripheral address, and execute the IO instruction by reading from or writing to a register on the IO device's interface.

The hardware used to connect peripherals to computers is called interface hardware. Using regular memory addresses alone tells us peripherals are special cases of memory. ALL peripherals have interfaces with on-board registers that are written to or read from by the CPU when executing IO instructions whether or not the addresses of the IO devices share main memory addresses or are on separate busses that are identical in function and operation to regular memory busses.

Absolutely all computer peripherals have switches that can be read from and written to using ordinary load and store type instructions. This is how peripherals are controlled by the programmer. IN, input "loads" duplicates switch setting(s) of a memory on the addressed device into a CPU register. OUT, output "stores" duplicates switch settings in a CPU register in memory on the device being addressed. The memory on the device can be and often is a single switch. It only takes one switch-on to launch the missile that destroys the world.

IO instructions like all types of instructions consists of a code that's usually the first few bits of the instruction identifying it to the CPU as an IO instruction, next bit(s) identify a register that contains the output data for output or receives the data input. The last bits are the address of the device itself. Data, switch settings are input to and output from CPU registers the same way data in memory is loaded into and stored from CPU registers.

IO instruction – IO code, register, device address.

You didn't forget the basic computer FIRE cycle, Fetch, Increment the IP, Resolve the address and Execute the instruction? IO instructions are no different than all other instructions. The CPU fetches the instruction, adds 1 to the instruction pointer register, resolves the address and executes the instruction by doing what it says. In the case of IO that's either input from or output to the IO device addressed by the address portion of the instruction. Inputting and outputting are the same as loading and storing that is the duplication of switch settings.

All instructions are sets of switches. Here's a typical instructions layout for a 32 bit machine:

iiii mmmm rrrr aaa aaa aaa aaa aaa

I broke the 32 bits up into sets of 4 to make it easier to read and count bits/switches. The first 4 bits, iiii indicate one of 16 possible instructions or words from the computer's vocabulary. A computer with a 4 bit instruction code has but 16 words to remember to know all of its vocabulary. The average person can memorize a vocabulary that short in about 10 seconds.

The next 4 bits, mmmm modifies the base instruction. Remember, we have different addressing modes that require address resolution. We also have both add and add with carry instruction. The iiii bits select the major category and the mmmm bits particularize it. That's what adverbs do, particularize verbs? Speak loudly. Add with-carry. Loudly and with-carry particularize speak and add.

The next 4 bits, rrrr select a register for storing to the particular IO device or loading from, receiving data from the particular IO device. Load and store means make duplicates of switch setting. Being 4 bits wide rrrr implies the CPU has a bank of 16 registers which is about the minimum for CPU's in use at this time, 2017. The rrrr switches selects one of 16 possible registers.

The rest of the instruction, aaaa's is the address of the particular IO device. The address of a given IO device is determined at manufacturing time. The CPU has a set of IO addresses corresponding to positions that are the equal of memory locations on an IO interface.

A typical input from keyboard program:

```
Wait    IN,3  7            read the keyboard control switch
        NI,3  1            test the control switch for on
        JZ    Wait         jump if off, go back and try again
        IN,3  8            read the key
```

Some from of the above works on all computers. IN says input. The ,3 says use register 3 implying there are several registers in the particular CPU. NI,3 says AND the contents of register 3 with the address part of the instruction which is the number 1.

AND 1 AND 0 → 0
    0 AND 1 → 0
    1 AND 1 → 1

The least significant bit of register 3 gets the key-ready switch when IN,3 is executed. If the switch is on, 1 then a key is ready to be input. If it is off, 0 no key has been hit. The NI,3 instruction AND's the switch with the number 1. If the switch is on then the Zero flag will be 1, 1 AND 1 is 1. 1 is not 0. If the switch is off the, 0 AND 1 is zero and the Zero flag is set, 1. JZ says test the Zero flag and if it is zero jump. If not zero then continue with next instruction. Jumping causes the program to stop execution and continue execution at the address in the address portion of the instruction.

The above is the most primitive method for inputting from a keyboard or other device. As written the computer would set in a tight loop waiting for a key to be hit. There is another way of inputting called interrupt driven. Interrupts allow the program to do other things while waiting for a key to be hit.

An interrupt is exactly what the word implies. You're doing something and you get interrupted. If the pilot is relaxing with the plane at cruising altitude and in autopilot interrupting him is innocent. If the plane is landing and the pilot is interrupted there's a chance the plane will crash. Interrupts come at random times based upon external stimulus, i.e. the operator hits a key on the keyboard for example.

When an interrupt happens any process in progress is stopped and control is turned over to the interrupter. Thus all processes must be interruptible without causing a problem. This is an area where caution is advised. Many a poor boy has hung himself on the interrupt cross creating bugs that he never manages to rid himself of.

In the interrupt driven system instead of the keyboard routine being called by the user program it is called via an interrupt when a key is ready to be read. Here's what happens:

Some program is running, a key is hit on the keyboard, an interrupt is executed, (Executed – killed, put to death) and the keyboard input routine is activated. Instead of the computer taking the next instruction from the location pointed to by the contents of the instruction pointer register the contents of the instruction pointer register is saved, (stored somewhere to be retrieved later) and it is then set to the first location of the keyboard input routine. This "turns on" the keyboard input routine that now knows a key is ready to be read, reads it, stores it in a buffer, (buffer - set of consecutive memory locations) does some housekeeping like adding 1 to the number-of-keys in buffer counter and a pointer to the next etc. Then it "returns" to the location where the running program was at the time of the interrupt.

Why are we talking about interrupts? They are employed by just about all so-called operating systems. I'm not aware of one in use today that isn't interrupt driven. I want you to know there's another way of doing the same thing. I've only written a couple dozen multitasking systems controller programs myself. None of them ever failed. In my world Windows is an April fool's day prank not serious computer software.

You'll quickly discover writing your own system for either Windows or Apple based computers is right next door to impossible. That's an implied patent, a patent by difficulty to replace. PC's are no more programmable by the average person than the dishwashing machine under the counter in the kitchen that too is a computer system with an electronic brain. Bet you didn't know it takes brains to wash dirty dishes. Since all is done by the programmer computer scientist students are being trained to wash dishes.

We're talking about methods for "feeding" stuff into the computer and catching computer excrement's from the computer usually referred to as input/output shortened to IO. We've taken a glimpse at inputting/outputting two ways, directly one byte at a time and interrupt driven one byte at a time. Now we'll take a glance at the DMA, the Direct Memory Access method that employs one or both of the above.

Direct Memory Access or DMA as its commonly known does what the nomenclature implies. Inputs and outputs go directly from DMA operated devices to memory and from memory to the DMA operated devices. DMA devices are not read/written one byte at a time via program control but rather they time-share the memory with the CPU with blocks of data being read and written in parallel with running programs. The programmer sets up the DMA by outputting a memory address for the first byte and relative to the particular device and control data. If the device is both input and output such as a hard drive then the setup program specifies which by setting a read/write flag bit in the DMA controller. Once the DMA controller is set up and given a final "do-it" signal amounting to turning still another bit/switch on the operation proceeds with no further instructing.

Hard drives are memories, collections of switches arranged in units of measure called sectors. Sector – a string of bits/switches of a given length. A particular hard drive has a specific number of sectors with each sector being a specific number of bits/switches long. Reading and writing the hard drive involves reading and writing entire sectors. Sectors 4096 bits long are fairly common. 4096 bits is 512, 8bit bytes. Sectors are usually specified in bytes rather than bits. Hard drives are most always on DMA channels. A DMA channel is the equal of another CPU sharing the same memory as the main CPU. Modern hard drives often have on-board processors and memories.

Of course CPUs have registers. DMA channels have registers that must be set prior to initiating a DMA input or output. It's rather obvious a particular sector must be selected. Sectors are numbered from zero to the last one possible. Those registers have IO addresses just like programmed controlled IO devices that are assigned at the time the computer system is manufactured. A register containing the particular sector that will be read or written must be set with an output instruction. If the device allows for multiple sector operations then the number of sectors will be in a register on the device's DAM controller. An output instruction is used to set it to the desired number of sectors. Read and write devices will have a direction bit/flag that must be set. An output instruction is required to set it.

Once the starting sector register, the number of sectors register and the direction, (input or output) flag is set we're half way there. The DMA must be given the memory address to store input data if inputting or find data to output when outputting. That's still another register that is set by an output instruction. The last step is an output instruction to turn the DMA on starting the operation.

Let's recap setting up a DMA operation of the hard drive. 1 set the starting sector address. 2 set the number of sectors. 3 set the direction flag bit for read or write. 4 set the starting address for the location of data in the computer's memory. 5. Output the do-it command.

The DMA controller will now either read from the data/switch settings or write to the number of sectors worth of data/switches into or out of the memory locations specified, first byte going into or coming from the first location the second byte to or from the second and so on until all the sectors specified are read or written. If it is a read operation the contents of the hard drive is duplicated in the memory. If it is a write operation then the contents of the memory are duplicated on the hard drive. It almost goes without saying the first piece of official literature you pick up on DMA will insist data is moved to and from the hard drive. You're going to be a good student of mine and thumb your nose at the author of that fable aren't you else

I'm giving you a failing grade, D for dumb. Remember, bowels move data is duplicated.

The DMA "steals" CPU cycles to read and store data directly into and read data directly out of memory. If the IO device is fast enough the DMA could stop the CPU altogether blitzing the operation. Stick memories used as hard drives could be, should be lightning fast.

IO devices "blitzing" DMA operations are a source of system's crashes. If the system uses DRAM memory that needs refreshing halting the CPU can halt refreshing. Ordinarily the DMA is fast enough the DRAM stays refreshed. One little hard drive read fail and automatic retry can crash the system by keeping the CPU turned off too long.

We're almost done, finished with DMA. At the end of the DMA operation there can be an interrupt. As part of the setup some if not all DMA controllers now in use, have a possible interrupt to signal the end of the operation. I say possible because it must be enabled as part of the setup operation. All DMA controllers have a "finished" bit/flag at a regular IO address. An interrupt can be used but is not necessary.

A last method of peripheral access is shared memory. Display screens have memory identical to computer memory. Again we're talking about off/on switching. The picture on the screen is determined by the contents of the display's memory. Displays are sized in pixels with a pixel being itself a set of switches. Pixels correspond to dots on the screen. Displays usually have one bit or one byte of memory for every dot. A 256 by 256 display has 65,536 pixels and 65,536 bits or bytes of memory with one for each pixel. The picture is determined by the contents of the display's memory. Putting and changing pictures on the display is as simple as using the ST, store instruction to change all or part of the display's memory that is part of the computer's memory.

The display's memory is a part of the main memory and accessed with ordinary instructions. The display reads the contents of memory to create the picture on its screen. To change the picture simply change the display's memory using ordinary instructions.

Those interested in making motion pictures, cartoons or editing video camera footage will find it a simple process once they become computer literate, learn how to read and write in computer language. Changing the picture is as simple as changing the display's memory using easy to understand instructions. Realization it's a matter of changing switch settings to create a new picture is the first step.

ALL IO input devices are read-from them while ALL IO output devices are controlled by writing-to them. Reading is looking at switch settings and duplication them in CPU registers while writing is duplicating CPU register switch settings in IO controller registers. It's always duplicating meaning make identical copies of.

Chapter 8, computer vocabularies…

…are made of words just like people vocabularies. The nicest part about computers vocabularies versus those of humans is their simplicity. Not only are they small in number of words but those words have straight forward meanings. Oops, forgot about the universal, "do what I mean" MOV instruction deemed to be the standard by an official committee for duplicating data. Oh well, I can't remember everything.

I hope by now you've given up your prejudice and accepted the fact that computers are nothing more than sets of switches. Absolutely nothing is going on other than turning switches on and off. Now we'll address computer programming, turning switches on and off in an orderly fashion to accomplish goals.

You guessed it. Computer programs are nothing more than lists of switch settings done in groupings called words and also called instructions. Requests, commands and operations are other ways of saying instructions. Words and instructions as well as commands mean the same thing. A computer word is a set of switches the width of the CPU's instruction register. In 16 bit machines those words are 16 switches wide. The number of bits/switches needed to make computer words varies from one make and model of central processing unit to another. CPU's have special memories called registers. An 8 bit CPU has 8 bit wide words that are also called bytes. 16 bit CPU's have 16 bit wide words. 32 bit CPU's have 32 bit wide words and on and on to any number of switches side by side.

New word, clock. We know what clocks are. They keep time and they time events as well. Another way of looking at computer clocks is timing in music done by a continuous drum beat. CPU's do things to the beat of their clock-drums.

Computers operate in "FIRE" cycles. FIRE – Fetch the next instruction, Increment the IP, Resolve the address, and Execute the instruction. Firing is orchestrated by a clock, the CPU's clock. Clocks go tic toc. Tic is switch on. Toc is switch off. CPU clocks are switches that are continuously turned on and off. With each clock cycle all or part of the next FIRE step is done until the presently executing instruction is finished. Then the next FIRE cycle begins.

Instructions are written using CPU wide words that are sentences for all practical purposes. What do instructions do? But of course, instructions instruct. In the case of computer instructions, instructions are words, sets of switches that cause switches settings in memory and registers to change, to be turned on and off. We seldom need to think about individual switches with whole words being the usual case.

"Load Register with the contents of memory at address" is a frequently used instruction. The instruction itself is a word that resides in memory. It has three parts, the operation code for load register, the number of the register to be loaded if the CPU has more than one register and the memory address of the switch settings to be loaded into the specified register. Load – make an identical copy of. At the end of a load instruction the switch settings in the "loaded" register will be identically the same as the switch settings in the "addressed" memory location.

If there is anything mentally taxing about programming it's getting straight in one's mind what happens when instructions are executed. That is why I keep emphasizing the basic computing cycle, FIRE. What happens when a load register instruction is executed? All instructions and data are stored in memory, meaning written on memory in the form of switch settings. The instruction itself is written on memory in switch settings the same as the data to be loaded into one of several possible registers. The register to be loaded is a part of the CPU. Most CPU's have multiple registers thus one must be specified else the CPU cannot know which one is to be loaded. Lastly the address of the data to load into the register must be specified. Addresses can be simple meaning the actual address or they can be complex meaning they are the contents of either another register or memory location.

Example instruction:
L,5   Address
The instruction is L, load register. The register to be loaded is number 5. The data to load into register 5 is located in memory at Address. Address can be simple or complex.

Example of simple addressing:
L,5   George

The data is in memory at a location the programmer named George. Elsewhere in the program George must be defined.

Example of complex addressing:

LI,7   George
L,5   (7)

L says load. LI says the data to be loaded is the address field of the instruction. Together L and I along with the number 7 says, load the address field into register 7. The address field has the address of George. After the LI instruction is executed register 7 "points" to George. For example if George's address is 377 then register 7 will have 377 in it.

L,5   (7)

The above instruction has a complex address. Addresses in parentheses says the contents of and not the thing itself. The address field does not point to the data but rather points to where the CPU will find the address of the data to be loaded. In this example the CPU uses the contents of register number 7 to resolve the address. George is a simple address. (7) is a complex address requiring resolution to simple before it can be used. Resolving is as simple in this case as using the contents of register 7 rather than the address field of the instruction.

Direct addressing is simple. The CPU uses the address specified. Indirect addressing, using an address that is somewhere else the CPU must Resolve the address before executing the instruction.

I've written thousands of computer programs. The very first program I wrote I did with pencil and paper and keyed one switch setting at a time into the computer's memory. I had learned how to program in less than an hour. It was my first day at work fresh out of college. My job title was engineer. The job was designing RARAR systems. The program was secret so I had to get a security clearance before given access to my actual work place. While I waited for the FBI to investigate me I was told by my boss to take a look at a somewhat strange looking piece of equipment called computer. He implied we only had it because it was made by our company, North American Aviation. He introduced me to the one person in the group who knew anything at all about it, an engineer assigned to it and known by the group as its keeper.

The boss introduced us and explained to keeper he would be helped with the computer by me while I waited for my security clearance. Keeper handed me the computer's manual and with a few words of encouragement left me to read it. It began with a statement attributed to the computer's inventor that went something like, "how convenient that data and instructions share the same memory." I remember thinking, "he's invented a board game with an electronic board." Soon I discovered I could write numbers on that electronic paper and I could write sequences of operations using numbers to do arithmetic using sets of numbers. The computer did all the grunt work of adding, subtracting, multiplying and dividing.

Being only 4,096 words long the machine's memory would make one laugh when compared to today's gigabyte size memories. The 40 millisecond clock cycle time, 25 hertz is even more amusing by comparison to the several gigahertz clock speeds of modern processors.

That puny by comparison to today's computers had something today's don't have. It had a control panel that I could use to look in its memory and write on its memory. It was a little clumsy to program with absolutely no software at all, no operating system, no C++, no Windows, no nothing. It could be programmed and was programmed by me a fresh out of college beginner and I wrote my first ever program in less than an hour from the time I even knew there was such a thing as a computer.

This, the first digital computer I ever saw did have an operating capability else it would have been completely worthless. It had a control panel that I could use to write data and instructions one set of switch settings at a time on the computer's memory.

First I took a mimeographed form used for "coding" and wrote my first little program out. It included a couple of numbers I put in memory at locations 100 and 101. Then at location 0, I put, L,A 100, (load the A register, the accumulator with the contents of location 100). At location 1, I put A,A 101, (Add the contents of location 101 to the contents of the accumulator). At location 2, I put, ST,A 102, (Store the contents of the accumulator in memory at location 102). At location 3 I put a STOP instruction which as I recall was all 0's. I translated all of that four line program and my 2 data words into 0's and 1's, selected each memory address using a set of switches on the computer's control panel, using another set of switches I put the contents of that location and toggled a load memory switch. I did that for the 6 words of memory my little program occupied, loaded all 0's into the instruction pointer register to start running at location zero, hit the start button and to my amazement nothing seemed to happen except the instruction pointer register now had 4, 100 binary in it.

Keeper had been looking over my shoulder. He said look at memory location 102. I did by flipping the address switches and again to my amazement there was the sum of the numbers I had put in 100 and 101. I changed the numbers in 100 and 101 and did it again a few times, added multiply and divide steps and before long I had a dozen word program that executed a simple formula.

What did that do for me? It gave me a 100% understanding of how digital computers work, how to work them and make them a part of me through programming. My mind was stored in the computer giving me the mental power to calculate, add, subtract, multiply and divide any numbers I pleased pencil and paper not required.

Program are the thoughts of programmers inside the computer just like a books are the thoughts of their authors. Big difference in program and book. Push button and program author comes to life, runs doing calculation and goes back to dead, stops running. Add to doing big calculation anything the human mind can think of doing. Don't you wish you had one of them so you could write programs and try them out like I did?

We were in a large room with rows of desks and people banging away on Frieden brand mechanical calculators. I said to keeper, "why don't they put those numbers in this computer and let it do all that grunt work." He replied, "They're doing a piece by piece polynomial divisions on reams of test data and polynomial division can't be done on the computer."

That was before lunch. After lunch I wrote the "can't be done" program to do polynomial division and tested it by manually entering it and test data in the computer's memory one switch setting at a time. That program allowed the computer with my little program in it to replace 16 people using calculators. It was not the computer. It was me doing the calculations using the computer as an extension of my mind. Through the computer my power to calculate was increased to greater than that of 16 people using calculators. This is a fine but necessary point to get straight in one's mind. Computers are mind amplifiers.

Everyone has a mind therefore everyone qualifies to amplify their mind by programming computers. English, art, social scientists, geographers, historians, and people of every discipline even athletes have minds. All are qualified to amplify their minds but are presently shut out by an implied patent, a patent by difficulty.

My soon to be fellow engineers designing a RADAR used my program to analyze their test data taking an hour or less where before it had taken 16 people a week or more using calculators doing one arithmetic operation at a time writing the results on paper using pencils "with eraser." I did that without the aid of an operating system, assembler, or compiler or system's software of any kind. Most significantly I had no formal computer education.

Does my learning experience suggest anything to you? Maybe how to go about teaching computer? Maybe I'm a little quicker than the average. I learned the basic computer FIRE cycle is a few seconds. I also realized memories and registers were nothing more than sets of switches and I instinctively knew switches are memories. They remember off and on.

It's a pity but a handful of big billion dollar corporations have shut you out form having my learning experience. I learned everything possible to know about computers in a few hours at most. In less than 10 minutes I knew the basic FIRE cycle and understood sets of switches were the equal of paper. Paper is written on and so are switches.

I had a big advantage over you. My brain was as clean of computer as it could possibly be. No one had ever told me about all the things computers do or how I had to get myself a genuine IBM-machine with an IBM sanctified operating system and go back to college, study computer science and learn how to make the computer say, "hello world." And prepare my emotions for failure signaled by, "Aw snap."

Of course I cheated. I wrote my first programs in a language known as machine language. Machine language is the natural language of the computer and therefore the easiest to learn and most of all it's the most exacting. Programs written in machine language are hand assembled one switch setting at a time. That's tedious to say the least but it didn't take all that long or frustrate me that much. Agreed, it's not a job for the impatient. In my opinion it's mandatory to do at least once for those who want to know all there is to know about computers. We'll do the next best thing later using a theoretical paper computer. And we'll do it in decimal so we can read it. Computers are independent of number systems because they can be programmed to calculate in any system.

Learning computer from books is doing it the hard way. Using a computer with a control panel takes all the imagination out of it. Beginning programming in high level compile language is like trying to learn how to writing books without first learning how to read and write. I plan to learn how to read and write myself one of these days provided I live that long.

If you've managed to understand the fact that computers have but two "invisible" parts, a CPU and memory and they operate in cycles orchestrated by a clocked switch you already know more than PhD's in computer science if all they know is how to "make" the computer say things. We're going to learn how to make the computer an extension of ourselves through a process known as programming. Computers do nothing. They are tools just like monkey wrenches.

What did I do when I wrote my first program? I put myself inside the computer. The engineer started me up. Then we had a conversation. I spoke first by typing on the computer's only peripheral, a teletype, a carriage-return line-fee and the message, "Start a new analysis" followed by a carriage return and line feed. Then the engineer spoke to me by typing his test data one number at a time. With the last number I did the calculations taking as long as a second and then I wrote the results on the teletype.

It was me and him working as a team. He "fed" me the numbers, I did the calculations and "regurgitated" the results. I had a big advantage over you. I didn't know computers were so hard they had to be studied before they could be used.

Software comes under two general headings, systems software and application software. Operating systems are systems software. "Apps" are application software. The I-phone is misnamed. It's not a phone with a computer. It's a computer with a telephone peripheral. Telephoning is in reality an application. It's not the phone and it's not the computer doing whatever, its programmer(s).

We all know what an operating system is. It's the thing that slows the computer to a crawl and quits altogether at the most inopportune time. In reality operating systems are relatively simple programs and when properly done are like well-behaved children, seen but not heard.

Assemblers are systems programs that translate instructions written using letters of the alphabet, punctuation marks and numbers into machine language. Assemblers are programs that allow us to write statements instead of switch settings. They take a lot of the tedium out of programming.

In the beginning there were no assemblers, compilers or systems software to use. That made learning all there is to know about computers easy. The learning process must begin at the no software help at all while stressing the fundamentals.

We're going to learn assembly language programming and as a byproduct firm up what we've already learned especially machine language programming. You didn't know you've already learned how to program in machine language did you? You can operate a light switch? Congratulations you're a computer programmer. All that's left is get you a computer. That rules out Apple computers and PC's.

Every program possible can be written in machine language. Not true for any and all high level compiler languages such as C++, D, Algol, COBOL, FORTRAN, you name it. Every computer language will allow you to say something expressing computer ignorance like "make" the computer say, "hello world." Repeat after me, Computers do not do things. People do things using computers." You are a people therefore you qualify to do things using computers.

Doing things using computers is a literary art, writing to be exact. Writing requires one to know words and how to

84

arrange those words to make meaningful statements. That means learning vocabulary and grammatical structure.

Different computers have different vocabularies. The vocabulary of the computer is the individual instructions its CPU can execute. With every different brand of computer we must relearn the machine language instruction set that includes all its CPU's possible instructions. Then we learn its assembly language that includes all machine language instructions plus assembler control instructions. Knowing the instructions of any CPU is paramount to knowing the instructions sets of them all.

We will learn grammar before vocabulary. Vocabulary varies while grammatical structure is a constant. With every new computer one must learn a new vocabulary. Once any computer's vocabulary is learned learning a new one is a nothing, provided it's documented of course. Learning how to write computer sentences for any computer is knowing how for all computers. And, most importantly those sentences are really simple ones.

There are two types of instructions. Some instructions require a memory address while others do not. The word address means the same thing here it does at the post office. Some instructions have memory addresses and some don't. That's about all the variation there be, those with addresses and those without addresses. They are the equal of mail and interoffice memos. Mail must have an address otherwise the postman doesn't know where to deliver it. Interoffice memos do not require an address only an addressee.

Examples of addressing types:

L,r   address ← "load direct" has the address
                        where the data is located.
LI,r   data   ← "load immediate" the data is
                        part of the instruction
L,r   (x)   ← "load indirect" the address
                        of the date is in register x.
INC,r   ← "add one" the number one
                        is inherent, a part of the verb.

If you don't know what the above means you'll be finding out shortly. We're talking about word/instruction types that differ only in how one says where the data is located. The word address here is no different in concept than the address where you live. Maybe I should have said some instructions don't have data associated with them. Program control instructions have addresses but no data.

We must first learn to read before we can write. That requires us to both know the vocabulary and know the grammatical structure of sentences. Assembly language computer programs are written in sentences commonly known as lines of code using shorthand. Lines of code roughly equal sentences.

All programs are sets of statements made by the programmer talking to him/herself. "I will now _____ the _____ using the data at address _____." When writing my first instruction as a matter of the subconscious I said to myself, I will <u>load</u> the <u>accumulator</u> with the contents of memory address <u>100</u>. Programming is filling in the blanks. The equal for writing sentences is subject, verb and object. Computers use foreign language sentence structure with verb first.

A programmer writing:

L,r   address

Should have said to him/herself, "I will now <u>Load register</u> r using <u>the contents of the memory location at address</u>." The verb is Load. The subject is the r register and the object is the data/switch settings written in memory at address. Most computers today have multiple accumulator/index registers. The small r is a number zero through the highest number register. My first ever computer only had one accumulator register. In machine language the address is the number address of the specific memory location. In assembly language the address is a name made up by the programmer.

Example:

L,7   count   Load register 7 with the contents of
                       a memory location named count.

"count" is a word made up by the programmer to identify a particular memory location like a mother naming her baby. Somewhere else in the program "count" is defined making it a new word added to the vocabulary of the program.

The vocabulary of the computer is its instruction set. Assemblers are programs that translate instructions into switch settings. Assemblers have additional instructions called pseudo instructions that are used to define data and name program locations etc. The vocabulary of the program is the vocabulary of the computer plus the assembler program's pseudo instructions and all new words added by the programmer. DATA is a common pseudo instruction for defining data.

Label   DATA   the actual number

In the above example, (L,7 count) the programmer must define count. A DATA instruction can be used:

count   DATA   a number, label or text string

Labels are one word names thought up by the programmer. In the above example the label was count. Labels can have both letters of the alphabet and numbers. Letters of the alphabet such as X are possible labels. Letters of the alphabet combined with numbers such as A1 are also possible labels. One can also use real names like Fred or George. The shorter the name the less likely it will be misspelled when using it. Those who don't want to get yelled at by the assembler, actually the programmer who wrote the assembler program will not misspell their baby's names. Assemblers are stricter than English teachers when it comes to misspelling.

You didn't forget computers do nothing. Shame on you if you did. Who's doing something in the above instructions? The programmer and not the computer. Computers allow mental work to be done. An old programmer joke, "people should work and let computers do the thinking." Who's doing the thinking the computer or the programmer? If you can think then you can program any computer. If it can't be programmed by you it's not a computer.

Again, instruction sets are unique to different makes of computers. All have a couple of things in common or they are not computers. They all operate in FIRE cycles, fetching the present instruction form memory, incrementing the instruction pointer getting ready to fetch the next instruction, resolving the address, executing the instruction and then doing it all over again as fast as possible.

All computers are programmable. Technically PC's and Apple computers are not actually computers because they cannot be programmed by us ordinary people. This is absolutely so for I-phones. We're forced to buy our programs with names like Windows and Apps to get our Burger King coupons. We've already discussed the insanity in doing that.

We can't use Intel's or AMD's microprocessors with pet names like Acceleron and i5 for example because they are not properly documented. Instead of one of them for our example computer we will use the people programmable people friendly DC-3 that's superior to any and all microprocessors by bunches. Most of all it can be programmed by anyone. Isn't that lovely?

The DC-3 is a third generation computer designed by myself and John Larsen, 1972. It was manufactured and sold commercially by several companies under licensing agreements. We will use some of the DC-3 instruction set as an example along with its assembler's pseudo instructions. I wrote the assembler. That was 45 years ago. I have a fairly good memory. I'm working form my people memory as I have been unable to find my DC-3 reference manual that I also wrote.

Once one learns the instruction set of any computer learning that of any other computer is reduced to a 15 minute task. Provided it's properly documented of course.

DC-3 Instruction set:

How to read my writing first. The following is the meanings of symbols I use:

r any one of 16 registers, i.e. 0,1,2,,15

( ) means contents of. Your mail box is written mail box. Your mail is the contents of your mail box written, (mail box). (mail box) means mail while mail box is the location where your mail is delivered with a unique address. An item in parentheses reads "the contents of the item." Learn to say it that way as you read along.

-----L, Load and ST, Store instructions------------------

L,r   address ← load (register r) with (address)

Reads, "load, make the <u>contents of</u> register r identical to the <u>contents of</u> the memory location at address." Load – duplicate.

LI,r   data   ← load immediate, data becomes new (register r)

ST,r   address ← store duplicate (register r) in (address)

----- Arithmetic and Logic instructions------------

A,r   address   ← Add (address) to (register r)

AI,r   data   ← Add data to (register r)

AC,r address   ← Add (address) + carry to

(register r)
ACI,r data   ← Add data + carry to (register r)
INC,r   ← add 1 to (register r)
S,r   address ← Subtract (address) from (register r)
SI,r   data   ← Subtract data from (register r)
SC,r   address ← Subtract (address) + carry from (r)
SCI,r data   ← Subtract data + carry from (register r)
DEC,r   ← subtract 1 from (register r)
N,r   address ← AND (register r) with (address)
NI,r   data   ← AND (register r) with data
O,r   address ← OR (register r) with (address)
OI,r   data   ← OR (register r) with data
X,r   address ← Exclusive or (reg r) with (address)
XI,r   data   ← Exclusive or (register r) with data
CP,r address   ← Compare (address) to (register r)
CPI,r data   ← Compare data to (register r)

----- Program flow-control instructions----------
CALL,r address ← Subroutine call, return address is (r)
JT   address   ← Jump to address
JZ   address   ← Jump IF Zero flag 1
JNZ address   ← Jump IF Zero flag 0
JG   address   ← Jump IF Minus flag 0 and Zero flag 0
JGE address   ← Jump IF Zero flag 1 or Minus flag 0
JL   address   ← Jump IF Minus flag 1
JLE address   ← Jump IF Minus flag 1 or Zero flag 1
JE   address   ← Jump IF equal flag 1
JNE address   ← Jump IF equal flag 0
JC   address   ← Jump IF carry bit is 1
JNC address   ← Jump IF carry bit is 0

----- INput and OUTput instructions
IN,r   IOaddress ← load (register r) from (IOaddress)
OUT,r IOaddress ← store (register r) at (IOaddress)

----- Shift and rotate instructions
SHL,r   ← Shift (r) 1 position left
SHLC,r   ← Shift (r) 1 position left through carry
SHR,r   ← Shift (r) 1 position right
SHRC,r   ← Shift (r) 1 position right through carry

```
RL,r       ← Rotate (r) 1 position left
RLC,r      ← Rotate (r) 1 position left through carry
RR,r       ← Rotate (r) 1 position right
RRC,r      ← Rotate (r) 1 position right through carry
```

```
---------DC-3 assembler pseudo instructions------------
Label  EQU   address      ← Label and address same
       ORG   address      ← locate the next instruction
       DATA  address/data ← define data-pointers/data
       END                ← that's all folks
```

The DC-3 has 3 flag bits that are changed with every arithmetic, logical and compare instruction. The Zero flag is set to 1 if the results of the operation are zero or in the case of a compare the two items being compared to each other are identically the same. The Zero flag is set to zero if the results of an arithmetic or logical operation are not zero or not identically the same when doing a compare. The Minus flag bit is a duplicate of the most significant bit of the results. The carry bit is also the overflow bit. When overflow/carry is set it indicates the results of an arithmetic instruction are too large to fit in the register or in the case of multi precision arithmetic, two or more words side by side to make a single number it means there was a carry. These three flags are typical of all makes of CPU's.

I agree, my literary capabilities are limited to say the least. But anyhow I do believe we've reached what is known as the pregnant moment. Count them. How many words are in the DC-3's and its assembler's vocabularies added together? I went cross-eyed counting them myself. I saw a measly 45 or so. But that's counting the same instruction with different addressing modes more than once. In reality A, AI, AC, ACI, and INC are but one instruction, add. The register with contents "added to" is the same for all. It's where to find the number to add to the contents of the register that differs one from the other. A, by itself means add the contents of a memory location or the contents of another register. AI, means the number to add is a part of the instruction. Counting instructions again we only have, 17 and that's counting shifting and rotation for both left one bit and right one bit/switch.

I understand if you have a problem. Did I hear you gasp, "How in the name of Fred Finklebaum can one possibly make cartoon characters like Pac Man move about the television screen eating everything in his path with nothing more than those instructions?" Believe it or not the original Pac Man computer's instruction set is a really sick sister compared the DC-3's instruction set above. Let's see if I can explain it to you, how to make Pac Man and make him move. It's so easy once you "get it" you'll gasp even louder, "Why didn't I think of that?"

The television screen is a peripheral device, a part of the computer system and not a part of the computer. You've always described the compute as a television with bugs in it? Cut that out! It's a sign of ignorance like saying, "I ain't got no money" or "that's where it's at." Television screens and computers are two different things. It's mandatory to get that straight in one's mind. That means the picture making element in Pac Man is the television and not the computer. We must know how television screens work before we can "make" them do anything. And, we don't make screens make pictures we make pictures using televisions screens.

Once one knows how computers are programmed and how television screens are programmed putting the two together is a nothing. All television screens used as computer peripherals are identically the same in the most important aspects. They are the same in that they turn switch settings into pictures. Did I hear you mumble, "There's those bleeping switches again?" Yep, we've bumped into that high tech light switch in a rather strange place. Different television screens attached to computers differ only in how they get the switch settings from you the programmer. Just like the computer the television screen has a memory where the switches to make the "next" picture are stored. You did know moving pictures are sets of still pictures, photographs presented one after the other?

All pictures on television screens are made of dots known by the name pixel. Pixels are pixels and dots are dots and never the twain shall part. Television screens are rated by how many dots they use to make a picture. You may have noticed something like 300 by 400 to describe a television when shopping for one. That means the particular unit has 300 dots per line across the screen and 400 lines from the top to the bottom of the screen. That's an amazing 120,000 dots total required to make a single picture. The more pixels the screen has the higher the resolution.

What any dot will be is determined by the contents of the television screen's memory. Mechanical switches set by you one at a time would work. And you got to do it again for the next frame. Maybe you should use a computer instead. You'll wear blisters on your fingers setting 120,000 switches manually as well as wear yourself out. Television screens do nothing people can't do just like computers do nothing people can't do. All is done by people either painfully slow one switch at a time or at 5,000,000 per second using a DC-3 type computer to do the heavy lifting.

Most all color television screens have sets of 8 bits to make each dot that are no more technical than sets of 8 light switches per dot. 8 switches have 256 different possible settings ranging from all off to all on and every combination in between. The highest quality color television screens use all 8 bits and thus they have 256 different possible colors etc. for every dot. The actual color, intensity etc. for a given set of 8 bits is unique to the particular make of television screen. Thus one must first find that out. That means reading the manual for the particular screen. I'm trying to encourage you, you can read and understand what that manual says. A lot of experimenting to actually find out how a particular screen is programmed is usually needed. Been my experience.

The original Apple computer with Pac Man had a two color CRT, (Cathode Ray Tube) screen commonly known as black and white. As I recall they were amber and white. I do not know the resolution, how many dots per line and how many lines the original Apple CRT screen had. Most likely it was some power of two in both dimensions, 256 X 256 for example.

The television screen has control electronics that reads its memory one dot at a time setting that dot on the screen accordingly. Making a picture on the screen is as simple as "storing" individual dot values in the television screen's memory. For Pac Man that's zeroes and ones, zero amber, one white or maybe black. All that's needed to do that is L, loading and ST, storing on/in the screen's memory using IN and OUT instructions. And you thought it was hard.

Off the top of my head putting a picture on the screen takes as few as a dozen instructions. To change the picture, make Pac Man "appear" to move it's only a matter of changing the television screen's memory where Pac Man be at the moment. Of course Pac Man eating things is simply changing the memory where things are eaten by replacing things eaten with the background, set all the bits to zeros no doubt. Read the manual and above all experiment, try different numbers and see what happens. Anyone can make moving pictures using computers with a screen attachment. Don't forget the documentation. Good luck in a world where a handful of greedy corporations control what you will be allowed to do.

Artistic talent is a greater requirement than technical skill to make pictures on television screens whether those screens are attached to computers or otherwise. I was told by the computer expert who showed me my first computer, "The engineers, (I was one of them) need to do polynomial division but it can't be done on the computer." His problem was lack of knowledge of polynomials. I learned programming in a minute or two. The last time I saw him he was still wrestling with polynomials and losing every bout. I still remember the look on his face when he saw that I had done the impossible. It took me all day to do it. Thus the expression, "the difficult we do right away while the impossible takes a little longer."

All instructions have 4 possible parts. 1, there can be a label, a name thought up by the programmer. 2, there must be an operation. 3, relative to the instruction type there may or may not be an address. 4, the programmer can but is not required to make a note to him/herself commonly known as a comment. Easy to remember, label, operation, address and comment. That's all there is to know about the grammatical structure, the syntax requirements of the DC-3 assembler written by me and the syntax of many other computers and assemblers written by others than me. This is true for most all assembly languages. Well, maybe not for official BAL with the all-inclusive MOV instruction.

Before we define, label, operation, address and comment let's look at the format of an instruction. Programs are made up of lines of code with one line being one instruction.

Lines of code are the equals of sentences. The format of a line of code for the DC-3 is typical of most all assemblers:
LABEL OPERATION ADDRESS COMMENT

Let's take them from the top. Make that left to right.

A LABEL is a set of letters and numbers, a name given a location in the program. If I want to reference a location then I must first give it a name. We cannot know "who's on first" without knowing his name else we drive ourselves mad. In computer programming names are made up by the programmer. They need not spell anything in particular but once defined must be spelled correctly when using. Typically, labels must begin with a letter of the alphabet, made of letters of the alphabet and numbers in any combination and can be no longer than 10 letters/numbers long. You will discover as I did that the shorter the names the easier they are to write. Using a simple A for Adamson takes the writing out of writing. Its exchanging writing with memory - must remember A means Adamson.

The OPEREATION field consists of a mnemonic, (operation code) for the particular instruction. If the instruction has a register it is followed by a comma and then the number of the register. Example: L,7 says load register 7. L is the mnemonic for the load operation and 7 is the register number to be loaded. Computers with but one register usually use the mnemonic, LDA. Jump instructions do not have source or destination registers thus no comma and no register number is specified.

The ADDRESS field locates the data or place in the program to transfer control in subroutine calls and jump instructions. In data definitions the address field has the value of the data. Some instructions do not have addresses. Example: INC,5 says add 1 to the contents of register 5. Some instructions do require an address. Addresses are names made up by the programmer. Example: L,3 X says load register 3 with the contents of memory location X. Elsewhere in the program: X DATA [actual number, address, or text string] the contents of address X. At the end of the instruction, L,3 X, register 3's switch settings will be identically the same as those memory at location X.

But of course we write numbers in assembly language in decimal and the assembler converts them to binary for us. Big relief? Not necessary to use binary unless we want to look directly into the computer's memory commonly known in the trades as doing electronic brain surgery. Yes indeed, when brain surgery is necessary it's usually means big trouble. Does your computer running "under" Windows need a little brain surgery just to get started? It will keep needing it until you do something about it like throw Windows in the trash.

All computers have addressing modes. I can't think of one that is singular, a model of computer having only one addressing mode. The DC-3 has 5 addressing modes, no address required, direct memory, immediate, indirect memory and indirect register. Indirect register is commonly known as indexing or indexed addressing. Some instruction types require no address at all. That's the easiest case with all cases being easy to understand, in time perhaps.

Instructions with direct memory addressing must state the address. Addresses always translate into switch settings. They can be stated using names made up by the programmer or they can be absolute values, numbers. Example: L,3 237 says make the contents of register 3 identical to the contents of memory location 237. Or. We can write L,3 A, with A being defined elsewhere in the program.

Do not to confuse L,r 237 with LI,r 237. In the case of L,r 237 the data loaded into register r is the contents of memory at address 237. In the case of LI,3 237 the data loaded into register 3 is the number 237. LI uses immediate addressing meaning the data is the address.

Indirect addressing is done using the contents of a register for the address. Example: L,3 (5) reads, Load register 3 with the contents of the memory at the address addressed by the contents of register 5. This facilitates copying a lot of data located in consecutive memory locations to another set of consecutive memory locations. To make Pac Man move for example of use:

```
LI,1      A       address  A→(r1) Pac Man's image
LI,2      B       address  B→(r2) TV memory
LI,3      216     lengths of A and B, Pac Man size in bytes
CL L,0    (1)     data addressed by (r1) to (r0)
```

```
ST,0      (2)      data in r0 to display address in r2
INC,1              add 1 to (1) - point to next byte of A
INC,2              add 1 to (2) - point to next byte of B
DEC,3              count down length counter
JNZ       CL       go to CL if length count not zero
     …             Falls through when length counter goes to
```
zero. That means the copy is finished and Pac Man's image is on the screen at location B. At this point 216 words, the contents of a string of words the programmer named B have been made identical to the contents of a string of words in the screen's memory the programmer named A. You didn't forget that contents of means "the switch settings of?"

We used immediate addressing above. Indirect addressing and immediate addressing are likely found together. Immediate addressing shortcuts having to define addresses using DATA statements.

Registers used in indirect addressing are commonly known as index registers. The above copy program uses indexing which is a one word way of saying indirectly addressing individual data words in strings of data words pointed to by the contents of registers.

The last element of a line of code a COMMENT is an optional note the programmer makes to refresh his/her memory later. Single instructions are like rabbit hairs in felt hats. It takes a lot of hairs to make a hat and a lot of instructions to make a program. Since little is done with any single instruction it's easy to confuse one's self thus comments are used to refresh ones memory later. Comments also make it easier for another person to understand your program. If you want to keep it confidential then don't make comments and force copiers to earn their ill-gotten goods.

Lines of source code may be comments-only without an instruction. This is done when one wishes to do things like identify what the program does and copyright it. In DC-3 syntax whole line comments begin with an asterisk, * in the first position. It's not unusual for programmers to make fancy headings using whole line comments. Example:

```
*******************************************************
*      This program slows the computer       *
*   causing Windows to time out very cycle    *
*        until they buy a new computer        *
*        I plan to sell billions of copies    *
*  to nerds who hack their way into Windows   *
*  install it and slow computers to a crawl for  *
*                  BIG HA HA                  *
*        © Copyright, 2017 by A Slock         *
*              All rights reserved.           *
*******************************************************
LOOP  JT  LOOP          loop-d-loop
          END
```

Way back when, I taught a junior high class how to program a theoretical computer we designed. The cheapest computer at the time costs $40,000, (40 million in today's dollars) well beyond any school's budget. I was a volunteer collared by their math teacher who himself wanted to learn about computers. It wasn't a regular class. It was a fun event for the kids and a one hour a day break in the action for me.

We created an instruction set, marked off columns and rows on the chalkboard for memory and registers, wrote instruction codes in the squares, set the instruction pointer to zero, took the first step and copied the first word from memory to the instruction register, added 1 to the instruction pointer and then played CPU executing the instruction.

We had fun. The kids and especially the math teacher caught on very quickly. Computing is a game like chess. We played computer the way chess is played, one move at a time. Chess is played on a checkered board with tokens. We played computer on a chalk board. Chess has rules. So does computer. Not a lot of rules but just a few. And like chess it's one move at a time. The next move is yours.

Chapter 9, grouping switches is…

…so common it's the norm. Any book on computers will almost immediately start using hexadecimal. More often than not the author will make some relatively meaningless statement about what hexadecimal is all about and leave the uninitiated dangling. Let's not do that. Let's take hexadecimal apart at the seams and see what it's all about. While we're at it we'll learn a little more about number systems.

We already know that computers are the simplest and easiest machines to know all there is to know about only requiring brains enough to understand the light switch. It's a matter of dragging that knowledge out of the subconscious mind to the forefront. Most of all it's overcoming a mental attitude, changing one's mind about how hard it is to stuff computers. See what I mean?

We know binary is the natural number system of computers. That's because the binary system has but two symbols that correspond one for one with light switches having but two positions. Light switches can be off or on and must be one or the other at all times. Bits, the name given computer switches are always zero or one and must be one or the other at all times.

Saying things in binary is clumsy to say the least. It takes as much effort to write a zero or one as it does to write any decimal digit from zero through nine. It takes 4 zeros and ones to represent zero through nine decimal. Let's write them out and verify that's so.

Binary	Same number in decimal
0000	0
0001	1
0010	2
0011	3
0100	4
0101	5
0110	6
0111	7
1000	8
1001	9

Binary requires writing 4 things where only one is required to write the same number in decimal. As numbers grow in size the number of switches needed to represent them grows and at a much faster rate. It takes 20 zeros and ones to represent 1,234,567. Writing large numbers using switches like say the national debt would be torturous. It's bad enough to do it using ordinary decimal numbering. We don't need that.

The number system that corresponds one for one with switches has but two digits, 0 and 1. That's the binary number system. Binary has its place especially in the description of the instruction set of any given machine. Hexadecimal is a short hand way to say the same thing. Like all things it requires a little thought. Not too much thought but some that's well worth the effort. Its value will become obvious as we go.

There are actually three popular groupings of switches, binary, octal and hexadecimal are their names. Binary is taking just one switch at a time. Octal is the grouping of switches in sets of 3. Hexadecimal is grouping switches in sets of 4. There is no grouping of switches that exactly matches decimal.

Octal was the first employed by computer programmers to lighten the load when writing out the contents of registers and memory locations. In the early days of computing memories were made in multiples of 6. 6 is evenly divisible by 3. Thus a memory address and/or its contents could be expressed, written in symbols representing sets of 3 bits. The IBM 7090 has 36 bit wide memory and registers making it a 36 bit word machine. In case I haven't told you or you've forgotten a computer word is the width in bits/switches of the CPU's accumulator(s) and index register(s). 3 divides evenly into 36. So does 6. Printouts of the contents of memory known as core, (memories were made of cores) dumps were in octal. Instead of 36 0's and 1's they had 12 0's through 7's. The largest number that can be represented by 3 switches is 7, i.e. using decimal digit symbols, 0,1,2,3,4,5,6, and 7.

By some process similar to osmosis or gravitation but likely because computers with 8 bit wide register and memory words became popular hexadecimal has become the norm. Hexadecimal is the grouping of bits/switches in sets of 4. You may have noticed I did that above when I described the DC-3 instruction set. I showed the individual bit settings in groups of

4 bits so you could count them without going cross-eyed. For example the store instruction in switch settings/binary:

ST, 0000 1100 rrrr aaaa aaaa aaaa aaaa aaaa

I could have written:

ST, 0Craaaaa

$0000 \rightarrow 0$

$1100 \rightarrow C$

$rrrr \rightarrow r$

$aaaa \rightarrow a$

Right away there's ambiguity. The capital C represents the binary number, 1100. The letters r, and a, represent variables and not actual numbers. Small r, and small a, can be any combination of 4 bits/switches. Have I adequately explained one of the reasons you find it impossible to read computer literature?

Let's make an observation about us. We were taught to count and do arithmetic in decimal. Decimal is the base 10 number system. Did you ever wonder why we have 10 symbols, 0 through 9 to represent numbers? Some great thinker from my past surmised that's because we have 10 fingers. Standing hillbilly joke, "he has to take his shoes off to count and even then he can't count higher than 20." If we had but 8 fingers we would only have 8 symbols, 0 through 7 and we would have learned to count and calculate in octal. It's easier to imagine only having 4 fingers on our hands than it is to imagine we have 8 fingers on each hand. If we were 16 fingered, 8 fingers on each hand we would have been taught to count and do arithmetic in hexadecimal.

The number of possible bases for number systems is unlimited. We'll cut the crop down to 4 total, binary-2, octal-8, decimal-10 and hexadecimal-16. To make it easy for you to learn I'm going to point something out you already know but never think about. Decimal is the base 10 number system. You know that but never think about it because in your world it's useless information. Now you need it, maybe.

The base of a number system is the number of different symbols needed to write a given number. In decimal, base 10, 10 symbols, 0, 1, 2, 3, 4, 5, 6, 7, 8 and 9 to be exact are needed. When the "count" goes beyond the highest symbol's count-value we add a one on the left and start counting again at zero. The number 14 is 10 + 4. In decimal it has a count value of 14. In octal a count of 14 is written 16. 16 octal is 14 decimal. In hexadecimal 14 is written with a single symbol, E. 14 written in binary is, 1110.

Counting is deciding how many. Numbering, attaching numbers to individual items is done relative to the number system. I have some capital X's that I lay out one after the other. The count value is the number of X's.

	Decimal	Binary	Octal	Hexadecimal
No X's	0	0	0	0
X	1	1	1	1
X	2	10	2	2
X	3	11	3	3
X	4	100	4	4
X	5	101	5	5
X	6	110	6	6
X	7	111	7	7
X	8	1000	10	8
X	9	1001	11	9
X	10	1010	12	A
X	11	1011	13	B
X	12	1100	14	C
X	13	1101	15	D
X	14	1110	16	E
X	15	1111	17	F
X	16	10000	20	10

We're breaking counts down to how they are written. In Binary we can only count to 1 before we get to 10, must add a 1 on the left and start again with zero on the right. 0 + 1 is 1 +1 is 10 +1 is 11 + 1 is 100…

In octal 0 + 1 is 1 + 1 is 2 + 1 is 3 + 1 is 4 + 1 is 5 + 1 is 6 + 1 is 7 + 1 is 10 +1….16 + 1 is 17 +1 is 20 + 1 is 21…26 + 1 is 27 + 1 is 30…76 + 1 is 77 + 1 is 100…

Of course in decimal we add 1 until we get to 9 and then the count becomes 10 and keep counting until we get to 20 and on to 99. Add one to 99 and get 100. It's always stat counting with none at zero adding 1 until every symbol in the set of possible symbols is used.

In hexadecimal we count to 15 before we run out of symbols. That means we exhaust our supply of decimal digits and must add 6 new ones. The great thinkers decide to use capital letters of the alphabet instead of inventing new symbols. Thus the digits of hexadecimal are, 0, 1, 2, 3, 4, 5, 6, 7, 8, 9, A, B, C, D, E, and F. After we count to F we begin again at 10, i.e. F + 1 = 10 in hexadecimal as indicated by the above conversion table.

736 in decimal is 6 + (10 times 3) + (100 times 7).

736 in octal is 6 + (8 times 3) + (64 times 7).

736 in hexadecimal is 6 + (16 times 3) + (256 times 7).

The first symbol in all systems is that count. Every symbol to the left of the first symbol is multiplied by the base as many times as the symbol is places from the rightmost symbol minus 1, i.e. 2nd by the base, 3rd by base times the base, (squared) 4th by base times the base times the base, (tripled) and so on for as many digits as there are in the number.

In decimal:

736 is

6 times 1 =   6

3 times 10 =   30

7 times 100 = 700

6 + 30 + 700 = 736 decimal

In octal:

736 is

6 times 1 =   6

3 times 8 =   24

7 times 64 = 448

6 + 24 + 448 = 478 decimal

In hexadecimal:

736 is

6 times 1 =   6

3 times 16 =   48

7 times 256 = 1792

6 + 48 + 1792 = 1846 decimal

The above is converting numbers in different based number systems with the final value stated in decimal. The base of a number system is the number of symbols used in the system. We're concerned with four here, binary, octal, decimal and hexadecimal. And we're really not concerned with octal because it's rarely if ever used. Hexadecimal is the common base representing groupings of 4 bits/switches in a single symbol.

In the set of symbols to represent numbers, 0 through 9 there's enough to do binary, octal and decimal. Binary needs 2 so we use 0 and 1. Octal needs 8 so we use 0, 1, 2, 3, 4, 5, 6 and 7. Decimal needs all 10 symbols 0 through 9. Hexadecimal needs 16 symbols. New number symbols to represent counts 10 through 15 could have been defined but they were not. The obvious and very compelling argument for not creating new number symbols is the fact the existing population of typewriters wouldn't have the new symbols and new typewriters would have to have them added. The great thinkers choose instead to use existing symbols specifically letters of the alphabet for the additional 6 beyond the first 10. The first 10 are taken from the decimal set, 0 through 9. To them are added, A, B, C, D, E and F.

Binary   0, 1
Octal   0, 1, 2, 3, 4, 5, 6, 7
Decimal   0, 1, 2, 3, 4, 5, 6, 7, 8, 9
Hexadecimal 0, 1, 2, 3, 4, 5, 6, 7, 8, 9, A, B, C, D, E, F

At the present time hexadecimal is the system of choice for most all if not all computers in use today. This is because all have 8 bit wide memories and multiples of 8 bits wide registers. Of course 8 is an even multiple of both 2, and 4. Binary, base 2 fits all memory/register widths corresponding to a single switch that can be either off or on and must be one or the other at all times. Hexadecimal represents 4 switches in sets.

Now we need to convince ourselves that all base 16 symbols represent all possible settings of 4 switches. 0 is off, 1 is on.

switches	octal	decimal	hexadecimal
0000	0	0	0
0001	1	1	1
0010	2	2	2
0011	3	3	3
0100	4	4	4
0101	5	5	5
0110	6	6	6
0111	7	7	7
1000	10	8	8

1001	11	9	9
1010	12	10	A
1011	13	11	B
1100	14	12	C
1101	15	13	D
1110	16	14	E
1111	17	15	F

You may be wondering why we're going over this. It has everything to do with reading the contents of memory and making sense out of it. You should also be getting a feel for how numbers are written using switches. Binary, one of two possible symbols correspond one for one with switches that have one of two possible settings, either off or on. Binary is the simplest of all the number systems but it is also the clumsiest. It takes 8 zeros/ones to display the contents of a memory location in binary while it only takes 2 symbols, zero through F to do the same thing in hexadecimal. This is true when looking at numbers but not exactly so when deciphering instructions.

Letters of the alphabet are Morse-type coded in zeroes and ones corresponding to a telegraph message coded in dots and dashes. When sending and receiving data via the USB, Universal Serial Bus one is actually telegraphing it in dots and dashes equivalences. Everything that happens in the computer is done using dots and dashes, switches open or closed, off or on. We can write those dots and dashes in individual dots and dashes or we can take them is sets and use sets to represent symbols. Writing in hexadecimal is doing that. Letters of the alphabet are coded:

Letter	binary	hexadecimal
A	01000001	41
B	01000010	42
.		
.		
Y	01011001	59
Z	01011010	5A
.		
.		
a	01100001	61
b	01100010	62
.		

y	01111001	79
z	01111010	7A

You may have noticed that we get from any letter of the alphabet to the next by adding 1 to the previous. A = 41. B = 41 +1 = 42, etc. Also and it's very important to remember capital letters and lower case letter are not coded the same. To go from caps to lower case add 32decimal or 20hex or 00100000binary to the cap's code to get the lower case code for the letter.

A	01000001	41hex 65decimal
a	01100001	61hex 97decimal

You may wonder if you will ever be able to use what we're learning here. The ticket at the checkout stand is always in decimal and never any other number system and you have decimal down pat. Me too. I retired from the world of computer hardware/software development many years ago and haven't had a need for anything but decimal ever since. I don't expect St Peter tests souls on knowledge of hexadecimal before opening the pearly gates and hopefully he's not so much as giving math tests.

My main goal is your entertainment. Don't you find it entertaining to know more than PhD's in computer science? You'd be amazed at how many of them there be that don't know what a number system is, only memorized enough to pass a test and have now forgotten most all of it.

Chapter 10, programming is the art…

…of carrying on a conversation with a stranger given the handicap of having to say everything in advance you will be able to say. Programming is writing a play with an optional plot. Happy endings are up to the reader. In the case of cook books the only difference is how one looks in the index to find a specific recipe and how it's presented. Instead of looking in the index and thumbing through pages to find the recipe in a book one types, or speaks it if the computer has voice decoding the name of the dish. The programmer looks its recipe up and outputs it to a display device of some kind. It's the programmer using the computer and not the computer doing it. You didn't forget computers do nothing? To do is human on all occasions.

Computers do nothing. Programmers do everything. Computers are no more capable of doing things than books are capable of writing themselves. Did you ever read a book-written book? Let me assure you, you will never see a computer-programmed computer. A computer without a program is as useless as and more harmless than a gun without bullets.

Programming is a literary art. Its imagining plots to stories and then writing them using tools totally unsuited to the task. Books are one-way conversations with strangers. Programs are two-way conversations with strangers. And, you must give the stranger control over the conversation. It's not all bad. You get to decide what the subject matter will be. Will be means will happen in the future. Programs are conversations that will take place later than when they are written. Say the wrong thing and the stranger will shut you up.

You didn't forget that computers do nothing? Relearn it if you did. Programming is making the computer appear to do things. People are pretty easy to fool. You're in the perfect position inside the computer looking out at strangers to make the computer seem to do some incredible things.

You always want to do something. Approach that with a bit of self-examination. "How do I _____" is the only way to be a successful programmer. It's never how do I make the computer do that. Ask yourself how do I use the computer to do that? Who's doing that? You are. It's a tricky point but it's the difference in being a good writer and a stumble bum. You don't say, "How do I get the pen to write a letter?" It's what will I say. It's always you and never the equipment that's doing the duty.

I never met a programmer who hadn't heard, "Every program has three parts, input, compute, and output the results of the computation." It's rare to find one who realizes it's the programmer and not the computer doing that. The programmer uses the computer to input the data, do the computation and output the results of the computation. The computer is an extension of the programmer's mind. Computer peripherals are extensions of the programmer's hands, arms and legs.

Inputting is using a peripheral to get information from a user/operator. Computing is doing what was requested using the computer itself to do the computation. Outputting is using one of the computer system's peripherals to show the user the results of the computation. Example: the user types a search word. You first input that word using a keyboard or other input device. You search a file looking for the word. You present the results of the search to the user using the display screen or other output device. In the case of looking things up the programmer becomes a Liberian. Library scientists are much better trained for the look-things-up task than computer scientists.

By now you should be giving up some of your prejudice and have accepted the fact that computers do nothing. My first assessment of what a computer be was a mathematical monkey wrench. Of course the task at hand was analyzing reams of data amounting to numbers only. 4 years later I was given an assignment to write a library cataloging program. I was teamed up with a library scientists. Bottom line I had to learn library science which I found to be relatively simple. Instead of hiring me to do the programming they could have taught the library scientist to program.

Today the computer is at the same primitive state writing was when Scribe was a profession. Universal computer literacy is the natural path from where we are to where we must go.

Let me encourage you, you can do it. You can carry on a conversation with someone you have never met. When a computer is turned on it always comes to a place where that stranger must decide what to do by saying something. This is the one constant from the very first ever computer program to what will be the last should that ever happen. A human being called a user or operator must do something else the computer just sets there.

If only I had a nickel for every call I got from friends and acquaintances who knew I was a "computer type" with the complaint, "I just bought a brand new IBM-machine and it don't do nothing." More often than not I would reply, "Does that change your opinion about IBM-machines a little?" As you may recall if you're that old the original Microsoft operating system blessed by and made official by IBM called DOS came on with a prompt amounting to *> and that was all there was on the screen. It was necessary to type something making a selection from a hidden menu to get anything more. That meant learning the hidden menu of operations that could be done using DOS.

The only change from *> is a screen full of funny looking things that one can "click on" instead of having to type something that made little to no sense. Those funny looking things are hints at what they're for. Some are even in boxes with English language statements. That's the answer from the world of nerds to, "I just bought a brand new IBM-machine and it don't do nothing." Now the reply is, "Click on one of them icons" with "stupid" at a whisper level added.

Of course, "But I don't want the computer to do none of that" is still a popular complaint. Now the answer to making the computer do something besides what the big computer corporations allow is to write your own programs. You'll never do that as long as you think programming is making the computer do things. You must understand programming is you doing things using the computer.

Need a reason to learn how to program and write your own operating system? Maybe you'd like a little security, a little privacy? The software world is controlled by a handful of corporations with but one purpose in life, making money. They're doing a good job at making piles of money selling very amateurish products. Their products are open doors for crooks to invade your computer. Imagine if you can a bank with no doors or windows, a wide open vault and the only requirement to get in is knowing a 4 digit number.

Names like viruses, malware and spyware are used to identify programs you don't know about that are running all the time in your computer. It's maddening but you cannot get rid of them once they get in without buying a new computer. Do that, buy a new computer, turn around twice and they're right back.

Later we'll take a crack at designing a "safe" operating system that comes on when turned on, runs at speeds relative to what the user does and not crook-speed. Look there I've invented a new word to describe how fast your computer runs, crook-speed. Cyber crook-speed anyone?

The dog has great difficulty catching the rabbit because the rabbit has a much better reason to run. I hope I've done two similar things, given you a reason to program and the courage to believe you can. Remember, they have billions of dollars' worth of reasons to stop you from replacing them. Like I've said many times if I can do it then so can you. I never do anything anyone can't do as well.

Haste makes waste in most situations. In programming it makes do it again until you get it right. The very first step in writing is vocabulary. No, not a lot of high-power words but just a handful of hairs from the sheep's back that are pressed together to make you a brand new felt hat.

Machine language programs are the easiest to write and the most difficult to get from mind to the computer's memory. Machine language is the language of zeroes and ones taken in sets. First step up from machine language is employing a combination of programs. There's 3 you'll need, a text editor to aid you when doing the actual writing, an assembler to translate your writing into machine language and a loader program to install the machine language version of your program in the computer's memory.

A text editor is nothing more than a word processor with aids to format instructions. Usually the tab key gets one form one field, label, operation, address and comment to the next and the ENTER key to get to the next line.

An assembler is a computer program that inputs lines of code and translates them into zeroes and ones for you. A line of code compares favorably with a sentence. I will now load register 7 with the contents of memory location XYZ is written:

L,7   XZY

When composing the above the programmer should have said to him/herself, "I will now/next load register 7 with the contents of memory at address XYZ."

Lines of code are a shorthand way of writing sentences. Every line of code comes from the programmer's mind. Thus the proper translation is into something that makes sense to the English professor specifically a sentence. You didn't forget computers don't do things. They aren't trainable either. They by definition are programmable. Programming is talking in sentences to one's self in an imaginary conversation with a stranger that always begin, "I will now and/or I will next…"

In our example above we used XYZ to identify a memory location. Our example computer is the DC-3 that is a 16 bit computer. 16 bits means taking switches is sets of 16 at a time. Not only that those switches must point to locations somewhere else. The assembler does all that work for you but you must do something for the assembler. You must identify where in your program you want XYZ to be. That's done with a pseudo operation. Somewhere in your program you say, "I will now define XYZ by writing a DATA statement." That somewhere can be anywhere outside of the range of the program's instructions themselves. Usually data is located at the end after all lines of machine instructions. The pseudo instruction, DATA. (Pseudo instructions are assembler instructions) is used to define and assign an initial value to variables. All data in writable memory is variable meaning the programmer can change what's in them via the program.

Data values are switch settings. Changing data values is changing switch settings. Programs do nothing but change switch settings.

Example of data defining/initiating statement:
XYZ   DATA a value

XYZ is a label. Label - a name given a location in memory thought up by the programmer. Cans of peaches have peaches written on them, their labels. Both program locations and data locations can have labels to locate them. If there are more than one data item then only the first need be labeled. For example, multi precision numbers say 64 bits or 4, 16 bit words per number might be identified by:

110

```
A          DATA 0
           DATA 0
           DATA 0
           DATA 0
B          DATA 0
           DATA 0
           DATA 0
           DATA 0
C          DATA 0
           DATA 0
           DATA 0
           DATA 0
```
Alternately in DC-3 assembly language and most all:
```
A          DATA 0,0,0,0
B          DATA 0,0,0,0
C          DATA 0,0,0,0
```
Numbers other than zero can be used. If a data value other than zero is required it's written in any of the number systems, binary, decimal or hexadecimal. Binary and hexadecimal require indicators while decimal is simply written.

Examples of writing number in data statements:
```
DATA    hFE              hex says hexadecimal
DATA    b11111110        small b says binary
DATA    254              just plain number - decimal
```
All the above assemble to the binary 11111110. I prefer writing 254 myself letting the assembler do the work of converting 254 to binary.

Subroutines to do quad, (4) word precision arithmetic might have three, 4-word data locations. I discovered years ago it's a lot easier to spell one letter names so I usually use single letters as often as possible. Misspell and get yelled at. CPU registers are often named, A, B and X. I think of multi precision data locations as CPU like registers making single letter naming appropriate.

For lack of people readable documentation of other computers we're using the very regular people friendly DC-3 instruction set and assembler. We had a brief look at its instruction set and syntax for writing in assembly language earlier. There's one last bit to learn, program listings.

A program listing is a printout of the assembled program. It allows the programmer to review the program and see where errors have been made. The programmer wrote:

L,3   Tom   looking for Tom

The assembler prints:

1 0000 1003 0000   L,3   Tom   looking for Tom
*********ERROR***VARIABLE Tom NOT DEFINED*****

From left to right top to bottom: 1 - the number of the line of code; 0000 - the memory location where the instruction goes; 1030 – 10 load register instruction, 03 – register to be loaded and 0000 the location of Tom set to all zeros because Tom wasn't defined. The rest is the original line of code.

The programmer looks at the listing and realizes he hasn't identified a data location labeled Tom. He/she now adds a statement like:

Tom   DATA   0,0   I need 2 words for 3 letters.

Let's expand a little and do something useful.

Nextry CALL,0 KEY2   Get 2 keys (r3)
       CPI,3   "To"   First 2 letters = To?
       JNE   Nextry   Jump if not To
       ST,3   Tom   Save first 2 letters

       .

       .
Tom   DATA   0,0

The listing:

1 0000 8030 002A Nextry CALL,0 KEY2   Get 2 keys (r3)
2 0002 1403 546F   CPI,3   "To"   First 2 letters = To?
3 0004 9130 0000   JNE   Nextry Jump if not "To"
4 0006 2003 0014   ST,3   Tom   Save first 2

                    .
9 0014 0000 0000   Tom   DATA   0,0

Nextry is at location 0000. Subroutine KEY2, (not shown) begins in memory at location 2A. Items enclosed in quotation marks translate into Morse type code ASCII code equivalents – 54 for capital T and 6F is small o. The variable Tom is in memory locations 14 and 15. CALL,0 KEY2 causes the contents of the updated instruction pointer register to be stored in register 0 and the address of KEY2, where KEY2 begins in memory is stored in the instruction pointer register. Thus the next instruction after the CALL will be taken from the first location of KEY2. KEY2 gets back to the next instruction after the CALL with the instruction JT (0) instruction that stores the contents of register 0 in the instruction pointer register thus "returning" to the first instruction after the CALL instruction. KEY2 is a subroutine that inputs 2 keys from the keyboard and returns them in register 3. The registers to use are at the pleasure of the programmer. Any of the 16 general register may be used instead of registers 0 and 3 that I used in this example. The register specified with the CALL instruction gets the "return" address so the subroutine CALLed can return control to the CALLing routine/program. The data obtained from KEY2 is "returned" meaning passed back to the CALLer in register 3. The 2 keys could be returned in any register or a memory location equally well, all choices made by the programmer. The second line of code consists of a compare instruction, CPI,3 "To." CP says compare two things. The 3 says one of the things to compare is in register 3. The capital I after CP says the other thing to compare is the address portion of the instruction. This reads, "I will now compare the contents of register 3 with the letters To." Another way to do the same thing is define location with some name like To DATA "To". In that case the instruction is, CP,3 To. In either case the instruction subtracts the two from one another, discards the results and sets the CPU's Zero flag according to whether or not they are identical to each other. Two equal anything's subtracted from each other yield a zero result. We're looking for the person keying, the one the programmer is conversing with to type cap T and small o. The combination of the instructions CP and JNE tests to see if he/she did. JNE says go back to Nextry if it wasn't "To" to get 2 more keys and try again.

Think of memory as post office boxes. Programs are little slips of paper in them. Executing/running the program is going to the first box, pulling out the little slip of paper, reading it and doing what it says. Then going to the next box and doing the same thing. This process continues indefinitely. What is said on those little slips of paper is limited to the instruction set of the computer and numbers. Letters of the alphabet, punctuation marks and other characters found on typewriter keyboards are numbered so they are written on those little slips of paper as numbers. There's one line of code per slip of paper.

There's just one number ranging from zero to the max per slip of paper. Instructions are lines of code that are numbers.

Think of it as a party game. Instructions are written on little slips of paper and put in the wine rack where bottles of wine usually go. The one who's "it" takes the next slip of paper from the next wine rack cubby and dose what it says. Programming is filling out those little slips of paper. One thinking up funny things for people to do at parties must think about what will be done. It's talking to one's self, "Next "victim" will have to _____." Of course little slips of paper for party fun can call for a lot to be done. The equivalent little slips of paper in the computer's wine rack are limited to incredibly simple things.

Chapter 11, programming is poison...

...take in in small doses or it will kill you. That's what my math professor said about math. Famous WW2 General Patton was heard to say, "I don't like paying for the same ground twice." When his army pushed them back, took their ground their ground stayed took. This is one of those rare cases where two birds can be killed with a single stone. We can take their ground and hold it and we can do it in steps so small we'll live through it. You didn't know this was about military science did you? Programming is war.

Of course you know this means war with the established monopolizes of the computer. They don't want you to program. They know you'll wipe them out of your life. Our weapons are tiny little bullets called instructions. The ground that must be taken is obvious.

Ground must be taken and done in steps so small we live through it. The stone that fells those two birds is called, subroutine. Subroutine – substitute routine. Routine – program.

Subroutines are made of small steps that allow us to take giant steps without fear of falling down. They also allow one to do the work, write programs just one time. That's taking ground and holding it.

We start from nothing but once. Break the problem up into small pieces. Look for pieces that are identical to each other. Write one subroutine that does that one thing, debug it and then we can do that thing as quickly as we can write, CALL,r subroutine-name.

The most important instruction in the computer's vocabulary is the CALL instruction. Call goes by other names. BAL for branch and link and JSR for jump to subroutine. Subroutines allow us to use ground previously taken so we need not take it again.

I've started out from scratch, not a single piece of software of any kind to help me several times. Step 1, I wrote input and output subroutines for my input output devices. Once written they never need to be written again. In a previous chapter using a sample program we examined "calling" a subroutine named KEY2. KEY2 called another subroutine called KEYIN. KEYIN did the actual inputting of just 1 key.

KEY2 "called" KEYIN twice to get 2 keys. Write once use as many times as one pleases. It's the equal of writing paragraphs that can be inserted in one's paper by reference.

There's nothing sacred about the names KEYIN and KEY2 to name those two subroutines. I could have named them George and Fred. Using KEY was done to give me a hint. Had I have used George I'd have to remember what I used George to do. Key is descriptive, sort of, more descriptive than George for inputting from keyboards.

Operating systems use subroutines written for the particular brand of computer. Programs are written to run "under" an operating system. If you wonder about the use of the word under I've been looking at it for well over 50 years and still wonder whose bright idea it was in the first place. All programs are extensions of a human being's mind thus all are autonomous. You don't even need an operating system. I'm sure the first time someone told me about running programs under an operating system I inquired, "How far under it do I have to crawl before my program will run?"

Operating systems are the children of input/output control systems known by the acronym, IOCS. IOCS's consists of subroutines that do exactly as advertised, they do the work of inputting the inputs and outputting the outputs. I've only written fifty to one hundred of them so I'm vaguely familiar with their longs and shorts-comings. And they do have shortcomings as I'm sure you have experienced using their rude unruly children named DOS and Windows and the like.

I believe everyone should write their own input and output routines at least once as a part of the learning process. They're real simple in most cases. Difficulties arise with the incredibly poor documentation of most peripheral devices available today. Every peripheral should come with a clear description including coding sequence for using it. The manufacturer didn't make it without knowing how to use it did he? How was it tested at time of manufacture to see if it works at all without a test program?

I've noticed that over the years the documentation for peripheral devices and in particular hard drives at the input and output levels has gone from easy to read and understand to missing altogether. I believe there is an untapped billion dollar market for a simple straight forward computer with 4 or 5 peripherals and a minimum of systems software. I'm talking about a programmable computer the English major can learn to program in an afternoon. Above all it must have secure, no eavesdroppers communications. I'll wager that English major will do the latter given the former. Telling English majors they're just too dumb to write is as ridiculous as it gets. What are they learning to do if not write?

Every computer system should have a few standard peripherals AKA IO devices including, a time of day clock, a keyboard, a display, a printer and a bulk storage device. With the capacities of memory chips now in the gigabit range and nonvolatile as well so they remember when the lights go out bulk storage is unnecessary. Let's take them from the top.

The great breakthrough in human thinking came with the realization everything happens with respect to time. A computer without a clock is like a cowboy without a horse. The cattle can be rounded up on foot but its worlds easier and less tiring to do riding a horse. There are many things that need to be timed. For easy example, program generated movies and music need relatively exacting timing. Inexact timing can be done by knowing the execution times of instructions and doing count-up-down loops. Early computers did not have clocks. I did a program that played "What Lola Wants Lola Gets" using do-nothing delay loops for timing a computer without a clock. Very accurate clocks are available in chips for pennies each. Every computer system should have one.

Don't confuse time of day clocks with CPU clocks. The CPU's clock is usable for time delays via programmed delay loops. The clock peripheral is another clock altogether that can and often does have actual time down to the microsecond level. Microsecond accuracy is necessary to time events in many disciplines. Movies and music are two obvious ones.

The ideal computer will have a keyboard. Keyboards are readily available for peanuts including wireless ones. PC's have USB chips that are matched to a counterpart in the keyboard itself. When a key is struck the keyboard encodes the key and passes it to the matching USB chip that does what a 19th century telegraph operator did, clicks it out in dots and dashes. Those dots and dashes make their way either over wires or through the air to a mating chip in the computer system that does exactly what the telegraph operator on the other end of the line did back then, converts the dots and dashes back into sets of 8 bits representing keys on the keyboard. When 8 bits have been assembled a flag bit indicating a key is ready to be read is turned on, set to 1. You don't need to know all this.

All you need to know is the address of the flag bit and the address of the data. You get that from the manual that came with the computer. No manual came with your computer? It not a computer. It's an appliance like your dishwasher with a computer controller. Does your computer do things? How about your dishwasher? You are your dishwasher? Sorry.

Get it yet? A handful of corporations have the world of computers cornered. The actual world of computers is empty, a vacuum just waiting to be filled. All you need to know to tell you where to start is to just look at the sick bordering on criminal Windows and Apple operating systems. Do you have updates enabled? Is your computer running slower and slower? Need I say more? Thank you, I'll go on.

Let's see what's involved in the IO control system, the father of the operating system. It's just a handful of simple subroutines, write once and all done forever.
** Get a key from the keyboard. Data ready flag in the
** least significant bit at IO address 0.
** Keyboard data at IO address 1.
** The key is returned in reg. 1
** The return address is in register 0
** Calling sequence:
**   CALL,0   Keyin
** Control returned here with key on r1.
Keyin   IN,1   0   ready flag to reg. 1
         NI,1   1   masking flag bit sets CPU Zero flag
         JZ   Keyin   key not ready for input, try again
         IN,1   1   input the key to reg. 1
         JT   (0)   return to caller
A form of the above works on all computers. Take it to the computer science department and ask the professor what he/she thinks about it. You'll be told it will work but it is "nonstandard" with the killing attribute that only one program can run at a time. You reply, "That takes care of all them

viruses and Russian spies and crooks looking for my personal information, bangs them right out of the saddle. The only program I want running at any time is mine."

Absolutely, the above sequence stops the computer until a key is hit. Say the program is started at 10:00AM and then the operator notices its coffee break time. The program will advance to the point where Keyin is called. It will stay there until the operator returns from coffee break and hits a key.

We'll discuss multi-tasking, more than one program seeming to run at the same time variety of operating system later. There's several ways to do that with at least one being compatible with subroutine Keyin as written. Others require a simple modification. Learn to crawl before waking. Not letting the poison kill us is the order of business at the moment.

The conversation is about the ideal computer for personal use that can be programmed by regular folks. We must also have at least one display device for the user/operator to converse with the programmer. You didn't forget all programs are conversations between two people, a programmer and a computer operator? It's identical to telephone conversations. Both parties both listen and talk. Of course it goes without saying but I'll say it anyhow, debugging programs involves programmers talking to themselves. A little like "Home on the Range" except frequently heard are discouraging words.

Keyboards are more or less standard. Displays are more like flowers with a multitude of different varieties. Thus it is necessary to resort to a theoretical display here. All have several things in common. Displays have memories where the last picture is kept. Changing the picture amounts to writing in/on that memory. I say in/on because either is correct with displays being like paper. One doesn't write in paper. Writing on the display screen amounts to changing the contents of the switch settings in the display's memory.

Two color type displays commonly known as black and white displays are changed by setting individual dots to 0 making them black and 1 making them white. That means there's one bit per dot on the screen that is by the very nature of memories always either 0 or 1 thus the screen is always something.

The dots make the picture the same way one would make a picture using pencil and graph paper by filling in or leaving blank squares on the graph paper. I'm not sure how but it's an odds on favorite Pac Man was created using graph paper. Using sets of 8 squares with filled in squares being 1's and blank squares 0's the picture was digitized and input by hand. That gave the programmer a string of 8 bit wide binary numbers that made the image of Pac Man. They could have been entered using a keyboard and the 0 and 1 keys. Most likely the 8 bit bytes were broken into 2 sets of 4 bits each and converted to hexadecimal so it could be typed into the computer using a keyboard and 0 through F keys.

No matter how the flow of information is from the programmer's mind to the graph paper to a list of binary numbers to the computer's memory and on to the display screen. That's a few easy steps. Try to do it all in one step and fail. It takes artistic talent and a lot of patience to create characters like Pac Man and get them from the mind to the display. The simple part of the problem is writing the programs to input the dot settings and copy them to the display. We know how to get keys into the computer already with a simple Keyin subroutine. Subroutine – write once use for the rest of your life. It's alright to copy someone else's just ask Microsoft if you don't believe me.

The contents of the display's memory determines the picture on the screen. That's the critical technical information. Changing the picture is changing the contents of the display's memory. Once a figure like Pac Man is in the computer's memory putting it on the screen at any position desired is storing it in the display's memory at particular locations. Everything that can be done with the display is broken up into individual actions and programmed in subroutines. The first and easiest is clearing the display, making it all black or all white or with some repeating pattern. When power is first applied the display's memory will likely have random 0's and 1's creating a nonsense display on the screen and cause the uninitiated to think it's broken.
** Subroutine to make all of the displays dots the same.
** Calling sequence:
** r1 contains the 8 bits to for all display bytes

** r1 can have any 8 bits.
** all 8 bits 0's or 1's makes all black or all white.
** 01010101 puts a pin-stripe pattern on screen
** 11001100 makes wider stripes
** 11110000 makes even wider stripes.
** the display has 256 dots per line and 256 lines
**   CALL,0 FillD Fill the display with same bits
** Upon return the display has been changed to a pattern
**

```
FillD   LI,2   8192        65,536/8 dots total
**                         (256 X 256 = 65,536)
** each 8 bit byte has 8 dots. 65,536/8 = 8192 bytes
        LI,3   DispA       Memory address of the
** first 8 dots in the display's memory
*DispA must be defined elsewhere with a DATA or
** other data defining statement.
Next    ST,1  (3)          Set next byte of display memory
        INC,3              Add 1 to index – point to next byte
        DEC,2              Sub 1 from countdown counter
        JNZ    Next        Not 0 then do next 8 dots
** We get here after 8192 bytes have been stored in
** display's memory changing the entire screen.
        JT     (0)         Returns to caller
```

It takes 7 lines of code to clear the display or fill it with a repeating pattern using the above subroutine. The calling program could have done the same thing by putting the code in line within the program. That means repeating it every time one needs to clear the display. By using a subroutine one need write the program but once. From that point forward it's a matter of calling it.

A program to alternately "flip" pinstripes and background giving the appearance they are dancing back and forth:

```
Dance LI,1          1111000       large stripes, white left
      CALL,0        FillD         fill entire screen
      LI,1          100           load decimal 100 in r1
      CALL,0        MSdelay       delay 100 milliseconds
      LI,1          0000111       large stripes, white right
      CALL,0        FillD         fill entire screen
      LI,1          100           load decimal 100 in r1
      CALL,0        MSdelay       delay 100 milliseconds
```

        JT   Dance   go back and do it again
        What the screen can be made to look like is limited only
by your imagination, and, a little trial and error.
        Let's suppose we want to change the display to an
entirely new picture. We must have that picture in the
computer's memory first. For easy example suppose we
scanned a picture into memory. We write a subroutine that
"fills" the entire screen.
** This subroutine changes the entire picture
** Calling sequence:
** r1 contains the address of new picture in memory
** Calling sequence. After loading address of new picture in r1
**   CALL,0   Newpix   complete new picture
** Returns here with entire screen changed
Newpix   LI,2   8192   65,536/8 total bytes
         LI,3   DispA   address of first display's byte
Nextb   L,4   (1)   Next set of 8 dots of new pix
         ST,4   (3)   Set next byte of display
         INC,1   Add 1 to index
         INC,3   Add 1 to index
         DEC,2   Sub 1 from countdown
         JNZ   Nextb   Not 0 then do next 8 dots
         JT   (0)   this instruction returns to caller
        Moving figures like Pac Man around on the screen calls
for slightly more complex subroutines but well beneath the
abilities of anyone of average intelligence. A couple of
subroutines allows us to suffer through the mental exercise of
locating the figure on the screen and working on those dots all
by themselves to make the figure appear to do things, make
faces and more around for example.
** This subroutine copies a string of bytes in computer
** memory to an area on the display.
** Calling sequence:
** r1 has the 8 bits for new 8 dots in 8 bit sets
** r2 has the address of the first byte to display
** r3 has the dot number locus of upper left corner
** r5 has the line number locus of upper left corner
** (r3,r5) has (x,y) location of upper left hand corner
** screen is 256 bits wide 256 lines tall
** r6 has the number of dots across of the area to fill.

                            122

```
** r7 has the number of lines tall of the area to fill.
** Calling sequence:
** load registers 1,3,5,6,7 and then:
**          CALL,0   FillDA   fill area on display
** returns to this location
FillDA  ST,0       SvretA        save the return address
        ST,2       SVr2          save (r2) Address of outputs
        ST,3       SVr3          save (r3) dot number
        ST,5       SVr5          save (r5) line number
        ST,6       SVr6          save (r6) # dots across
        ST,7       SVr7          save (r7) # lines down
NxtByt  CPI,6      8             8 bits more to go?
        JL         NxtLn         jumps if # bits to do < 8
        L,1        (2)           next byte to display
        INC,2                    point to next byte
        CALL,0     FillDBy       go fill next byte across
** FillDBy stores (r1) in next 8 bits of display memory
** the next 8 bits may not be on an even byte boundary
** FillDBy adds 8 to (r3) pointing to next 8 bits and
** subtracts 8 from (r6) number of dots across.
        JT         NxtByt        go back and do next byte
** At this point a line across has been filled.
** Now we move to the next line if we're not finished.
NxtLn   L,3        SVr3          restore (r3)
        L,6        SVr6          restore (r6)
        INC,5                    point to next line
        DEC,7                    sub 1 from # lines to go
        JG         NxtByt        jump if more lines to do
** all done. Restore registers and
** return to calling program
        L,0        SvretA        restore the return address
        L,2        SVr2 restore (r2) area address
        L,3        SVr3 restore (r3) dot number
        L,5        SVr5 restore (r5) line number
        L,6        SVr6 restore (r6) # dots across
        L,7        SVr7 restore (r7) # lines down
        JT         (0)           return to caller
SVretA  DATA       0,0
SVr2    DATA       0,0
SVr3    DATA       0,0
```

```
SVr5     DATA      0,0
SVr6     DATA      0,0
SVr7     DATA      0,0
```

In less than 3 dozen instructions I can put a figure like Pac Man on the display anywhere I please. I simply load registers with the location of the upper left hand corner dot, the width and height of the figure and a pointer to the switch settings known as bits in the computer's memory representing my figure and the subroutine does the work. Once the subroutine has been written it's forever written. That's capturing ground and holding it. With a handful of similarly difficult to do once and done forever subroutines we can create moving pictures. Sound like fun?

Here's how to make your figure move. Fill the screen with your background. Then put your figure somewhere on the screen writing over the background where your figure goes. To make your figure move restore the background where your figure is presently located and then put your figure in the same place plus or minus a dot or two across and/or a line or two up or down. The hard work is creating the background and figure(s) and converting them to dots, 0's and 1's.

Turning pictures into 0's and 1's is what scanners do. Sketch your background and scan it. It's just a string of 0's and 1's. They're really complicated, salugated, emancipated and sophisticated, really high tech, the stuff rocket scientists do, you know, turning light switches on and off. You got to be a real brain to operate light switches. Maybe there should be a degree in light switch science. There is, it's called computer science. Where does the picture come from? Try the mind of the artist. Did I mention being an artist is a much greater requirement to make pictures worth looking at than knowing how to mix paint?

Computers are modern day paint brushes for the artist. Computers are a room full of professional calculator operators to the engineer with data to analyze. Computers are the file clerks, the check writers, the bill writers and the bookkeeper for the accounting department. My very first impression of a digital computer is a math crescent wrench adjustable to fit all problems. It's a crescent wrench in all fields of endeavor. Computers are crescent wrenches of the mind.

Once upon a time reading and writing was done by a very few. One who read and wrote must have been a literate scientist. Now everyone except for mental cases reads and writes. We're just literate not literate scientists. It makes zero sense to me there is such a thing as computer science. I see no reason computer by itself leaving the scare word scientist out isn't a subject for grammar school just like reading and writing and arithmetic. Computer is a matter of learning an extremely small vocabulary and understanding the meanings of the words. It's thousands of times less difficult than learning a foreign language with a dictionary filled with words.

How great is the need for sound, hack-proof computer operating systems? In reply to a criticism comparing GM to Microsoft the president of GM said, "If I made cars that quit ever two or three miles and ran themselves into the ditch I couldn't give them away." Explaining that I said say, "Driving computers using Windows is like putting the steering wheel in the trunk and using a periscope looking into a mirror to see where one is going." Let's put the computer's steering wheel where it belongs in the hands of the common man and add windshield wipers for it's sure to rain now and again. We're talking about the most desirable computer for the computer literate with things to do not easily doable by hand.

The third desirable peripheral is a printer. In case you haven't noticed they come in all sorts of varieties. There's even printers that one can use to make things, objects one can hold in one's hands. There are printers that print edible ink on human consumable film making it possible to print one's picture on one's birthday cake along with words like, "Happy Birthday George." Of course there's the common write-a-letter kind of printer. All three varieties on the market today do the printing the same way pictures are displayed using a TV type display. It's done in dots. You didn't forget dots are switches? The same routines for displaying on television type screens also apply to all forms of printing with the addition of a third dimension for 3D, actual object printers.

Last but far from least is some form of removable storage device so we can save our work and even take it with us to use on another computer. Stick memories are the removable storage device of choice at present. They have the handicap of being on the USB bus which is patented. It should be a snap to defeat any patent on the telegraph in court but that's an expensive maybe. Evidently saying the word computer at the patent office is all that's necessary to be awarded a patent on anything. I wouldn't be surprised to find out both Microsoft and Apple have separate patents on the light switch calling it the computer wand or something like that.

With the advent of gigabyte integrated circuit memories mechanical devices such as floppy disks and hard drives are as obsolete as ox drawn covered wagons to get from New York to San Francisco. Not only is there tons of space on modern integrated circuit type memories they also never forget. The number one hazard of IC memories is forgetting. The technology has advanced to the point solid state portable bulk storage is the only way to fly with no conceivable threat of it being obsoleted any time soon. The problem to be solved by software is locating data one wishes to save and retrieve.

Bulk storage devices are usually setup in units called files with an access protocol. There are 4 subroutines required. One to identify files by name, create them and open them. A subroutine to write to the file. A subroutine to read from the file. And, a fourth to say I'm finished with the file.

One way to access date on the bulk storage device is to make the first file an index with pointers to all other files. When the device is new it must be initialized before using. Initializing amounts to setting the data for the index file to no files at all. That's as simple as defining the first set of bits to be the "files on this device counter" and loading it with zero. It's always write before read beginning with writing zero in the number of files counter. With the creation of every new file the counter has 1 added to it, the file name put in a list of files known as the index along with its particulars all beginning at zero, the length of the file for example.

A program to open or create a file is used to access the particular file by name. When called this subroutine searches the index for the file name. If it is there it returns a flag saying the file was found and is open. If the file is not there it is optionally created and the file open flag set to indicate open. Suppose I want to create and use a file containing information on patients at a doctor's office. I must think up a name. The word, "Patients" seems to me to be a relatively good one. I call the open/create with an address pointer to data with "Patients" in it. The first time I call this subroutine before I have any patients file the file will be created amounting to storing the name "Patients" in the index file and setting the first data pointer to zero. And, setting a flag indicating the file is open.

```
** Open/create file on bulk storage device.
** calling sequence
**        LI,1      Fname          points to file name
** other particulars of the file follow the name.
**        CALL,0  OpenF           open or create file
** returns here with file ready to be accessed
OpenF      ST,0      SVr0      save return address
           ST,2      SVr2      save (r2)
           LI,2      Index     address of first byte of index
           CALL,0    Asrch     Search for (r1) at (r2)
** if the name is found (r2) points to first word in file header
** and the return address (r0) is incremented to skip next
** instruction. If name not found returns to next instruction
           CALL,0    NewF      sets up new file
           L,0       SVr0      restore (r0) – return address
           L,2       SVr2      restore (r2)
           JT        (0)       return to caller
```

The write and read subroutines are equally simple. They require knowledge of how the particular device is accessed. All they do is copy data from the computer's memory to the bulk storage device, (writing) and copy data from the bulk storage device to computer's memory, (reading).

The last subroutine closes open files. In single user situations accessing it serves no purpose. In multi user situations where more than one person can access a file and that is not allowed the open subroutine first checks the open flag to see if someone else is already using it and returns a "busy" indicator if the file is in use. This also applies and even more so to individual records within a file. Easy to understand example: The add charges clerk accesses John Doe's record to add a new charge. While she is doing that the setup clerk also accesses John Doe's file to change his phone number. Both have "copies" of John Doe's record. The add charges clerk finishes first and writes the record with charges added in the file. Later the setup clerk get finished entering the new phone number and she too writes the record back to the file wiping out the old record and the new charges at the same time. The solution to the problem is a record busy flag.

When the first clerk accessed the record the busy flag is set. Anyone else attempting to access the same record will be denied. This is incredibly simple to do.

```
** Read patient record
** Calling sequence:
**      LI,1        Filename    r2 points to file name
**      LI,2        PatID       r3 points to patient's ID
**      LI,5        Buffer r1    points to where record goes
**      CALL,0      DiskRd      Go to read record sr
** returns here if there was a problem
** returns to 2nd instruction after call if got it
DiskRD  ST,0        SVr0            save registers
        ST,1        SVr1
        ST,2        SVr2
        ST,5        SVr5
        CALL,0      FindF       does this file exists?
        JT          NoFile      returns here if file not found
** returns here if file found
        L,1         SVr1        points to ID
        L,2         SVr5        points to where data goes
        CALL,0      FindR       Does this record exist?
        JT          NoRec       returns here if problem
** returns here if record found. Record copied from file to calling
program's record area known as buffer.
        L,0         SVr0        return address to r0
        INC,0                   add I to skip one instruction
        JT          NoRec+1     skip next instruction
NoRec   L,0         SVr0        error return address to r0
        L,1         SVr1        restore registers
        L,2         SVr2
        L,5         SVr5
        JT          (0)         return to caller
```

Programming is one of those things that either one can't do at all or it's a matter of practice and endurance. Either one can ride a bike, swim and the like or one cannot. Knowing the principals involved is easy while doing it is a matter of talent. In my mind programming is more akin to writing cook books than anything else. It's communicating remote control with another human being. The only difference between cookbooks and computer books is how the recipe is presented, on paper or on a display screen with all else involved being equals. Pens equal keyboards, paper equals computer memory, library equals bulk storage device and on and on. No matter how good a writer one be if one cannot communicate with the cook, instruct the cook on what to do next one is not qualified to write cook books. Of course the goodness of writing ordinary papers is how well one communicates with ones readers.

All programs are predetermined conversations between a programmer and a computer operator. In the creation and proofing phase of programming the operator and the programmer are the same person. Acting alone programmers write and test programs. This is the special case of programmers having to carry on meaningful conversations with themselves. Shakespeare wrote, "To thine own self be true." You don't suppose he was talking about computer program development? Those who lie to themselves will find program development impossible. The 11th commandment, "Thou shalt not believe thy own lies."

Chapter 12, IO control systems…

…have children that are all named Operating System. They solve the problem exemplified by, "I just bought my first IBM machine and it don't do nothing." This has led to the computer becoming what the operating system suppliers wants it to be and nothing more. It's no longer a computer but rather it's an appliance with a computer controller programmed to control everything its owner does.

You may have heard the term, "Closed architecture." That says everything possible will come from the computer manufacturer. Apple is a closed architecture system. You can use Apple everything or do without. In the beginning the PC was open architecture. Many million airs and a few billion airs were made with add-ons for the PC. Over time the PC has become de-facto closed architecture. In simple terms what you get is what a handful of corporations want you to get. It's get that or get nothing.

You did register your computer with the manufacturer and open an account with Microsoft? Bought any improvements, patched up a few holes yet? Have you been faithfully automatically updating getting all the latest patches? Have any idea how many holes are left that need patching? Anything personal like your social security number or bank account numbers showing through one of those giant size holes? Buying pants full of holes must be high fashion.

For many years Microsoft has dominated the PC "operating system" world through a universal mental condition that sprang from IBM attempting to make "IBM-machine" synonymous with "computer." Ask the average person at the time and be told an IBM-machine was better than a computer. And, the official operating system blessed by IBM was Microsoft's DOS, Disk Operating System.

The PC being open architecture literally thousands of competitors making PC's identical to IBM like flies swarming about a fresh cow pile. Almost instantly faster CPU's with more memory made by upstarts in garages and bedrooms could be bought for half the price of an IBM-machine. Turns out all issues are economic. Computer illiterate John Q was penny wise, willing to settle for more at a lower price suffering the embarrassment of it not being an official IBM-machine. Thousands manufactured IBM-machines that were better than IBM-machines. Eventually computer won the "what am I" contest defeating IBM-machine at the lowest bidder auction. The IBM-machine has gone the way of the dinosaur. IBM seems to be following close behind.

At the same time several operating systems far superior to Microsoft's DOS became available. A few of the little people making computers in their garages included them with their PC's. A saturated market and businessman prejudice cause a handful of major manufacturers to emerge and corner the PC market. Once upon a time there were 10,000 PC makers. Now it's a handful, the ones who managed to get theirs sold at established retail outlets like Office Max and Staples.

I wrote the equal of Windows in 1972. Necessity was the usual mother of invention. The task at hand was automating the cash register function for retailers. POS, Point Of Sale was the name of the game. With a single minicomputer I handled 16 cash registers all at the same time multi-tasking and without interrupts too. The minicomputer had 8,192 bytes of main memory and a 49,152 byte drum hard drive. Not only that when the computer failed and they failed, we had the first ever microprocessor based computer using the Intel 4004. It was programmed by me alone to detect system's failure. When the main system failed I automatically dial a "sister" computer at our facility and keep the store open over the phone lines.

It was me inside three computers doing the cash register function. Two computers were at the grocery store. One did the point of sale function and the other was an automatic failure detector with telephone calling capability. When systems failures occurred and they did I disconnected the local computer and reconnected a substitute over the phone. Notice it was me doing it and the computers.

You haven't forgotten computers do nothing. People use computers to do things. Over a 50 year career I did many things using computers. The best I ever did was confuse people about who was doing what. Not one ever fully gave up the idea it wasn't the computer. Are you still there?

My automatic backup system worked like a charm. The year was 1972. You know I chuckled at the Internet being sold as the latest and greatest thing since bottled beer, 1995. It only took computer scientists 23 more years to finally at last send, "hello world" or some other equally ridiculous message over the phone from one computer to another computer. The sad part is those doing it didn't know it was not computer to computer but rather it was programmer to programmer. No matter the message it was certainly earth shattering. Don't you imagine?

Evolution being a slow process we are now evolved to sending and receiving messages with the greatest of ease. With just a little effort on the part of Russian computer scientists, former Soviet IBM machinists with us sending our messages "under" the latest operating system our messages get to Moscow first. All roads lead to Rome but all phone lines lead to Moscow. The lack of communications privacy is a major feature of Windows and Apple's closed architecture operating systems. Ask an official computer scientist if you don't believe me.

It's hard to say those super-duper operating systems even have a front door or even windows filling in the holes in the walls. If they do have doors and windows rather than holes in the wall they're wide open. With battery power it's not necessary to turn your computer on before the crooks come marching in. At Microsoft headquarters there's someone with a program running in your computer scanning your computer's storage devices while you sleep. They only want to update your system, your computer may be running dangerously fast. The Microsoft motto, "Speed kills."

We have choices. We can let the crooks in. We can buy a virus detector program and hope it stops them from getting in. We can buy scanning software and try to find and remove them. We can buy a new computer and enjoy a few minutes without them. Or, we can write our own operating systems and slam the door in the crooks faces.

We've had a peek at IO control systems while pondering programming. The whole idea behind an IO control system is to control peripheral devices and not control either the programmer or the program user. Expressions like, "Off the shelf" and "canned" apply. I like, "do once and use as often as needed." Another and perhaps the best is, "Let someone else do the driving." Inventing one's own recipes isn't necessary, cook books sold everywhere. At both libraries and bookstores recipes are "lifted" from cook books making cook book purchase unnecessary.

Lots if not most people me included find writing IO subroutines and especially bulk storage ones tedious. Defining a filing system on the computer is as mentally taxing as defining a filing system for an office and more like an indexing system for a library. The librarian is the best trained person for the job. The display peripheral has now bubbled to the top of the list of the mentally taxing to implement. That's so we can make and show moving pictures and operate several programs at the same time.

The operating system began as a *> prompt and has evolved to "point and click." All else remains the same. The user should decide what programs to run. In the beginning that was done by typing the name of the program followed by the "enter" key. Now it's move the mouse pointer to an area on the screen and click. Two major changes, new steering wheel and the ability to drive more than one car at a time. Instead of typing a program name we use a device called mouse to move the cursor to an icon on the screen and click. Once a program is running we can "open" another screen and do the same thing again.

Now let's say something good about Microsoft. The Windows operating system is top drawer in that department. I can "run" the Ford.com program on one screen and Chevy's on another and ping-pong back and forth. If I like I can run the program of all auto makers at the same time with each having its own screen. I can't look at but one screen at a time so there has to be a way to select which one I want at any given time. This is the act of time-sharing both the computer and the display screen. There's more than one way to skin that cat.

Let's see if I can make you understand how incredibly easy it is to make more than one program seem to be running at the same time. I call it the "baseball Bugs" effect. There is a Bugs Bunny cartoon where Bugs got himself collared into playing baseball all by himself against a team of ruffians. Bugs pitched, caught, played first, second and third base, played short stop and all three outfield positions at the same time. Bugs is so fast he could throw a fastball and get to the catchers position and catch it. He pitched, caught the pitch and when the ball was hit made it to the defensive position and fielded it. Computers are equal to Bugs Bunny in the speed department.

Bugs played all position but only one at a time. Computers can run an indefinite number of programs but only one at a time. Bugs appeared to be playing all positions at the same time. The computer appears to be running all programs at the same time. Bugs played one position at a time. He played the next position as demanded by the progress of the game. The computer executes one program at a time. It executes the next program as demanded by the progress of the computing.

The very first theory of multi programming operation relied on every program immediately advancing to the state where an input was required. Take our several automaker's programs for example. We start them all. The only one running is the one we "clicked on" last. However, we can ask for a lot of information from one program it must get from the Internet for example. It will take a few seconds, minutes even. In the meantime we can click on another program while the information slowly comes in. We can have several programs "stalled" while obtaining data.

One program is always running. That's the user interface program. The user decides what to do. No matter how many programs are running the user interface program is also running giving the user the option to start still another program and stop programs that are running. Thus in the simplest possible scenario there's always the user interface program running. The proper name for this is multiplexing.

Windows has one maddening failure mode. The operator controls stop working altogether. Programs cannot be closed. The cure is ctrl-alt-del at the same time and "killing" all running programs causing all work done to be lost. Windows also has an even more aggravating failure mode where ctrl-alt-del doesn't work only unplugging the computer will do. They've only had 37 years to get it right. The atom bomb was done is less than 5 years. Nuclear scientists they're not.

Multi-programming and/or multi-tasking is simple. The computer user/operator is effectively carrying on conversations with two or more people known as programmers at the same time. Easy to understand example: There's a professor and 5 students discussing a subject. The professor allows each student to speak a word or two one after the other. All the words from any one student as a set make a whole statement. All students appear to be talking at the same time because all keep adding to what they are saying when they get a turn that only allows them to say one or two words.

In the computer there are any number of programs that appear to be running at the same time. A program called a monitor controls how long each will be allowed to run, how many words a given student will be allowed to speak in our people do the same thing example above. First program is given a few millionths of a second run time. Then the next is allowed to run for a similar period of time. Then the next and the next to the last program in the que, (que – list of running programs). The monitor then begins again with the first program. This way all get a little done each time they get a turn making all appear to be running at the same time. The computer executes one instruction at a time thus at any moment it's executing an instruction from one and only one of the three programs.

The notion of programs running "under" an operating system comes from the main system's program being called a monitor. The monitor is the equal of the professor in the above example of multiplexing. All programs are executed through the user communicating with the programmer(s) who wrote the monitor program. In the case of Windows the user clicks on an icon on the display screen.

Let's get back to the theory all programs will immediately advance to a state where they will have to wait for an input or an output to become ready. That makes the ideal place to stop one program and let another have control. Of course the next program will also instantly advance to the IO required state. Thus it's your turn, it's your turn, it's your turn and on and on in a circle made of a string that is as long as the number of programs running. It's program 1, program 2,, last program and start all over again giving program 1 a short actual run time.

Neither boasting nor bragging but I wrote a multiplexing system with a max of 17 programs running at the same time as well as an operator program, accounting programs to do sales reports etc. and a telephone modem to send reports to headquarters, 1972. They all appeared to be running at the same time with terminals clicking and jingling and the front office console, a teletype clanking away while the lights on the modem blinked as I sent reports to another computer I had programmed at company headquarters to receive the reports and print them out.

After all is said and done I'm a fairly regular college graduate. I have never taken a class in computer science. Get the idea? If I can do it so can you. Monitors are truly simple programs so it makes sense it took 10,000 computer scientists at Microsoft many years to almost get to the level of 1970's software done by one officially unqualified by university standards programmer, me. And of course they forgot to put doors and windows, pun intended, in their futuristic Windows operating system. Windows runs with windows open letting all sorts of buzzards fly right in.

Let's take a crack at that wonderful world of high tech art known as an operating system. In the real world when computers with operating systems are powered-on a thing called a bootstrap loader loads the operating system and transfers control, does JT, (jump to) its first instruction. Keep in mind that if it truly is an 8 gigahertz computer then it's executing 50,000,000 instructions each second. My old DC-3 only did 5,000,000 instructions per second. With a slow floppy disc it was hardly more than a blink of the eye to roll in the operating system and away we go, screen filled with a menu for an operator to choose from just like Windows only 20+ years earlier. Yes indeed I wonder what Windows is doing during power-on and restart that takes it so long.

In the real world operating computers are turned on and operating systems loaded and "turned on" meaning the loader executed a jump to its first line of code faster than the on/off switch can be released.

A more or less standard part of every program that usually comes in the first instructions is initialization. In our subroutine examples the first thing done is saving registers for an example of the kind of things done during initialization. It's not unusual for main programs such as operating systems to have no initialization to do. All counters, counts, pointers and so on are initialized by the loader. Anyhow a usual initialization can be measured in a handful of instruction that execute in millionths of seconds. What kind of masturbations Windows does when it's started and restarted is a wonderment to me.

I like to use descriptive names for different functions of operating systems. There's a director that turns programs off and on. It uses a table to decide where to restart running programs that are waiting their next turn. Say there's two programs running. The director starts the first program that runs until it reaches a break point usually having to wait for a peripheral to come ready. At that point the user program calls a subroutine in the directors set call HOLD which marks the place by putting it in the user's table as the place to restart execution next cycle.

```
** user program relinquishes control by:
        CALL,15    HOLD        give up control
** The director uses the return address in r15 as the place
** to turn the program back on. Turn on = jump to.
** The HOLD routine simply stores all registers in the user
** program's entry in the execution table.
** Since we get to HOLD with a CALL the contents of the
** specified register, r15 is the location of its next inst.
** The director program has a table, a que to tell it which
** program will be run next, a counter to tell it how many
** programs are in the execution chain, and a pointer to the
** first word of the executing program's table.
```

The big boss is called monitor. Technically it is the operating system with all programs loaded and execution started by it. It can also be called the "main" program. A part of the monitor is the user/operator interface, the steering wheel for all practical purposes. I call it "Control."

```
** After Monitor is loaded it executes:
Monitor LI,1 1            contents of r1 set to 1
        ST,1   NPgms      number of programs in the
**                        execution chain. All begins with
**                        one program running "Control"
        LI,1 Control      address of operator control
**                        program part of monitor. At
**                        power on Control is the
**                        only program running.
```

```
            ST,1        XTab+15       Where to enter Control
**                                    the first time.
**
** Start execution chain from the top – run first program.
NextC   LI, 1       0             contents of r1 zeroed
        ST,1        PgmXN         number of next program
        LI,1        Xectab        Address of execution table
        ST,1        Xecptr        First program's pointer
Director LI,15      Xecptr        Address of next pgm's table
        L,0         (15)          restore r0
        INC,15                    point to next entry in tab.
        L,1         (15)          restore r1
** repeat for all r's through r14
        L,15 (15)                 return address to r15
        JT          (15)          go to where pgm last "held"
Hold    ST,15       SVr15         save (r15)
** We're saving (r15) in a temporary location so we can
** use r15 as an index and not lose its contents
        L,15        Xecptr        points to first entry in table
        ST,0        (15)          save r0 in user pgm table
        INC,15                    add 1 to (15) point to next
        ST,1        (15)          save r1 in user pgm table
        INC,15                    add 1 to (15) point to next
** repeat ST and INC until r14 done then
        L,0         SVr15         restore r15 from table
        ST,0        (15)          save r15 in user pgm table
** At this point we've saved all the registers of our calling
** program with r15 pointing to where to restart it.
        L,0         Xecptr        points to this pgm's table
        AI,0        16            point to next pgm's table
        L,0         PgmXN         execution no. of this program
        INC,0                     add 1 for next pgm's no.
        ST,0        PgmXN         updated program number
** Now we set things up to execute the next program in
** our execution chain.
** But first we must see if we've just finished the last
** program in the chain.
** NPgms is total number of running programs.
        S,0         NPgms         Is this end of list?
        JL          Director      Another pgm in chain
```

138

```
** If we get here we've just reached the end of the list of
** programs executing.
        JT          NextC        start again from the top.
SVr15  DATA    0           temp for saving (r15)
NPgms DATA    0           no. pgms in que
PgmXN DATA    0           no. of pgm running
Xecptr  DATA    0           points to next pgm's table
XTab    ORG     XTab+512    room for 32 programs, 16ea
```

We only saved the registers in the execution table. This is an example program to show you how incredibly simple multitasking operating systems truly be. Other datum such as memory space used is usually kept in the program's data table and when a program is turned off that space is made available for other programs to use. When a program starts it is allocated memory space. When it's terminated that space is deallocated. I have the funny feeling this is a tender spot in Windows that causes systems stoppages.

We're looking at the monitor program that interfaces with the user. Monitors have loaders. The user indicates a program to run using the keyboard, mouse or other means and the monitor does the loading and puts the program in the execution chain. When the user/operator says all done with that one it's taken out of the execution chain.

User programs can be operating systems that run "under" a main operating system. For example, a computer could have several groups of people using them at the same time. A store has a main operating system. It also has an operating system for cash registers. The main operating system relinquishes control to the cash register operating system that cycles one time through all registers and then "HOLDs" waiting for its next turn in the main multiplexer's chain of running programs. There is only a time-of-execution and memory size limit to how many operating systems can be imbedded inside each other.

The above Operating System, OS for short is non-interrupt driven. Take it to the computer science professor and watch him shake his head. Never heard of such a thing. And for sure one program will hog the machine and all the others will just set there. So you say, "What if I stand over the programmers with a shotgun" adding, "and I say put breakpoints in your program or I'll put breakpoints in you." You can't shoot people for making mistakes. You can add just 1 little interrupt, a watchdog timer with a shotgun that blows hogging programs right out of the computer.

A watchdog timer is hardware, a countdown clock. As the execution of each program in the chain begins the director program sets it to a given time, the maximum time the program will be allowed to run. If the executing program does not "HOLD" within that time the timer "goes off" generating an interrupt.

What's an interrupt? The CPU inserts in the executing program a CALL to a subroutine that's a part of the operating system. Traditionally interrupt subroutines save all registers and flags so the interrupted program can be reentered at the point of interruption. The interrupt is serviced meaning whatever it calls for is done. An interrupt from the keyboard means a key is ready to be read for example. An interrupt from a watchdog timer says the running program is stuck in a rut.

Thus we can add a watchdog timer to our very well behaved non-interrupt driven operating system and weed out hogs or at a minimum give the user operator an opportunity to say kill it or let it run.

Do you see how crooks and bakers get "in" your computer and slow it down? Without knowing anything else about Windows I know that since they can "get in" Windows allows programs from the internet to get in its execution que. Having a virus says some program was put in the execution que by Windows. Once there the program disabled the interrupt system effectively shutting windows down. Did your computer stop? Its 90+% a case of malware disabling the interrupt system with a single instruction, DISI. DISI is cyanide to an interrupt driven system.

Here's how "they" get you. Back at home base the crooks modify Windows to do their dirty deed. Then Windows lets them execute a harmless looking program that disables the interrupt system. At their leisure, no interrupt to stop them possible they download their contaminated version of Windows and write it over your existing system. They also write over your backups so restoring the system doesn't get rid of them. Once they got you they got you. Goodbye Columbus to their world.

There is no defense against it. Be as careful as you can possibly be and accidently go to one of those web sites or open an e-mail from Russia. We aren't allowed to have secure communications because the FBI needs to wiretap us. We can't get rid of unknown programs in our execution chain because some of those folks only want to help whether or now we want any help. They watch us all the time, are in the execution chain eating up time. When we Google "hotel" the internet reservation sites swarm like flies around a fresh cow pile. How do they know? They're in the execution chain watching every keystroke and mouse click. No matter how fast the computer or how little time they take with enough of them and the fastest computer sputters and pops like starting an old car on a cold morning.

Can you see an obvious cure once you've been stung? How to get rid of them be it only for a little while. All computers should come with the operating system on a read only device, disk, stick memory etc. and the loader also in read only memory in the computer with no way of altering either one. To get rid of all the parasites that have invaded your computer restore it to right out of the box state by reloading the original operating system. You didn't get an operating system on a disk? You had to download it? I see.

IO control subroutines are a part of the operating system. Traditionally that is done using dedicated memory locations. The user program accesses them with absolute addressing. Suppose memory location 10 has a pointer to the keyboard input subroutine. That's the address of the subroutine put there by the loader when loading the operating system. The user programmer must know the dedicated address of pointers to all IO subroutines used. Thus the list must be included as a part of the operating system's documentation. Windows isn't documented or its documentation is effectively secret.

In my operating system's documentation I included the list with all the peripherals we had at the time. Calling my subroutines was as simple as first reading my documentation and then:

```
L,ra          absolute address    a decimal number
CALL,rb    (ra)
```

The first instruction uses the absolute address of the peripheral driver duplicating it in register a, one of the general purpose registers. The second is a call to the driver using the contents of register a as the address.

Example: Suppose the keyin subroutine's address is in memory at absolute address, 10.

```
        L,15      10          the contents of mem loc 10 to r15
        CALL,0  (15)          make the call to keyin
```

There's a thing called parameterizing. Huge word tiny meaning. Instead of using 10 in our instruction:

```
KEYIN       EQU     10          EQU makes
**                              KEYIN and 10 same thing
            L,15    KEYIN
```

Let me suggest:

```
KEYIN       ST,0    Ret+1       Put return in address of JT
            L,15    10
            CALL,0  (15)
Ret         JT      0           Instruction will be modified
```

When a key-in is to be done:

```
        CALL,0  KEYIN
```

Since we cannot anticipate new devices or their interface requirements we must have the ability to add driver subroutines to a basic set. That means "installing" drivers in the field. Don't you imagine it takes a wizard to do that? Nah, just load it into the next open space and put a pointer to it in the IO subroutine pointer table. Of course this modifies the system, a clear path for unwanted people to get in. This is especially so for drivers downloaded over the Internet. As far as I know no crooks have thought of sending some innocent looking "add on" through the regular mail that when added on gives them control of your computer.

My mother told me more than once, "There's more in managing than there is in making." One of the first things I was told in the world of programming was, "Knowing why is a lot more valuable than knowing how." The president of mini computer maker, Computer Automation, Dave Methvin's favorite expression was, "If the job calls for one person with a 170 IQ 10,000 with 150 IQ's will never get it done." Let me add one, "It takes one programmer to do it right and only two to make a mess of it." Evidently Windows is the work of thousands.

The best approach to large scale program development is to give the entire job to several programmers. The one with the 170 IQ will do it right away while the rest will make excuses for it taking longer than they originally thought.

Did I mention computers are just a bunch of switches no more difficult to understand than an ordinary light switch? How many light switches in a set of light switches does it take before you throw up your hands and say it's just too complicated for me to ever understand? One bad apple spoils all the others in the barrel. One bad switch setting spoils the whole program.

Chapter 13, the awesome power...

...of the light switch was understood thousands of years ago by the author of the first book of the Holy Bible, Genesis.
Genesis 1:3

And God said, Let there be **light**: and there was **light**.

The most dramatic event ever was God flipping the switch that turned on the big light bulb in the sky, the sun. Thus the power of the light switch operator is the power to "let there be light" that is the awesome power of Almighty God. Computing extends the power of God allowing the operation of billions and billions of light switches at speeds faster than the preacher can even in his wildest dreams pass the plate and have it lathered in a glorious foam of one hundred dollar bills.

Computers are collections of switches and nothing more or less. Thus computers do exactly what switches do, nothing at all. Switches don't turn lights on people use switches to turn lights on. I know what you're thinking, people use computers to do all sorts of things. At least I've gotten you past the point computers do all sorts of things. People do things using computers. If your computer starts doing things you had better unplug it. Won't work it's battery powered.

It's a fine point but necessary to understand point else we're back to the days when the average person was sure computers were thinking machines that made mistakes. "That was caused by a computer error" was the standard dodge of the truth. Now we know why computers don't make mistakes. It's because they are nothing more or less than a collection of switches and we know switches can neither think nor can they make mistakes.

People can leverage their thinking using light switches in collections called computers. The word is programming. The objective is to operate machinery, move material and create objects both mental and physical via though processes.

I think I mentioned earlier electrically operated computers are no different in all respects other than difficulty of operation than one with manually operated switches. We'd quickly wear blisters on our fingers throwing switches without the help of electricity. This brings us to electricity and magnetism and switches that are magnetically and electrically operated.

In my opinion the only subject more over rated than computers is electricity and magnetism, electricity and magnetism being but one thing in two different forms. Right off the bat we've cut the problem in half by noticing its but one subject.

There's but three words we must know the definition of to know all we **need to know** about electricity and magnetism. There's worlds more to it but we needn't bother with more than these three words. They're common words you hear all the time, voltage, current and resistance. That's the basics of and all of electricity and magnetism we'll bother with here. That's plenty enough to make switches we can turn on and off using mental processes.

Let us note, the world is smothered in electrical ignorance. For example, it's often heard on the television, "volts of electricity." "They is plum et up with ignorance" is no less ignorant. Volts is a measure of electrical force. It's, "currents of electricity" not "Volts of electricity." Here's a better analogy to, "volts of electricity." Try he was killed by "grams of gun powder." The gun powder didn't do the killing. It's the bullet the gun powder propelled at him that killed him. Gun powder is the force behind the bullet. Volts is the same class of things as gun powder. Volts is the force behind electrical bullets called electrons. Both gun powder and volts are measures of force.

A million grams of gun powder will not kill if there is no bullet. A million volts will not kill if there is no current. A tiny little 22 caliber slug propelled with a small powder charge can kill. As little as 90 volts pushing one tenth of an amp of current through the human body can kill. Volts equal gun powder. Current, amps equal bullets. Resistance equals the thickness of the armor. A little bullet, few amps propelled by a small powder charge, voltage, at one in the wide open can kill. A huge bullet, many amps propelled by a large powder charge, a lot of volts will not injure one behind a thick steel plate, with massive resistance. There's but one formula for those who care.

$$V = IR$$

V is in volts. I is in amps. R is resistance measured in ohms. This formula is known as Ohm's law. 90 volts will push

90 amps through the body of a sweaty person's giving the body zero resistance and instantly kill the person deader than a door knob. One million volts cannot push enough amps through the body of a person with a billion ohms of resistance to even be noticed. Do the arithmetic, plug the givens into the above equation. The fellow on TV talking about "volts of electricity" is, you know what I mean, just plain ignorant.

Only engineers designing electrical things need to know and use Ohm's law. Programmers have no need to know Ohm's law unless given the task of writing a program that uses it. Even then it's just another formula like, D=RT used to calculate how long it will take to get to grandma's house when the kids in a whiney tone of voice inquire, "Are we there yet?"

Now about that magnetism stuff. Wrap a wire around an iron rod, pass an electrical current through it and the iron rod becomes a temporary magnet. Leave the current there long enough and the rod becomes a permanent magnet, just plain magnet in the vernacular. If we add to the iron rod a spring loaded iron plate attached to a light switch's arm we can operate the switch electrically. When a current is passed through the wire the iron rod becomes a magnet and attracts the iron plate causing it to move and turn the light switch on. Removing the current demagnetizes the iron rod causing it to "turn loose of" the iron plate and the spring causes the iron plate to move back turning the switch off. When the current is on the iron rod becomes a magnet attracting the iron plate physically attached to the switch causing it to move and turn the switch on. The spring will turn the switch off when current is withdrawn from the coil of wire. This kind of electrically operated switch is called a relay. Early computers used relays for memories, registers and logic all three.

Another kind of electrically operable switch is the vacuum tube. The vacuum tube was invented, (discovered) by John Fleming, 1904. John discovered that burned out light bulbs still conducted tiny currents across the space between the dangling wires where the filament once was. Later it was discovered that heating one of the wires caused electrons to "boil off" it. This allowed significant unidirectional current flow between the wires from heated wire to cold wire. Devices that allow current flow in one direction and inhibit it in the other are called diodes.

The next breakthrough came with the invention of the triode. The hot wire that emits electrons is the tube's cathode. The cold wire that receives the electrons is the tube's anode. A third wire was inserted between the two and named grid. The grid is the equal of the lever used to operate a light switch. With no voltage on the grid the tube conducts electricity, switch on. If a negative voltage is applied to the grid current flow is "pinched off" switch off. Thus the grid is used to switch the tube on and off, i.e. allow current flow across it or inhibit current flow across it. Notice this is exactly what a light switch does. When the light switch is on current flows across it and when it is off current flow across it is pinched off, halted, stopped.

Recently I was surprised to find out high quality amplifiers used by musicians still had vacuum tubes. I thought vacuum tubes had been completely replaced by transistors. Vacuum tubes are the original non mechanical switches. They have three parts, a cathode, anode and grid. The grid is the lever used to operate the switch. Current flows from cathode to anode if the grid has a small enough voltage on it. If a large negative voltage is applied to the grid there will be no current flow. No voltage means current flow. No voltage on grid turns tube on negative voltage on grid turns tube off. Friends and neighbors that's a switch.

You don't need to know this but to avoid too much valid criticism vacuum tubes come is many variations. So do transistors that we'll discuss momentarily. Amplifier is the proper term for all embodiments of both vacuum tubes and transistors. Amplifiers are classified according to how they're used. I'm only talking about a class C amplifiers that are either "pinched off" meaning no or miniscule current flow across them or "saturated" meaning max possible current flow across them. Light switches are class C amplifiers by the definition of class C amplifiers. Off means no current while on allows max current flow.

The very first fast computers had vacuum tube based switches for registers and logic. Vacuum tubes have a couple of nasty problems. They need high voltages, consume large amounts of electrical power, generate a lot of heat and they have short life spans. But they were fast and brought about the possibility of large scale computing. Someone stood by with fire extinguisher in hand in during the early days of large scale computers.

I'm an old Navy ET, Electronic Technician. More correctly I'm a Naval Air Weapons Systems Technician. I was at the front in the cold war. We did the night watch in the skies over Korea and Japan in night fighters, F3D's to be exact. The F3D had gun aiming RADAR along with two search RADARs, one search RARAR looking forward to find the bad guys and one aft to see if anyone was sneaking up behind us. Total weight of the RADAR system was around two tons. By the probability of parts failure it had so many parts one would always be failed thus the system would never be 100% operable. In spite of it all we managed to down over a dozen Russian made counterparts in the night skies over Korea. Correct, I was a cop in the big Korean police action, a high tech Marine with a bullet launcher rather than a rifle. We kept those "can never work" RADAR's working and received a unit citation for our efforts. I'm a decorated war hero, lol.

Memory switches developed more slowly than logic switches. You didn't forget computers are nothing but a pile of switches? The huge memory breakthrough came with the invention of core memories. The first major CPU breakthrough came with the development of the transistor.

Transistors make extremely friendly switches compared to vacuum tubes. Anode voltages as high as 500volts are necessary for some vacuum tubes. Transistors operate on flashlight battery voltages. 5 volts became the standard for all second generation computers. Transistors make switches just like vacuum tubes.

The type of transistors we're concerned with here have 3 parts, emitters, collectors and gates. They're the equal in function to vacuum tubes but that's where the equal ends. Just like the light switches on your wall transistors are open circuit meaning off or closed circuit meaning on. When a transistor is on current flows from the emitter to the collector. When off no current flows. Putting 5 volts on the gate turns the transistor on and putting 0 volts on the gate turns it off. Fight it with all your mite there's no way to get around switches.

Transistor switches are inherently signal inverters. Invert - make the opposite of the given. The inversion of 0 is 1, the inversion of 1 is 0, the inversion of 0 volts is 5 volts and the inversion of 5 volts is 0 volts. When we put 5 volts on the gate of a transistor the voltage at the emitter appears on the collector. The emitter being grounded its voltage is zero volts. With the gate at zero volts the collector will be at 5 volts. With the gate at 5 volts the emitter voltage of zero will be on the collector. The output of the switch is the voltage on the collector. The input is the gate. Input 5 volts, output 0 volts. Input 0 volts, output 5 volts. Thus the output is inverted, meaning the opposite of the input. Think of it as the switch with the voltage on the output lug and ground on the input lug. Turning the switch on connects the output to the input grounding it.

If you care this is where Ohm's law comes into play. The collector is connected to the 5 volt power source using a resistor that limits the amount of current flowing across the transistor by the formula, V=IR. V is 5 volts. I is current that can destroy the transistor if it is too high. Thus R=5/I is used to pick the size of the resistor given a nominal value for I.

All we need to know here is the fact that transistors are used to make electrically operable switches. Electrically operating means turning switches on and off using electricity instead of our fingers.

5 volts

↑

Current limiting resistor

↑

Collector

↑→ Output

Input, **Gate** →|

Emitter

↑

Ground, 0 volts

Above we have a schematic of the fundamental transistor bases electrically operable switch as used in modern computers and computer memories.

Now let's take some of the wonderment out of how logic works. Computers use things called gates. There's two kinds of them, AND gates and OR gates. They do exactly what the words AND, and OR imply. If switch 1 is on AND switch 2 is on then the light is on. AND gate - 2 or more switches in series. All must be turned on for the light to go on. As a set, 2 or more switches are effectively a single switch. All must be on for the conglomerate switch to be on.

How about OR? Can you guess? We have 2 or more switches in parallel. If any one of the switches is on the light will be on. OR gates are a conglomerates of switches in parallel that as a set become a single switch.

Did you notice the use of the word gate? Transistors have three parts, emitter, collector and gate. Gating is turning the transistor switch on or off. A set of transistor switches are arranged in either series or parallel to operate still another transistor switch. That's what logic is all about.

AND, and OR is all there actually be. However they have compatibles known as NAND and NOR. NAND is identical to AND except the output is inverted. AND – if all switches are on then the output is on – if any switch is off then the output is off. NAND – if all switches are on then the output is off – if any switch is off then the output is on. NOR is identical to OR except the output is inverted. OR – if any switch is on the output is on – if all switches are off then the output is off. NOR – if any switch is on the output is off – if all switches are off the output is on. You may recall from above, signal inversion is natural with transistor switches thus NAND and NOR are the norm with AND, and OR requiring an additional inversion.

Registers are made of switches that stay set. They stay turned on or off. These switches are conglomerate sets of switches arranged in a configuration called latches. Electrical latches are latching switches. It takes a minimum of 2 transistors to make a latch. Let's call them transistors A and B. Both emitters are connected to ground and both collectors are at switchable 5 volts, (switchable – normally at 5 volts and have a current limiting resistor so they can be shorted to ground at 0 volts). A's collector is connected to B's gate and B's collector is connected to A's gate. A little though twister for you. If temporarily we put 5 volts on A's gate the voltage on A's collector goes to zero. That puts zero volts on B's gate causing B's collector to have 5 volts on it. B's collector is connected to

A's gate. When we take our 5 volts away A's gate still has the 5 volts from B's collector and therefore the output is, "latched." If we temporarily ground A's gate then A's collector will go to 5 volts and on to B's gate causing B's collector to go to 0 volts that's connected to A's gate latching that condition. Taking the input ground away changes nothing as the input of 0 volts has been "latched."

You should have noticed there's no new meaning for the word latch. Latch means the same thing in computer as it does in door knobs. Only difference is how the latching is done.

Registers are made of sets of latches with two transistors, A and B. When a register is "loaded" the loading element temporarily sets the voltage on the registers A transistor's gate that pass through inverted to the B transistor's gate that causes the B transistor's collector to be the same as the input on A's gate. The signal is latched and held at the voltage thus the register becomes a duplicate of the loading element. Notice that the output of transistor A is the inversion of the "setting" voltage while the output of transistor B is the same.

Voltages, 5Volts, 0Volts, translate into, on, off, and 1, 0. Think of memory as a set of registers. "Storing" a register's contents is temporarily putting the voltages at the register's latches-out on the corresponding latches-in of the memory. The terms for this is loading and storing. Loading is making a register's latches identical to a memory location's latches. Storing is the opposite of loading, a memory location's latches are made identical to the latches of the register being stored.

Don't be alarmed if thinking about transistor switches arranged in devices like AND, NAND, OR, NOR, inverters and latches makes your head hurt. The nice folks at Texas Instruments, Fairchild, Toshiba and a host of other companies have already done all the brain scrambling logic design for us. Did I leave Bell Labs out? Shame on me for their place is as holy as the manger. It's the birthplace of the transistor and a lot more. Having said that let me take some if not a lot of it back. Germany is the actual birthplace of both the transistor, 1909 and the integrated circuit, 1949. Integrated circuit – two or more transistors on a single substrate. With two or more transistors as single thing we can make a single part latch.

Who cares who invented transistors or integrated circuits either one? That's the attitude at Bell Labs for sure where a lot of R and D, "rob and duplicate" was done, patents filed and awarded, man exclaiming, "What has God wrought" and God exclaimed, "Let there be lawsuits." The most popular expression in the high tech world soon became, "prior art! You can't patent that it was invented in Germany, 1909." I got some really bad news for the greedy lot.

The switch was probably invented before the wheel. Any patent on the computer is a patent on something as old as the human brain itself. And most of all the arrangement of switches to make modern computers was done on contract to the US government and thus it belongs to us all. Adding more registers or as Digital Equipment Corporation did find the least amount of everything possible and still be a computer, PDP-8, no matter what is done it's still nothing more than a pile of switches. Make that a giant sized pile of glorified switches.

The makeup of the switch has changed dramatically over the very few years since the first computer was made and employed to do statistical analysis of census data, 1930's time frame. Having the proper attitude is a prerequisite to being a good programmer. Programming – carrying on a conversation with strangers saying everything that will ever be said by either in advance. That's what writing papers and books is all about is it not? Therefore computer programming must by its very nature be a literary art. Steps one and two, learn the vocabulary and the grammatical structure. Of course one must have something to say.

The topic is electrically operable switches. We've seen there's more than one variety. And we've taken a glimpse at how switches no matter the switch are arranged to make decisions, i.e. If A AND B then C otherwise D, or, If A OR B then C otherwise D. This brings us to a special switch known as the enabling switch. Enable means the same thing here it does everywhere else. Enable – allow to happen.

CPUs registers, all registers are sets of switches that as conglomerate switches are always either off or on. Any one register can be used at any one time to send or receive settings, have its contents added to or subtracted from or compared with any another register or memory location. Of course memory locations are sets of switches too. Picking one register out of all possible registers is done by an enabling switch commonly known as an enabling gate. Example: I want to "store" the contents of register 0 in memory at location 54. The switches comprising register 0 are enabled with all other register's switches not-enabled. The enabled switch is connected to the switches located in memory at location 54. Location 54 is also enabled with all other memory locations not-enabled at the same time. The output side of register 0's switches are physically connected to the input side of the latches at memory location 54 through two enabling gates. The settings of the latches at location 54 will become identical to the settings of register 0. That's called "storing." Loading is the opposite of storing with the inputs of register 0's latches being physically connected via enabling gates to the outputs of memory location 54's latches thus making the two identical to each other.

The word buss is the accepted name for the intersections where different registers are connected to each other and memory, one onto the buss and another off of the buss. It's always the contents of two sets of switches. One set is the source and the other the destination. All CPU registers, flags etc. that can be stored in memory have enabling gates to a buss also connected to memory. Ordinary buses carry many people. Computer busses carry many switch-in and switch-out wires. If the computer has 16 bit wide registers then the buss connecting registers to memory will be 16 wires wide. Computer busses are nothing but wires.

Not to belittle wires, busses being nothing but wires. Cyber space is the telephone wire connecting computers to each other over the phone. If it's cyber wire it just has to be so high-tech only geniuses can understand it. Don't you think?

An ordinary way of saying a memory cycle is, the address is gated, (all switches enabled) onto the memory address buss along with a read or write signal. The memory either accepts the settings, (write operation) copies the settings on the memory data buss or, (read operation) puts the contents of the memory location indicated by the contents of the memory address buss on the memory data buss. All registers etc. are connected to both the memory address buss and memory data buss via enabling gates. There may be IO address and data busses relative to the design of the CPU. If IO devices are addressed using the memory address buss then IO will also use the memory data buss as well and there are no separate IO busses.

The act of gating onto a buss or anywhere else is the act of enabling the conglomerate of a set of switches. Can this be done with ordinary light switches you ask? Absolutely with the following arrangement, the input side of the enabling switch is the hot side meaning if the output of the conglomerate of switches is 5 volts there will be 5 volts on the input lug of the enabling switch. With the enabling switch off there is no signal at all on the switches output lug. Any number of so arranged switches can be connected to a single point without interfering with each other provided only one is on at any given time. This arrangement of enabling switches has a special name. It's called tristate because the signal has three possibilities, on, off and not there. When the enabling switch is off it's as though it's not there. All switches must at all times be either off or on. Tristate says there's a third state, not there. We know it really is there making it "as though" it's not there.

Another common enable gating arrangement that is compatible with transistor switches is called open collector. Transistors are identical to switches in ordinary implementation. The emitter and collector terminals are the equals of the two lugs on ordinary light switches. The transistor's gate is the equal of the light switches little arm sticking out used to operate it. Ordinarily a resistor is used to connect the collector to 5 volts and the emitter is connected to ground. Thus when the gate is low and no current is flowing through the transistor there will be 5 volts on the collector's lug. This is the equal of an off light switch with voltage on the output lug. When the transistor has 5 volts on its gate current flows through it effectively connecting the emitter and collector to each other. If the input side of the enabling transistor switch is at ground the collector stays at 5 volts. It's as though the transistor was not there just like when a light switch is on it becomes the equal of a wire. Open collector means there is a single resistor between the collector and the 5 volt power supply for more than one gate. Using open collector enabling switches requires a "pull up" resistor on every bus line pulling-up all open collector enabling gates but only the gate that is enabled having the ability to pull it down. This is the way early buses were operated. Open collector gating is still valid.

Nothing happens in this world in zero time. It takes time for switches to be operated even incredibly fast transistor switches running in the 5 to 25 billionths of a second time frame. This is the speed of ordinary open collector and tristate implementations. Not fast enough to let every Tom, Dick and crooked Harry take a turn in your multi user Windows operating system and leave a little time for you. Enter the fastest thing since Speedy Gonzales the fastest mouse in all Mexico, the emitter follower. The time delay from when gating voltage is changed until the output at the collector is realized is shortened considerably by moving the pull-up resistor from the collector side to the emitter side of the transistor and changing its name from pullup to pulldown. It's no longer a pull-up resistor becoming a pull-down resistor instead. The results of the switching is realized much sooner at the emitter than at the collector. Thus the output of the switch is at the emitter.

During my 55 years and counting career in the wonderful world of computers I had many experiences. When my partner and I designed the DC-3 and fabricated the first prototype he worried needlessly how we would test it. We had no software or firmware or anything to try it out. I surprised him by making a memory using ordinary switches. I went to the electronic junk shop and bought 256 miniature toggle switches, (3 cents each) on to the lumber yard for a couple 8 foot long 1 by 2's and took all of it home. I cut 17, 10 inch long boards from the 1 by 2's, and two others for support. I also bought a couple boxes of #4 x 3/8 inch wood screws. In sets of 16 switches I screwed those switches between two of my 10 inch long 1 by 2's. In the end I had 16 rows with 16 switches each in a matrix with 17, 10 inch 1 by 2's and then stabilized the affair with two 1 by 2's along each side. I had made a 16 bit wide 16 word memory programmable by hand. This turned out to be the best possible solution to our test the new CPU problem.

In the end we had a one bit at a time programmable by hand 16 bits wide words, 16 words long memory that turned out to be just the right length to check every instruction in the set. I'll never forget the look on my partner's face when I showed him what had occupied me for the entire afternoon. I was supposed to be sweating like him worrying about how we were going to test the prototype. He got his tongue all tangled up when between words when it finally dawned on him the fact that memories cells were nothing more than switches and we could program my real switch memory by simply setting those switches one at a time by hand.

Know all there is to know about light switches and you already know all there is to know about how computers compute. Here's 8,000,000,000 switches that's surely enough to keep you busy for a while. Not to worry, all the hard work has already been done. They're called integrated circuits, lots of transistor switches on a single substrate arranged to accomplish given tasks. They're known as 7400 series integrated circuits. They have names like 7400, 7404, and 7474 and on and on always beginning with 74. Texas Instruments published/publishes a book with specs on every part in the latest set. It and most of those "chips" are available on line. Google the part number and get 500 or more potential sources including Amazon.com. You can also get really good data sheets on them too over the internet.

One of my associates over my long career was an engineer named Tony Robertsen. Tony's favorite expression was, "I refuse to be outsmarted by a tiny sliver of silicone." Of course it wasn't silicone at all but rather Tony was up against a handful of really smart light switches. Are you smarter than a light switch?

Chapter 14, code is…

…the most important word to get perfectly clear and perhaps the most difficult one to so do. Everybody knows what a code is, that's how secret agents send messages to MI5 headquarters. In computer CODE is everything. Code is everywhere. It's life itself with DNA being coded.

CODE – replacing one thing with another.

Everything in the computer is coded. Computers are nothing more than sets of switches. The coding begins with switch-off coded zero and switch-on coded one. There are no zeroes and ones in the computer only switches. Switch settings are coded as numbers thus from there everything in the computer is a code of one kind or the other. Writing programs is called coding.

Programs are made of lines of code. The measure of a programmer's productivity is measured by how many lines of code he/she writes on a periodic basis. It's been a while but the first ever survey showed the average programmer working for a contractor to the government produced 13 lines of code a year. A programmer earning $130,000 annually gets $10,000 per line of code written at the 13 per year rate. I wrote 1,000 lines per day many days with several days where I wrote 2,000 lines.

Way back when programs were written on punch cards one line of code per card. There were 2,000 cards in a new box. One year I wrote so many programs I had 73 boxes of cards at the end of the year. Those boxes weren't full but all had over 1,000 each. I had changed employer's mid-December. My new employer was a software contractor. Every box of cards represented a contract satisfied.

I understood I was writing code that caused things to happen inside the computer. Most importantly I understood there was nothing going on other than switches represented by zeros and ones being turned on and off. Thinking up space age sky wars' type names like cyber changes nothing. Computers begin as switches, nothing ever happens other than switches being flipped on and off yet computers are capable of causing some amazing things to happen.

Replacing a room full of people with a single person and a computer is amazing is it not? That was my first ever program done my first day at work and my first ever hearing digital computer spoken. I immediately recognized it was nothing but switches and thought everyone else did the same. I have never seen the computer as anything other than a bunch of switches with a master switch that's continually flipped on and off. Most of all I've never thought of the computer as being anything other than a tool.

Programming, doing things using the computer is called coding because it's using numbers to set switches. Programs are sets of switch settings that cause switches including the program's switches to be turned on and off in an orderly fashion. For example, 0010011 is a number representing switch settings. That's code and that's code at the most fundamental level in computer coding, programming. The next step below zeroes and ones is physically putting finger on switch as in "turn the light on or off."

If the computer can be programmed one switch at a time via a control panel then programming really is setting switches. I had that advantage over today's beginners. Compared to today's computers the computer itself was a joke, 32,000 6bit bytes of memory compared to 32,000,000,000,000 8bit bytes of memories and a 25 hertz clock compared to an Intel i5 with a 3,200,000,000,000 hertz clock. Compared to my first computer today's computers are a joke because they are without control panel. Setting switches one at a time leaves no doubt whatsoever about what one is doing.

Switch-off is coded zero while switch-on is coded one. Zeroes and ones are machine language code for switch off or on. L,r is assembly language type code used to generate zeroes and ones that are code for switch on or off. A = B + C is compiler language code used to generate L,r type codes that in turn are used to generate zeroes and ones that are code for switch on or off.

Machine language programming requires one level of coding. Assembly language requires two levels of coding. Compiler language requires three levels of coding. In all cases the programmer only codes at one level.

We're at three levels of code yet we're just getting started with codes. Letters of the alphabet are codes representing sounds. We talk in codes to each other. That's why one always hears what is said but often misunderstands what it means. What it means is a matter of decoding whatever is said. I thought I'd mention this to give you confidence in your ability to code and decode. You may have noticed people are programmed in places called schools by teachers using codes.

Getting ABC codes from the classroom to computer's switch settings requires another level of coding. ABC's in the classroom are codes at one level. To represent them in the computer another level of coding is required.

A couple of standards for coding ABC's in switches have been established by committee no doubt. ASCII code is an international standard for arranging switch settings to represent ABC's. I may be wrong but I credit a gentleman named Morse for inventing the first coding of letters of the alphabet into switch settings. He did it with a single switch adding time to the equation. Switch-on-off making di and da sounds in sets using a single switch is the equal of a set of switches side by side. Coding messages has been going on as long as there has been people so Morse is a Johnny come lately no doubt. He is the first to use electricity to send messages of record. His codes for letters of the alphabet etc. are different but map one for one into ASCII.

ASCII seems to be the accepted standard at this time. There's another very similar code called EBCDIC blessed by IBM and maybe even originated by IBM. Don't know, who cares. ASCII is the first name in the coding game in today's computer world.

All information of any kind in the computer's memory is represented by switch settings. Nothing more is possible thus it is impossible to put the actual letter A in the computer's memory the way we can draw it out on paper. We type it in and later we see it printed out. We don't see what happens to it from the time we type the letter A on the keyboard until we see it back again printed or displayed. If we looked in the computer's memory and found the place where it's stored we'd see 01000001 representing 8 switch off-on settings. 01000001 is binary. Convert it to decimal and its 65. In hexadecimal the letter A is 41.

Just about all if not all CPU's today are single chip affairs with multiple registers. Those registers are numbered and appear in the computer's memory as parts of instructions in binary. In an effort to humanize the situation it's not uncommon for programmers to equate register numbers to names and write their programs using names instead of the register numbers.

> L,3   address

> Is written by some:

MACK EQU 3

> L,MACK addres

In most assemblers, all written by me anything can be substituted for anything else using the pseudo instruction, EQU that's short hand for equate. Equate – create a synonym for. Of course equating is re-coding the already coded. The 3 part of L,3 and the MACK part of L,MACK are both translated by the assembler into binary. 3 in binary is 11 and become two switches-on in the computer's memory. Two switches-on is code for the number 3.

Of course computers are made of switches so technically the binary digits, 0 and 1 are also coded – switch off is coded 0, switch on is coded 1. Both letters of the alphabet and the digits 0 through 9 are coded and appear in memory as 0's and 1's that are themselves code for switch off, switch on. Coding happens in multiples with codes also being coded. The assembler allows us to write letters and numbers in a more civilized manner, (syntax sugar sweet) and it translates them into 0's and 1's for us.

Assemblers aren't necessary. The first program I ever wrote I did the assembly part by hand. After writing in somewhat people readable writing I translated it into 0's and 1's one instruction at a time. I translate the zeroes and ones into switch settings using actual switches on the computer's control panel.

In the world of mini computers bootstrap loaders are input to the computer's memory one bit at a time using a bank of switches on the computer's control panel. Bootstrap loaders are simple programs, 10 to 20 instructions to read in, store in the computer's memory an initial program to get computing started. Bootstrap loaders are in ROM chips in today's computers. The entire system can be and is in many instances in ROM thus permanently installed.

The operation codes for different instructions are actually numbers. L, ST, A, S, N, O, X and all others are codes translated by the assembler into binary numbers. An instruction in memory might look like:

10011000

The operation "code" in the above is an 8 bits wide binary number ranging in decimal value from 0 to 255. A CPU with this instruction format has 256 possible operations. Usually the first 4 bits are the base operation code and the second 4 bits are base modifiers. Rarely will a CPU have many more than a dozen base instructions.

Cryptography, decoding coded information is one of my favorite subjects. I never tire of hearing about the Polish/British Enigma code breakers reading the German army's coded messages faster than the Germans themselves. Rommel could have gotten his orders from Hitler faster by ringing Blexly Park than waiting for his decoders. Of special interest to me is the computer they used. It had both relay logic and banks of relays making its memory. Relays are electrically operable switches, electromechanical transistors. In spite of the size of memory and the slow processing pace that primitive computer beat people speed by many miles per second.

Codes are critical in this world. Codes of all kinds are everywhere. The words we speak are themselves codes that translate into pictures and emotions and more in our minds. Above all else codes offer us a degree of privacy that seems to be in short supply in today's computer based world. Once upon a time not very long ago we were shielded from intrusion into our world by foreigners. Now we're being watched and every word written getting to Moscow faster than to our addressees.

I have the solution to that problem. It's called coding, that's encrypting in the stuffy formal world. What if all our information was coded. They'd just crack our codes and read it anyhow? I agree, there is no such thing as a code that can't be cracked and especially so using the computer to do the duty. There's a couple of things we can do to make it so difficult, so time consuming they give up.

Computers work both ways. Yes computers can be used to do the trial and error work needed to crack codes. They can also be used to create codes that are extremely difficult to crack, so difficult code crackers won't even try to crack them.

Let's start from the end and work backwards. How are codes cracked? Let's learn by example. I have a deck of cards. I shuffle them a lot. The problem for the code cracker is to identify the top card. It only takes a maximum of 52 guesses to get it. On average it only takes 26 guesses to identify the top card in a shuffled deck. Not only that all subsequent cards take fewer guesses with the last two cards being identified with a max of 1 guess. Instead of 52 cards let's take a deck with 52,000,000 cards all shuffled up, then we'll shuffle the deck over to the code crackers and watch them turn blue in the face.

Flooding the message with random nonsense works like a charm. Within a 52 million character message there's 1,000 or so that are the message and the rest are confusion factors. The combinations of 52,000,000 things is well beyond anyone's patients even using the fastest computer. We can hide the message in a pile of garbage and they will never find it because it's too difficult. That's what the Enigma inventor thought.

Those of us who know how to write letters in computer language have some tools of deception never dreamt of by 20th century code designers and not doable in any high level computer language presently in use without a lot of math. I have invented, implemented and deployed over a dozen high level languages one of which we will go over later that is perfect of coding messages. Coding messages in assembly language is a piece of cake to borrow an expression.

Let's look at an example of how to blind prying eyes. Suppose for example we have a simple 4 letter message, ABCD to encode. In the computer's memory that's:

0100 0001 0100 0010 0100 0011 0100 0100

Spaces are added between nibbles, (nibbles are half bytes) in the above to make it easier to read. There's no shortage of people who can translate the above to ABCD without so much as pencil and paper. Let's complicate it for them a little. One little bit shuffle and:

0010 0000 1010 0001 0010 0001 1010 0010

Compare this to the original above. Do you see what I did? I "rotated-right" the entire message 1 bit. They'll figure that out in no time at all so let's work on the rotated-right version of the message and give them a hobby:

1001 1010 0000 1011 1000 1011 0000 1000

Compare this second level coded version to the original and the rotated right version. Now what have I done? I inverted every other bit - if it was zero I made it one and if it was one I made it zero. Not every bit but every other bit. It'll take them a little longer but they'll figure that out too. Let's throw them a screwball and see how much confidence we can gain in foiling them. To show you what I'm doing I need to add a table, 0000 through 1111. And I need to shuffle that 16 long set of numbers like they were ordinary playing cards. Notice I have every possible combination of 4 switches but not in order. Let's suppose the shuffled version of my 16 card deck looks like this:

0111, 1000, 0100, 1111, 0010, 1100, 1010, 0110, 1101, 0101, 0001, 1011, 0000, 0011, 1001, 1110

Using 4bit sets of our shifted, inverted message as indexes we substitute from the table and get:
Original 1001 1010 0000 1011 1000 1011 0000 1000
Coded   0101 0001 0111 1011 0110 1011 0111 1101

What do I mean by indexes? Let's write the table out and see what indexing is all about.

Original → Indexed

Original	→	Indexed
0000	→	0111
0001	→	1000
0010	→	0100
0011	→	1111
0100	→	0010
0101	→	1100
0110	→	1010
0111	→	0110
1000	→	1101
1001	→	0101
1010	→	0001
1011	→	1011
1100	→	0000
1101	→	0011
1110	→	1001
1111	→	1110

The number on the right is substituted for the number on the left. The number on the left is from the message. It's like using zero through twenty five to represent A through Z and substituting the letter's number for the letter.

I don't believe there's a code cracker alive or a computer based code cracking technique capable of decoding the above as is without knowing the steps we took. They must know we did three things, know what they are and the order in which we did them. They must know we used a 16 long, 4bit indexed translation table as the third step. A bit inversion of every other bit before that, and a right rotate the entire message one position. Given our steps it's not all that difficult. Without the steps it's virtually impossible.

Why am I showing you this? I want to encourage you, you can become computer literate if you aren't already. Computer literate means you have the knowledge to compose, write, debug and use machine language programs. When you can do that you can invent your own code and communicate in private. No! I'm not promising you a high paying job but only the same thing being able to read and write in the English language brought you. What if you couldn't read and write? Would you expect to get a high paying job for almost learning how? There's more to having knowledge than high paying jobs.

If you looked inside our 17 government agencies involved in intelligence operations you'd find programming is a department. That's as silly as having illiterate English teachers with a literates department.

Did I hear we're in danger of a cyber attack from an enemy nation, Iran or Russia or someone unexpected? Now you know why "they're" all worried sick about a cyber attack. Do you even know what a cyber attack is other than someone somewhere in the world types something into a computer and, "bang" the lights go out in the white house. What idiot put the lights in the white house in that position? The same idiot who put the nuclear fired electric power generating plant "on line."

Our leaders don't know what they are doing because they're computer illiterates. What kind of an idiot would open the door and then worry about wolves getting in and eating the baby? Close the door stupid. Keep people out of your computer the same way. Don't rely on Microsoft to do it. They have both feet in the door keeping it open. Microsoft has got to go or the door stays open. Don't look for computer scientists to throw them out. Computer scientists are hoping to get high paying jobs at Microsoft writing 13 instructions, compute words per year.

Do you have any idea what a cyber is. If you had a cyber where would you keep it? The word cyber if it is a real word has no place in the world of computers. Cyber fits in the same place as "volts of electricity" in the real world, real close akin to "gun-powders of bullets."

Programming is a literary art not a science like physics or chemistry. The only science part if we can call it that is the fact that computers are sets of switches with one switch continually going off to on and back to off. The colleges and universities are already training writers and some of them manage to write sentences. They are qualified to write operating systems and encoders and decoders and most of what we use or should be using. Writing computer programs and especially games is more akin to play writing than writing scientific papers. Maybe the literate writer will give us definitions of words such as cyber that are now only insinuated. If it's an attack of any kind it must be bad. What is it?

What happens when a cyber attack takes place? It's a con with the setup happening over time. Programs are installed in computers by enemies with sneaky emails and other things where programs are allowed to be downloaded and executed. In this case they should be executed the way criminals are executer rather than the computer meaning of the word. The attacker modifies an innocent looking piece of the operating system. The clock update subroutine is a good place to hide a virus. They replace the system's clock updater with one their own that has other things it can do, like say erase all the files on the hard drive. It doesn't do it's dirty deed until it receives a signal from something. The simplest is to watch the date and time and go off like a time bomb. Now take the Michelangelo virus that sets there doing nothing watching the date and wipes the hard drive clean on Michelangelo's birthday.

Virus is a word used to name such things. The Michelangelo virus watches the date and time and does it dirty deed on his birthday. The cyber attacker is the same as a virus attacker for all practical purposes. You should have a good enough feel for how programs work to see all sorts of soft spots to attach "malware" when running "under" Windows.

At this very moment you should be wondering like me what kind of idiot created such a stupid system. A billion air idiot did it and he did it under license from IBM. Are you one of the better class of people insisting on having the "real McCoy" paying extra to get your very own IBM-machine? In other word did you fall for IBM's propaganda, make IBM-machine and computer synonyms? Whose fault is that, IBM's or yours? You're an Apple fan? Has your I-phone been hacked yet? How can you tell?

How does malware get in your computer and the big computer at the pentagon? The operating system allows programs to be downloaded and executed by people who are in the system. How do people get in the system? But of course with passwords. How does that work?

Over at the CIA agent 008 gets an e-mail and opens it. As a part of the email process programs are allowed to be downloaded and executed. While 008 is browsing through the email the program he inadvertently just downloaded via the email is busy modifying the operating system. It installs a program to shut the CIA's computer down that will execute on some future time and date. Do you see where the problem lies? What would you do if your car allowed people to modify your engine without you knowing it?

The president of General Motors replying to a criticism by Microsoft said something like, if my cars quit running for no reason at all I couldn't give them away. He could have added, "If my cars invited tin horns, crook and pranksters and allowed them to run my cars off the road into the ditch I'd get sued from hell to breakfast."

Why in the name of George do we let emails download and execute programs? Simple rule. No program will be downloaded ever. All modifications to the system will be done on site. Problem solved. That slams the door closed on cyber attacks.

Go to the computer science department and get the lecture on how really spiffy systems allow over the Internet updates and how embedded programs in emails causes nerds

166

to go into orgasm and stay there for hours on end. However would Microsoft update your computer right to the high tech recycle center without downloading the latest computer slowing updates? The words you are now reading were typed on a laptop vintage 2006. This is 2017 and soon to be 2018. It has never been updated and runs at the same speed it did the day I brought it home. There's "things" in it. Every time I turn it on I get urgent messages telling me I must update. I just chuckle.

Not allowing downloads of programs eliminates the possibility of so called cyber attacks, viruses, malware and hotels.com from installing a program to watch for you to look for a hotel. No downloaded programs eliminates that little aggravating bit of stupidity as well as all other crooks, bakers and candle stickups.

That leaves the problem of the Russians "hacking" their way into the DNC's computer and making Donald Trump president. Trump fans will temporarily say that was an act of God. Wait until it's a Democrat gets help from an enemy nation and listen to them roar. The Russians didn't hack their way into the DNC computer. They dummied their way in.

The Russians sent an email to a DNC operative saying there was a problem with his account and for him to log in and fix it before something really bad happens. They provided a convenient click-here for him to use. The "dummy" clicked there and up came a screen that was a duplicate of the one used by the DNC computer to log people in. He entered his security code and the rest is history. It wasn't the DNC computer but one at KGB headquarters in Moscow, (Actually Petersburg) he was "talking" to. They used his security code to gain access to all the data on the DNC computer and used interpretations of what the data said to defame Hillary thus helping Trump.

The Russians didn't hack their way in they dummied it. Hacking is trying one number after the other until one that works is found. It's very easy to write a program even in C to do that trying new security codes as fast as the Internet allows. How amateurish can a system's design get? That's how amateurish. They allow the same computer to keep trying one try after the other until finally at last it has "hacked" its way in. Let's slam the door shut on both hacking and dummying.

How do we stop dummying? Every valid pin number has an Internet address attached to it. When that pin is entered in the "get-in" procedure the caller is "in" the system. That's the problem. Instead of the pin number getting one in it only gets one called. The computer "calls" the addressee rather than just letting the caller in. They enter the pin number from a computer in Moscow. The system calls the person to whom it belongs in Hoboken because it has his address. Communications are always established by called computer hanging up and calling back. That stops both hacking and dummying dead in their tracks.

You won't believe the reasons given for not doing it that way. Maybe he's away from his desk and wants to use his cell phone. Easy to fix. Every instrument that can connect to the central computer must have a unique pin number. Got 5 computers and 10 cell phones. You're going to need 15 pin numbers. Oh there's good news tonight. You can write those pin numbers on billboards for other people having them is harmless. They call the computer and the computer calls you. They'll get the message and give up real fast.

The rule is simple. We never know who called us while we always know who we called. Therefore we never give out information to callers only to those we call. Get a call from the IRS. Say, "I can't talk to you right now. I'll call you back. I already have the IRS main number. What's your extension?" If it really is the IRS the caller will give you his/her extension? Hang up and call back that way you're sure who you're talking to. If you don't have the IRS's number it's readily available in phone books and on line.

Now it's time for you to get in on the mucho multibillion dollar computer market. Imagine if you can that you have an I-phone like phone ready for market and you run this ad on CNBC the business cable channel, "This phone allows you to communicate in absolute privacy. It is both tap proof and hack proof. Call this number to order yours." All the marketing phone services in the US of A together could not answer the calls. Communications security is the greatest need in today's world just begging for the next billion air to recognize it and solve the problem.

I hope I've given you the courage to "just do it." I'd do it myself but I'm a bit old and feeble to start a company and go through the hassle of raising capital, hiring people and setting up an organization. The actual product is almost as simple as making buggy whips. Take the half hour you'll need to become computer literate. There's a world full of experts that will flock to you once they find out you're starting a new company with the possibility of making them rich.

I learned to program in less than 5 minutes. Nobody told me it was hard. Maybe you need a half hour? I had a big advantage over you. I had a computer. You may think you have a computer but until you program it it's no more computer than your dishwashing machine. Maybe there's another billion dollar market for a bare bones computer with an old fashioned control panel so ordinary people can look in memory, change it, manually enter little ditty programs and learn to program like I did. Oh! Don't forget the manual with a description of the CPU, its registers, buss sizes etc. and above all else don't forget the instruction set with addressing modes. And a console with keyboard and display and the basic software development tools, text editor, assembler and loader are also in order. None of this is all that technical. It's just a bunch of switches and lists of switch settings.

Expecting a computer to do something is like expecting a wrench to start taking off nuts all by itself. Connect the wrench to the computer and through programming and take nuts off bolts with your thoughts. Think take nut off once, write doing it in computer language and do it as often as desired.

I have mentioned before computers do nothing? My very first boss when I was fresh out of college said it all not realizing it when he said, "it doesn't do anything." He didn't know he was making a statement of fact rather than what he thought he was doing, making an observation.

Chapter 15, control panels are…

…the most significant learning tools ever in the world of computers. It takes all of the imagination out of the most important things one must know. I'll try to make that point with a typical and minimal computer control panel for a paper computer.

```
---------------------------------------------------------
              CPU -Central Processing Unit
                        Address
              oo  oooo  oooo   Run
              ⇑⇑  ⇑⇑⇑⇑  ⇑⇑⇑⇑   ↓ o
                                Stop
                        Data
            oooo  oooo  oooo  oooo   Store
            ⇑⇑⇑⇑  ⇑⇑⇑⇑  ⇑⇑⇑⇑  ⇑⇑⇑⇑    ↓
---------------------------------------------------------
         Accumularor   oooo oooo oooo oooo
---------------------------------------------------------
              Index   oo oooo oooo
---------------------------------------------------------
            Carry o   Minus o   Zero o
---------------------------------------------------------
```

Above we have a minimal control panel for a computer that has one accumulator register and one index register. The small o's represent LED's. LED on says 1 and LED off says 0. The arrows represent switches. We have two sets of switches and LED's labeled Address and Data along with a Run/Stop switch, an LED to indicate the computer is running and a momentary, spring-loaded-off Store switch. We also have LED's to shows us the contents of the CPU's Accumulator register and Index register as well as flag LED's indicating Carry, Minus and Zero.

Address refers to memory address. We have but 10 address switches thus we can look at the contents of memory at no address larger than 2 to the 10th power minus 1. Thus 1023 is the largest address possible. Address 1023 is with all 10 switches on. Since the address switches are always at some setting between all off, 0 and all on, 1023 one memory location is always addressed by them.

The Data LED's always show the contents of the memory location addressed by the address switches. To see what's in a particular memory location one simply sets the Address switches to its address and its contents in bits are displayed in the Data LED's. Thus one can see what's in/on the entire memory by flipping the address switches from all off to all on and every combination in between.

This is one of those rare cases where knowing binary is helpful. It's still not necessary but takes a lot of mental anguish and wonderment out of what one is looking at. It turns out the control panel is an excellent tool for learning binary. I got an A in number systems in college math but had never put any base other than 10 (decimal) into practice. I found becoming familiar with binary a little difficult but using the control panel it became second nature in no time. I can now use it almost as well as decimal after years of using computers with control panels.

Using a control panel to enter and run small programs is the fastest way to learn all there is to know about computers. Of course one needs to know the vocabulary of the computer and the instruction format, what bits go where in the particular brand of computer's instructions. In the beginning the instruction format for individual instructions were always clearly stated in the manual that came with the machine. Computers don't have manuals anymore only registration and sign up for a Microsoft account "sketches" while going through the aggravating first time start up procedures. Sorry folks but it's not a computer if it's not programmable by you. They lied when they told you it was a computer.

By now you should know that loading is duplicating the contents of a selected memory location in a CPU register and storing is the opposite, the duplication of the contents of a CPU register in a specified memory location. The ordinary copy machine makes a good example of either operation. An original is duplicated. The most common mistake is to think something was moved. Thinking data is moved is a mistake so common it's being taught as factual in computer science.

To change the contents of a given memory location, commonly stated as "feeding to the computer" put its address in the Address switches, put the actual number in binary in the

Data switches and operate the Store switch that is a spring-loaded-off pushbutton type. Switch ↓ to store, switch ↑ is off. Simply depress and release the Store switch and the Data switches are duplicated in the memory at the Address indicated by the Address switches. For example, to look at location zero all Address switches are ↓ meaning turned off, 0. To change the contents of memory location zero turn all Address switches off, set the Data switches to the desired number and depress and release the Store switch. You will notice the Data LED's change to the same as the switches, switch on is indicated by LED on, and switch off is indicated by LED off.

As Address switches are flipped off and on the contents of the Data LED's will change showing the contents of memory selected by the different Address switch settings. Changing the Data switches does not change the contents of memory until the Store switch is operated at which time the switch settings of the Data switches are stored in memory at the location selected by the address switches. Thus we can look at memory without changing it. If the Store switch is operated the Data LED's will then be identical to the data switch settings.

I have already mentioned the fact computers are nothing but a bunch of switches? I thought so but just in case. You didn't forget did you? Now you can completely understand what the scientists did when he "fed" data to a computer in the early days when computer was simple. They're still feeding computers? "Feeding" data to the computer is nothing more than flipping switches and pushing the Store switch. The hungry computer eats switch setting all up as fast as you can flip switches and push the Store button. You determine the speed at which your computer gets fed.

Now you know how to enter your program and data into the computer's memory. The next step is to write a program, enter it and its associated data into the computer's memory, set the address switches to the memory location of your first instruction, operate the Run switch and see what happens. There is no better way to learn. And, most of all there is no punishment for getting it wrong. You can't damage a switch by setting it to an unintended position.

That goes more than double for paper computers. In our theoretical paper computer an instruction is the same width in bits as the Data and the Accumulator. Memory addresses in our instruction set are 10 bits wide making the max size memory 1024 words long. That limits the largest Address possible to all 10 bits on, (11 1111 1111) or 1023 in decimal. Address and Index registers are limited to 10 bits.

Instructions have formats, where different things are located within them. We're going to define a simple machine with as many as 64 instructions. From left to right the first 6 bits of the instruction has the operation code, a number 0000 00 through 1111 11. The next 10 bits of our 16 bit instruction have the address of the data for doing arithmetic etc. or program locations in the case of jump-to instructions.

We won't define all 64 possible instructions but just enough to see how the whole thing called computer actually works. At this time we'll only use direct addressing, i.e. the address is in the last 12 bits of the instruction.

Mnemonic - meaning	Switches
LA - Load accumulator	0001 00
ADD - Add to accumulator	0100 00
STA - Store accumulator	0010 00
SUB - Subtract	0101 00
JMP - Jump to	1001 00
CMP - Compare	0110 00
JE - Jump if equal	1000 01
JNE - Jump if not equal	1000 00
STOP	0000 00

Our first ever program:

Adr	Instruction		Switch settings
000	LA	100	0001 00 01 0000 0000
001	ADD	101	0100 00 01 0000 0001
010	STA	102	0010 00 01 0000 0010
011	STOP		0000 00 00 0000 0000

The above reads, load the accumulator with the contents of memory at location 100 (hexadecimal), add to the contents of the accumulator the contents of memory at location 101, and store the contents of the accumulator in memory at location 102 and then stop.

First we write it out in readable form, LA 100 for example. Next we translate that into switch settings using the operation code for the particular instruction from the table above, 0001 00 for LA, load accumulator. We set the Address switches to all off that is address zero, set the data switches to 0001 00 01 0000 0000, and operate the Store switch. This is repeated for all the instructions with the address being incremented, (1 added to the previous) each time. Then we set the Address switches to 100 hexadecimal, 01 0000 0000. Pick a number that we can translate into binary like say 9 which is 1001, set the Data switches and operate the store switch. Location 100 will contain 0000 0000 0000 1001 that is the number 9 in decimal. We do the same thing for Address 101 except we pick another number like say 7 which is 0000 0000 0000 0111 binary, set the Data switches and operate the Store switch. Lastly we put some number in address 102 so we can see it be changed by running the program. Try, 1111 1111 1111 1111 and see it change after running the program.

At this time we have a simple program loaded and ready to run. We also have test data, specifically 9 and 7 so we know the answer should be 16 decimal. Now we set the Address switches to zero, all Address switches off and operate the Run switch. It will be as though nothing happened. The address LED's will be 00 0000 0100.

The address LED's shows the contents of the "updated" instruction pointer register. Remember the FIRE cycle? The last instruction, STOP is in memory location, 00 0000 0011. When the CPU executes the STOP it, uses the contents of the instruction pointer register that are 00 0000 0011 to FETCH the STOP instruction. Then the CPU INCREMENTS the IP, instruction pointer register by adding 1 to its contents. The instruction pointer register will be 00 0000 0011 + 1 that is 00 0000 0100 after this step. The R step, Resolve address is skipped because the STOP instruction does not have an address only an operation code. The last step, Execution of the STOP instruction causes the CPU to stop running. It will stay stopped until the Run switch is operated.

When the computer stops the Accumulator LED's show the last number in the accumulator. The last thing our tiny program did was store the contents of the accumulator. Storing DOES NOT change that which is stored thus the computer ignorance expressed by renaming ST, store to MOV, move. The accumulator will have, 0000 0000 0001 0000 which just happens to be 16 in decimal, 9 + 7 = 16. If we look in memory at location 102 we'll see the same thing there as in the Accumulator, specifically 0000 0000 0001 0000.

This simple program adds the two numbers we put in memory at locations 100 and 101 and stores the results in memory at address 102. Now we're going to do a simple variation and learn a little about binary.

Adr	Instruction		Switch settings
000	LA	100	0001 00 01 0000 0000
001	ADD	101	0100 00 01 0000 0001
010	STA	100	0010 00 01 0000 0000
011	STOP		0000 00 00 0000 0000
100	JMP	000	1001 00 00 0000 0000

And we put:

0000 0000 0000 0000 in location 100

0000 0000 0000 0001 in location 101

We've changed where the results of the addition are stored from 102 to 100. Our original program added two numbers and put the results in a third memory location. This program adds one number to another and stores the results in the first number. It's like clearing the calculator and then adding 1 again and again without clearing it again. The first time the program is run both the Accumulator and location 100 will have 0000 0000 0000 0001 in them and the program will STOP with the Instruction Pointer register pointing to location 100binary, (4 decimal). If we simply push the Run switch again the instruction in memory location 4, JMP to 000 will be executed "Jumping to" location 000. Jumping amounts to setting the Instruction Pointer register's contents to the address portion of the jump instruction that is all 0's thus the next instruction will be taken from the fist location of our program and the load, add, store and stop will again be executed. You will notice the Accumulator increase by 1 every time we release and then push-down the Run switch. This is the equal of the INC instruction which adds 1 to the contents of the target location. The accumulator and memory location 100 count up in binary by 1 each time the start switch is operated.

Now we'll learn how we make decisions using the computer. Note: it's the programmer and not the computer making the decision. Only people make decisions. Animals act and react. Computers are extensions of the computer programmer's brains, making all the usual assumptions about brains.

Adr	Instruction		Switch settings
000	LA	100	0001 00 01 0000 0000
001	ADD	101	0100 00 01 0000 0001
010	STA	100	0010 00 01 0000 0000
011	CMP	102	0110 00 01 0000 0020
100	JNE	000	1001 00 00 0000 0000
101	STOP		0000 00 00 0000 0000
110	JMP	000	1001 00 00 0000 0000

And we put:

    0000 0000 0000 0000 in location 100, (01 0000)
    0000 0000 0000 0001 in location 101, (01 0001)
    0000 0001 0000 0000 in location 102, (01 0010)

We've added a CMP, compare instruction. When the CPU executes a CMP instruction it subtracts the contents of the memory location from the contents of the accumulator and discards it. Subtraction causes the Zero flags to be set according to the results of the subtraction. Any two identical numbers subtracted from each other will be zero. In the above program the accumulator has 1 added to it over and over again. The compare instruction sets the Zero flag to 1, LED on if and only if the two numbers are identical. If the two are not identical the Zero flag is set to 0. JNE, jump if not equal and JNZ, jump if not zero are the same instruction with two names.

When executing the JNE, jump if not equal instruction the CPU examines the Zero flag. If it is 0 indicating the most recent arithmetic or logical instruction yielded a non-zero result the jump is made. Jumping amounts to the CPU replacing the contents of the instruction pointer register with the address portion of the jump instruction. In the above program the address portion of the JNE is 00 0000 thus the program continues execution at location 00 0000.

The above program will add 1 to the contents of the Accumulator in a "loop" until the Accumulator reaches 0000 0001 0000 0000. As long as the Accumulator has any other switch settings the results of the CMP, (compare) instruction will be negative, Zero flag set to 0 and the JNE, (jump if not equal) will jump. When the Accumulator has exactly 0000 0001

0000 0000 the CMP, compare conditions will be met meaning in this case the two numbers tested are identical, the Zero flag is set, the jump not zero will not take place and the program will "fall through" to the STOP causing the computer to stop when the two numbers are identically the same. At this time the address will be 00 0000 0110 and the accumulator will be, 0000 0001 0000 0000. Memory location 100 will be identical to the accumulator and have 00 0001 0000 in it.

    The first time we run the program, when the beginning data values are at 100, and 102 are 0, 1, and 100hex the time to get to the stop will be near instantaneous, operating the Run switch on and the computer will appear to have done nothing counting from zero to 01 000 000 is so fast. If we again push the Run switch the program will pick up at location 000 and do it again with one difference. The count will begin where it left off, 0000 0001 0000 0000 at our compare number and the counting will go "around the horn" meaning count all the way to 1111 1111 1111 1111 and then to 0000 0000 0000 0000 where we initially set the beginning value and from there to 0001 0000 0000 0000. You will notice a delay from the time the Run is activated and the time the computer stops. That's because it takes over 195,000 instruction executions times to count from any number all the way back to that number by adding 1 to a 16 bit accumulated number. Remember, registers are odometers having max numbers they can hold.

Adr	Instruction		Switch settings
000	LA	100	0001 00 01 0000 0000
001	ADD	101	0100 00 01 0000 0001
010	STA	102	0010 00 01 0000 0010
011	STOP		0000 00 00 0000 0000
100	JMP	000	1001 00 00 0000 0000

    We will now come to a complete understanding of those mysterious flags bits, Carry, Minus and Zero. To do that we'll add numbers that will cause them to be turned on and off. Using our simple, load-add-store-stop program we put:

    At 100   0100 0000 0000 0000
    At 101   0100 0000 0000 0000

    After we Run the program the Accumulator will have, 1000 0000 0000 0000.

    And, the Minus flag's LED will be lit. The Carry and Zero

flag's LED's will both be off. The Minus flag is a copy of the "results of the operation's word's" most significant, left most bit. In this case the operation was ADD. Do you know the meaning of "most significant bit?" It's this simple:

Most significant bit → 0000 0000 0000 0000. It's the left most bit. The opposite, the right most bit is:

0000 0000 0000 0000 ← Least significant bit.

All flags are set according to the results of all arithmetic, logical and compare operations. The most significant bit is the sign bit. If it's 0 then the number is positive. If the most significant bit is 1 the number is a negative number. You don't need to know this only that if a small number has a larger one subtracted from it the most significant bit of the results will be a 1. And, if two numbers are added to each other and the most significant bit is turned on, 1 then the results are in error.

Now let's change our data to:

At 100   1111 1111 1111 1111

At 101   0000 0000 0000 0001

After we Run the program the Accumulator will have, 0000 0000 0000 0000

Both the Carry and Zero flag's LED's will be lit and the Minus flag's LED will be off. In this case the Carry is called Overflow. The Accumulator overflowed, had a number larger than it could handle. That's a problem that must be addressed when doing arithmetic operations else the computer will make mistakes. Computer or programmer's mistake to accept the results when the results are too large to be held in a single word? If it was the first part of a multi precision operation then it's the carry bit that will be added to the next word. It's obvious the meaning of this single flag is relative to context.

The Zero flag says all bits/switches/latches in the results were off. Note that zero is a positive number thus the Minus flag is off.

From the weakest to the strongest, from the slowest to the fastest, from the smallest memories to gigabyte memories all computers, absolutely no exception one and all operate exactly the way our paper computer operates doing all the same and nothing more. The basic cycle is the same for all no exceptions made for the latest whiz banging fancy named Intel or AMD chip or that of any other manufacturer.

Getting that basic cycle down pat is paramount to knowing all there is to know about computers because all computers, mini, maxi, micro, no matter are identical in this respect. Absolutely all without exception have the basic, fetch, increment instruction pointer, resolve address, execute the instruction and after that do the next instruction just as fast as possible. The art of programming is executing the basic computer cycle mentally as one writes.

If the computer could talk and would tell us what it's doing it would say, I will use the contents of my instruction pointer register and read the next instruction out of memory. Before doing what it says for me to do I'll add one to the instruction pointer? If the instruction has an address and the address is complex I will resolve the complex to simple. Now I'm doing what the instruction says for me to do. That was so much fun I'm going to do it again and again and again until a human being stops me by unplugging me. That won't work I'm battery powered. Computers can't talk. Authors called programmers must do their talking for them.

The basic control panel with rows of switches and "blinking lights" is the best training tool ever. The best we can do here is a paper version of the real deal. If I were 20 year younger I'd make a simple computer with a control panel similar to the one above dedicated to teaching 5th graders all about computers. By the time the child finished the 8th grade the child would be as computer literate as it is language literate. Computer literacy should be a requirement for college entry just like language literacy.

It's totally unnecessary to know binary as a prerequisite to becoming computer literate. I'll try to make that point with a typical and minimal computer control panel using the decimal number system. Try to remember the fact that two position switches are the simplest to implement in hardware is the only reason binary is used. Binary and two position switches have a one for one relationship. We could use 10 position rotary switches that correspond one for one with decimal.

Here's what a decimal computer control panel would look like:

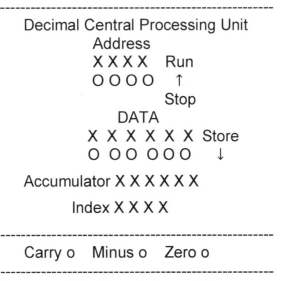

```
------------------------------------------------------
        Decimal Central Processing Unit
           Address
           X X X X    Run
           O O O O     ↑
                       Stop
           DATA
           X X X X X X Store
           O O O O O O   ↓

      Accumulator X X X X X X

         Index X X X X

------------------------------------------------------
      Carry o    Minus o    Zero o
------------------------------------------------------
```

Above we have a minimal control panel for a computer that has one accumulator register and one index register. The X's represent single digit decimal readouts. The small o's represent LED's. LED on says 1 and LED off says 0. The capital O's represent 10 position rotary switches, 0 through 9. We have two sets of switches and LED's labeled Address and Data along with a Run/Stop switch and a momentary, spring-loaded-off Store switch. We also have digital readouts to shows us the contents of the CPU's Accumulator register and Index register as well as flag LED's indicating Carry, Minus and Zero.

Address refers to memory address and always shows the contents of the memory location selected by the Address switches in the Data decimal readouts. To see what's in a particular memory location one simply dials the Address and its contents in decimal are displayed in the Data readouts. In this case we're looking at decimal, 0 through 9 numbers in the readouts and using decimal rotary 0 through 9 switches.

Knowing binary is not necessary. This computer is as valid as any other. The reason binary is used is because of the one for one relationship between two position switches and the binary number system. Make a note of it. We're still looking at switches. All that's changed is the complications of the switches themselves from simple light switches to dialers. There is a one for one relationship between decimal digits and 10 position switches.

Using a control panel to enter and run small programs is the fastest way to learn all there is to know about computers. Making the machine decimal instead of binary doesn't change that. Of course one needs to know the vocabulary of the computer and the instruction format, what digits go where in the particular make of computer's instructions. Good news, the vocabulary is the same no matter the number system.

The instruction format for our paper decimal computer is identically the same with binary numbers being replaced by decimal. Instead of 6 bit instruction codes we have 2 digit ones.

Mnemonic - meaning	number
LA - Load accumulator	04
ADD - Add to accumulator	16
STA - Store accumulator	08
SUB - Subtract	14
JMP - Jump to	36
CMP - Compare	24
JE - Jump if equal	33
JNE - Jump if not equal	32
STOP	00

Our first ever program in decimal:

Adr	Instruction		Switch settings
000	LA	200	04 0200
001	ADD	201	16 0201
002	STA	202	08 0202
003	STOP		00 0000

The above reads, load the accumulator with the contents of memory at location 200, add to the contents of the accumulator the contents of memory at location 201, store the contents of the accumulator in memory at location 202 and stop. All that's changed is the difficulty of learning and the difficulty of rotating switches rather than flipping switches.

We put numbers in memory to add by dialing up 200 and 201. When we run the program the accumulator will have the answer in decimal. We dial up 202 and see it's the same as the accumulator that is the sum of the two numbers we put in 200 and 201.

Is a decimal computer realistic? Let me say it like this. I made decimal computers using binary computers. Our next stop after learning all there is to know about computers is reviewing an ASCII computer I put into service, 1981. Not only is binary not necessary for ordinary people but its ever so clumsy. At the control panel level we've just gotten a demonstration of the difference between binary computers and decimal computers. The beauty of the ASCII computer is the contents of memory is in ABC's so we can read it with no translation at all. Now for a hint at the why of it all.

Why would a music major need or want to be computer literate, have the ability to write his/her own programs? Maybe he/she would like to invent a new musical instrument. The crescent wrench of machines, the digital computer is the perfect tool for doing that. It needs one or more speakers and the means of making them speak from inside the computer. With that the music expert with computer literacy can invent any number of new musical instruments, compose etc.

We're uncovering a wide open billion dollar market. There is a crying need for real computer literacy training tools. Every child should have one, should learn how to program in machine language and in the end be computer literate. If one does not know the basic computer cycle, FIRE - Fetch, Increment instruction pointer, Resolve address, Execute and do it again then one doesn't know beans about computers.

Chapter 16, from the land of dreams…

…comes the means through which all programs will run on all makes, models, sizes and shapes of computers. Dream on Simone. Never happen yet. Maybe we can make that dream come true? It's up to you and me. Waiting for those who now rake in the big bucks with trashy products will never do it because it will surely put them out of business.

The law of averages says we can make a standard computer platform on which programs can be moved from one computer to another without any modifications but the odds remain the same. Universal computer literacy is bound to improve the odds. Many have tried to create the machine independent software system and many have failed yet we find ourselves in a world where a few claim to have accomplished the goal. While failing miserably they still help themselves to the billions of dollars in prize money.

Terms like portable, machine independent, and universal software platform are often heard, seldom understood and never accomplished. Both portable and machine independent means I can take a program from one computer to another and have it run with no changes. That's why Microsoft is still shipping DOS.1 and Oracle is still downloading for free JAVA.1 and neither never ever need updating. Dream on say I, keep trying for surely there just has to be a mouthwatering peachy pie in that billion dollar sky. So far the rule has been, if you can't do it then fake it. Fakers rule the computer world.

We have two gorillas in this cage, high-level compiler language and software platform. The little darlings are holding hands and attracting multitudes willing to pay to see them not do what the showman says they do. They are not portable. They are not machine independent. They are software platforms with both legs, well, at least one leg that's broken trying to run the marathon with a rubber crutch for support. I do believe we've discovered the proverbial one legged man with a rubber crutch flopping about in the high tech world of nerds. He's making so much money laying there on the ground flopping around trying to get to his feet no one dares to pick him up. Let's give that filthy rich little fellow a helping hand, something else he can patent, you know like the patent recently issued on the latest high tech invention the telegraph. Did you know the telegraph has been renamed? New name, USB, universal serial bus.

I may have mentioned the notion of an ASCII based computer earlier. An ASCII computer's memory only contains symbols that display and print without any translation from a non-decimal number system to decimal. The whole idea here is machine independence and portability. Stop the computer and look into memory and see characters of the alphabet, Greek too and numbers in decimal. I made this machine, 1981 and made a good living selling and programming them. This is 2017. There is at least one of my computer systems still running that was built, installed and programmed by me acting alone, 1982. It runs the same speed today it did the day it was installed. The operating system hasn't been updated ever but the applications have grown to the point it would take an army of Computer Scientists years to duplicate it in C++ if they can at all. I designed the machine and wrote every line of code beginning with a bootstrapped assembler in machine language and I bootstrapped my way to a complete system with a programming platform on an ASCII pseudo computer.

What's a pseudo computer? A pseudo computer is a theoretical computer implemented on a real computer. All programs written in pseudo language run on all pseudo computers of the same kind. It's a computer program that simulates a theoretical machine. This is what computer platforms are loosely defined to be but to my knowledge and experience never stated as such. I say loosely defined because JAVA, the most popular platform is far from a pseudo computer. Look at their free download website and notice things like, "will not run on..."

Pseudo computers have rigorously defined instructions just like real computers. They have instruction formats, vocabularies, and all else. They operate in cycles just like real computers. The pseudo computer I'm defining here has the operating system built in, not a separate program but rather is a part of basic machine structure. And everything is in people readable international standard ASCII.

The word multi is often heard when talking about computer systems software. It's multi-tasking or multi-user or other multi-something. Most people don't know what "they" are talking about. It's this simple, they're talking about having a single-program machine seem to be running several programs at the same time. There is no way of getting around the pretend part of the situation. Computers execute one instruction at a time no exception. As we've seen that one thing is minuscule comparing favorably with a single hair out of all the hairs it takes to make a felt hat.

The pseudo computer has the multi-what-have-you built in. It's a multi-computer. Every program running has its own set of registers but can share data with other programs that appear to be running at the same time. Never forget the word appear because one computer can only execute one instruction at a time. Pseudo computers have the same basic FIRE execution cycle, Fetch, Increment the instruction pointer, Resolve the address, Execute the instruction and do it again. Every active program has its own independent instruction pointer register as well as all other registers, flags, whatever else.

The pseudo CPU does one instruction for every program running in a super cycle. A super cycle is executing the "next" instruction of every running program. Time sharing the CPU is automatic with no hardware or software needed other than the pseudo computer software. One program doesn't run until it's interrupted and put on hold while others get a turn. Every running program gets one instruction every super cycle. Thus all running programs progress at the same pace. It's OK to "hang" in a tight loop waiting for an operator gone on break to return and hit a key on the keyboard. Only that program is "hung up." All others still get a turn every super cycle.

Instead of having one instruction pointer register the pseudo computer I invented many years ago has a table of instruction pointer registers, one for each program running at the time. The pseudo CPU has a super cycle program pointer that points to the next program on the list of running programs.

The super cycle program pointer points to the next basic cycle instruction pointer. The super cycle operates identically to the basic cycle of all CPU's.

Super cycle: 1, use the super cycle program pointer to Fetch the next program's instruction pointer from the running programs instruction pointer table. 2, Increments, update the super cycle program pointer. 3, Resolve the address, 4, Execute one instruction for the presently selected program. This is done in a loop for every program. Thus every program gets to execute one instruction every super cycle.

I'm talking about running programs in source code. I have already mentioned I did this, 1981. I was shocked at how fast it ran. I expected programs to sputter and pop like they do in Windows based multi-tasking where the CPU is tied up by strangers in your computer scanning your disk and sending every keystroke you make to them. I did the first pseudo computer program as a matter of necessity.

I had small microcomputer manufacturing and programming shop doing custom systems for businesses. A religious organization wanted to do personalized mailings. They spent a lot of money on a fancy printer capable of fooling people into thinking the letter had been hand written and personally signed by Brother Jack. I had to put flags in the form letter for things like Miss or Mister and first names to be inserted from the mailing list. One thing led to another. I had no difficulty with that. Then I discovered I could do accounting functions, generate invoices and other forms and add up the bill if I simply added arithmetic and logic to my base word processor with flags telling me there was something to do other than print exactly what was written. Next thing, someone wanted to have several work stations with all doing different things. In the end I had the pseudo computer that is decades ahead of anything on the market today. No one has come close yet. The time is now for the need is overwhelming.

Why wasn't it accepted as the norm? Did I mention computer illiterate John Q Public just had to have an official IBM-machine? And, the most common expression that followed was, "I just bought a brand new IBM-machine and it don't do nothing?" I may have mentioned computers do nothing. I could have told them that before they wasted their money. If it isn't programmable by you it isn't a computer.

Having a computer as a part of it does not a computer it make. Programmable is the first requirement for IT to be a computer. IBM PC's were programmable and came with nothing but Microsoft's DOS operating system. John Q didn't know what programming was much less be able to do it. So the original personal IBM-machines ended up in the broom closet waiting for the next garage sale.

I named my multi everything pseudo computer, WIN, an acronym standing for Words, Information and Numbers and asked the question, "Is there anything else you want to do on the computer?" Yes, I did noticed it when several years later Microsoft came out with the latest and greatest operating system they called Windows with WIN as its pet name. Borrowing an expression from my Marine Corps DI who pointed out to me in words harshly spoken, "You wouldn't make a pimple on a Marine's ass" Windows and JAVA added together wouldn't amount to a pimple on WIN's ass.

The strongest selling point of WIN was the fact all programs were source only in ASCII and thus readable by people. There was but one type of file. There were no dot exe files or source files or jpg files. There was no text editor for writing programs as such. All programs were written using the word processor, note pad. Programs were documents with a special characters to identify instruction codes. In the original implementation I used FF hex which printed as a blacked-out vertical rectangle to signal instruction. Later I changed to the backslash, \. Turns out FF doesn't print or display in ASCII.

Example:

I want to personalize a form letter to a list of people in a file on the disk. I read the next person's record from the disk into memory and copied the name of the person to a variable I named, name. The variable is defined by,

\DV name: \E

The \ says code. The DV says I'm defining a variable. Variable names end with a colon, (:). The length of the variable itself, the maximum letters possible is determined by the number of spaces between the colon and the \E that says the end of the definition. Stop the program while it's running and see the name of the last person where the blanks are in the above. The letter was written with usual addresses and dates and then:

Dear \I name :

The \ says code. The, I after \ says insert the contents of a variable in the text. The variable's name is name. The blank after name says just one word, (first name). I could have put, \I3 and first name, middle initial, and last name all three would have printed. The pseudo computer, WIN printing the letter has just written Dear followed by a space. WIN finds the \, examines the next character and finds the, I saying insert text, sees a blank count for number of words and then it finds the variable name and after getting rid of spaces at the end etc. it prints the first word of the person's name. Then back to printing the rest of the letter with the colon being the next character printed. The printed results for a person with the name Jane would be:

Dear Jane:

Further on in the same letter it might say something like:

…now, \I name you know how much God loves a cheerful giver.

When printed:

…now, Jane you know how much God loves a cheerful giver.

It was nothing to train Brother Jack's volunteer help to write personalized letters using \I to insert names in place of a generic name used by him when composing it. My how the money rolled in along with letters in reply, way too many for any one person to read and respond to without a lot of both people and computer help.

I've had the past 37 years to think about pseudo computing. I also have a little experience implementing such things all by myself. You probably haven't so much as had the thought cross your mind. Wouldn't you like to have a computer you can program in English? I gave up years ago especially when I watched as the computer went over the cliff, lost its identity, was captured by mercenaries and turned into an appliance with no more intellectual attributes left than dishwashing machines. Turn this knob, push that button and get what you want, just as long as we already have what you want. Don't worry we have hundreds of app developers working on what you want. Wouldn't it be nice to do what you want rather than having to buy someone else's version of what they think you want?

Am I on a crusade? Yeah. I've appointed myself commander in chief. I'm ordering General Education to raise an army and take the computer back one misconception at a time. Old General Ed is recruiting them young, all the way down to preschool and kindergarten. The way to defeat them is education. The best tool for education is a simple real computer with a control panel to take all the imagination out of it.

The word is computer literacy. Computer literacy begins with the complete understanding of the basic computer cycle, FIRE - Fetch, Increment the instruction pointer, Resolve the address, Execute the instruction and do it again just as fast as possible.

It's my understanding we already have a literacy department. I was there when the first Computer Science department was created and thought it was nonsense at the time. At a minimum Computer belongs in Liberal Arts and for sure in Math. Algorithms are the equal of Matrix Algebra in terms of classroom study. Of course literacy, reading and writing no matter what is to be written or read is the function of the English teacher.

At present we are experiencing the slings and arrows of outrageous computer ignorance combined with corporate greed. No single word describes the problem better than the word update. The notions of machine independence is nothing but a dream, unless. Unless we can actually define and implement a truly universal computer that covers all bases, day one to dooms day. Above all security is the most pressing need. Is your country under threat of a cyber attack? Have hackers stolen your personal information from people you trusted with it such as credit rating companies?

Step one, get the crooks, bakers and candle stick sellers out of the computer and keep them out. Above all and as the most significant part of so doing, stabilize the operating system. The system in general and the operating system in particular may not be altered by outside programs of any kind. The "allow anyone to modify the operating system" problem has become a matter of national security adding an element of urgency to the task at hand.

Why would a pseudo computer be any more secure than an ordinary computer? Instead of attempting to give a general answer let me start with a simple particular one. When anything, disk, memory, anything at all is changed under control of the pseudo computer it's the pseudo computer doing it and not the potential criminal program. The way the crooks take over your computer under Windows or Apple is through the execution of downloaded programs attached to innocent looking things like email. "They" have books full of reason to not simply forbid the execution of downloaded programs. You don't want to hear them. Instead allow programs to be downloaded and run and mute them. Above all else never allow a downloaded program to alter the system.

OK, so you want to download and execute programs on my pseudo computer. No problem for me but I have a problem for you if you have evil intentions. You will NOT write over me, alter me in any way either in main memory or on the hard drive or other bulk storage device. I do mean me. It's me in there executing your program. If you do anything like attempt to delete files or any other mischievous looking thing I'm going to NOT let you and I'm telling the owner on you. How can I NOT let you? All instructions are executed by me including all store instructions of any kind and all write to disk etc. instructions. That's how pseudo computer work.

When the computer is a piece of hardware it's the hardware that has to do the things to stop the crooks. When its software stopping the crooks is a simple matter. For easy example: Every store instruction's address is tested for being out of range of the program running. Memory can only be altered by the program assigned the memory to be altered. The way it's now done the rogue program is allowed to run. It takes over the computer by turning off the interrupts. By the nature of the computer the operating system MUST turn the control of the computer over to any and all executing programs when they are executed. The interrupt system is the only means by which a rogue program can be stopped once it is allowed to run other than it voluntarily turning control back over to the operating system. The rogue turns control back to the main system after it has made changes to the main system. Those changes can be sleepers put there by the enemy nation that watch the clock or look for some other stimulus, a signal from over the Internet for example to come to life. This is known as a cyber attack. In the pseudo computer the operating system never gives control of the computer to any program. Problem solved.

Functions such as store-address limits testing can be and should be implemented in hardware. Other soft functions in pseudo computing necessary to make an ideal computer can also be implemented in the hardware giving the chip designers a new hobby. They mostly ran out of new good ideas many years ago.

Since in my WIN pseudo computer all computer codes are in people readable text there is no need for a specialized text editor program to compose new programs. Word processing is all that's needed. The basis of the pseudo computer is the word processor. Did it ever occur to you that people are word processors? Every word heard or read triggers a biological computer inside the person's head, words processed and action taken. WIN imitates, simulates the human though process.

In WIN there is also no need for translating programs, assemblers or compilers as such. When a program is started the operating system scans it collecting information to speed up execution. This is a behind the scenes activity, done in less than a second and it can totally be ignored by the programmer. It's done with every restart of the program. Programs are written the same way one writes a theme or term paper and for the ambitious the way books are written.

To my way of thinking play writing best describes programming. All programs are predetermined conversations between two people, the programmer and the user. Any author familiar with writing using word processing is already ahead of the game. All capable of writing a letter are authors. However, getting people to read what one has written is a different game altogether.

We discussed computer vocabularies earlier. Learning to program for one who is already language literate is a nothing. It amounts to memorizing a short vocabulary and the grammatical structure of computer instructions. In the case of my first pseudo computer I used the letters of the alphabet as the vocabulary. That takes misspelling out of spelling. I never misspell I or G or any other one letter word. The first thing the new programmer discovers will likely be the misspelling of words in computer is mentally far worse than in English class.

Let's take a glance at a few English language instructions. The heart and soul of the multi-processing system are the START and STOP instructions. Look at me. After praising the use of short, one letter instructions I've spelled out the two most important ones in multi-programming. And, adding to the misery I've spelled them with all caps. Old habits die hard. When I wrote my first program computers only had printers that printed in all caps. Lower case came a decade or more later. Nice part about it all, I usually allow synonyms to be added by the programmer for his/her program using the EQU instruction. Don't like START, STOP?

Start EQU START
Stop EQU STOP
        .or.
Go EQU START
XX EQU STOP
        .or.
Whatever EQU whichever
        .maybe.
Equ EQU EQU

Define your own language. All instructions can be equated to, given alternate names. Like to write things out then: DV EQU define variable. Shoot yourself I always say.

Instead of writing \DV you can write \define variable. The choice is yours. Misspell and get yelled at by the computer. That's not the computer yelling. That's me in there and I never yell. I do know who has the problem and it's not me.

What I'm doing is taking the pressure off me when defining my pseudo computer's vocabulary. You don't like the names I gave my babies then name them yourself. I have a relatively small family so you won't wear yourself out or strain your brain doing it.

START says exactly what start means, start a program running amounting to adding another program to the list of running programs. The thing that START doesn't do is more significant than what it does. START doesn't stop the program doing the STARTing.

Example:

I'm writing a game program like poker. On the screen I have places for players to take their seats. In the startup I START a program "looking" for new players. One shows up and "clicks" on an empty seat. The "looking" program START's a program that puts the player etc. on the screen and when it's finished it STARTs a program to service the player in the seat and when it finishes doing that it STOPs itself. The "looking" program keeps on running. Programs can START other programs and programs can START and STOP themselves.

The system has a user interface program that's always running. The user STARTs, IDLEs and STOPs programs via a keyboard, mouse of other input device. The actual STARTing, IDLEing and STOPing is done by the user interface program executing the requested instruction. Programs can start and stop other programs and operators can start and stop programs that start and stop programs. User interface and operating system are the same things in WIN world.

The IDLE instruction allows a program to be stopped on a temporary basis under control of the user/operator. This is a powerful debug tool. The screen has a tool bar icons indicating

START, STOP, IDLE and CONTINUE. The programmer has written a program and wants to try it out. All programs are written in word processing and appear on the screen as text. The programmer simply clicks on the START icon. That causes the system to start running the program on the screen at the time from the top. Then the programmer notices a problem.

The programmer clicks on the STOP icon and the program will reappear on the screen with the cursor pointing to the "next" instruction to be executed had the program not been STOPped. The programmer makes whatever changes and clicks on either START to begin from the top or another icon for CONTINUE for execution to pick up at the place in the program where it was STOPped.

My point here is simple. Anyone can be an expert programmer. As things now stand no computer I'm aware of is available on the market that can be programmed without, "knowing somebody." You need a full semester course to learn all the details of setting up, creating, compiling, loading and running programs where all is more mysterious than the chemical makeup of royal jelly.

In the real people world computers come on when turned on, may have a begin program that you setup yourself or may as they were when fresh from the box begin with a blank screen with a tool bar for you to START something. If you're going to compose a program then the blank screen is either there or a matter of clicking on an icon. From that point forward you have a blank piece of paper to write on.

Of course you'll need to know both vocabulary and the grammatical structure. We'll cover that in the next few chapters. In the meantime let's gain confidence there's nothing magic going on. And, we'll take a peek at a couple of mysterious computer instructions. We've already visited with START, STOP, IDLE and CONTINUE.

Let's see just how simple it is to "make" the computer say, "hello world". You had better not "make" the computer do anything! You USE the computer to say, "hello world" and you do it like this, type:

\KO @3,10 "hello world"

\IDLE

This is your program. It reads, instruction, Key-Out beginning at line 3, column 10 on the display screen all the text between the quotation marks. \IDLE says stop swimming and tread water, i.e. stop running and leave all as is. This is so the screen doesn't change.

After STARTing the screen will blank and hello world will appear on the screen three lines down from the top and ten spaces to the right. \IDLE causes the program to stop running without changing the screen. Click on STOP and the screen will blank and your program reappear.

Let's complicate it a little:

\DV name: \E
\KO @5,15 "Name: "
\KI name:
\IDLE

Variables can go anywhere. Here we've defined a Variable we've named, name with, \DV name: \E. It's as large in number of letters possible as the number of spaces between the colon ending the name and the \E that says End of definition.

All programs are conversations between a programmer and a user, programmer should speak first. In the above the programmer writes a prompt on the screen inviting the user to write a name. That is done with a /KO, (Key-Out) instruction. The reply is done using /KI meaning Key-In. The conversation goes like this:

Programmer, "What's the name?"

User, "The name is" what he/she types.

The programmer should have said to him/herself when writing the program, "Now I'll ask for the name. To do that I will write, Name: on the display at line 5 and 15 spaces to the right. Then I will use a key-in the name instruction after which I will IDLE until the operator clicks on the STOP icon."

When the program is run by clicking on START icon the screen will blank and Name: will appear 5 lines down the screen and 15 spaces from the left side of the screen and the cursor will be one space to the right of Name: inviting the operator to type a name. Type a name, any letters of the alphabet etc.

When the STOP is executed by you clicking on a control icon the program will reappear on the screen. You will see the name you typed in response to the prompt inside the variable name. Suppose you typed Fred and hit the enter key. When the program is STOPped the program will reappear on the screen and name will look like this:

```
\DV name:Fred        \E
\DV name:                 \E
\KO @5,15 "Name: "
\KI name:
\IDLE
```

At this point, assuming my writing abilities aren't too awfully wanton you should see how incredibly easy it to write and debug programs in my WIN pseudo computer system. The greatest requirement is the need. You must need a program first and foremost. My guess is there's a world of needed programs in the most unexpected places. Now take the music department for easy example.

With a WIN pseudo computer equipped with a speaker music majors can invent new musical instruments, make musical arrangements, create and conduct software based orchestras etc. How about the music teacher? How about the industrial arts professor with students struggling to learn how to program NC controllers? Anytime one must rely on someone else's program to do their job the likelihood of being disappointed is nearly absolute. Become computer literate and write your own programs. Nothing to it once you've learned a short vocabulary and the grammatical structure of the particular language.

I'm suggesting a fight for the control of the most important invention since the wheel. Shall a handful of greedy corporations hold the computer hostage or will you join the army of volunteers and rescue it? That is the question. I've shown you the weapons. They're easy to operate. The bar is low enough for grammar schoolers to get over. Do you have what it takes to get over that bar? What you do will decide the outcome. General Education is calling you. Borrowing an expression from days long past, "You have been selected so you need not feel neglected."

Chapter 17, the pseudo computer's...

…vocabulary is somewhat longer than the vocabulary of the computer's machine language or even that of the assembly language. Some pseudo computer instructions are also operator controls. START, STOP to name a couple are used by the operator to start and stop programs and can be used in programs as well. We'll look at operator controls first.

LOAD – load a program from bulk storage. The top of the program, the first screen full if it's longer than one screen will appear on the display screen with all of it being viewable by scrolling down the screen.

START – start a program. Click START and the program will begin running.

CONTINUE – continue running a STOPped program. A running program can be STOPped and later restarted where it left off with this command.

STOP – stops a running program with the text of the program on the display screen. If one suspects a malicious program is running then STOPping allows one to see its code.

IDLE – suspend a running program.

CLOSE – STOP and remove a program from memory.

HIDE – let program continue to run but don't show its screen(s).

SHOW – show a running hidden program's screens.

The above is a short list of operator instructions executable by clicking on icons in the tool bar. The name operating system means what it says, a system by which an operator selects and executes programs.

All programs are conversations between the programmer and the computer operator. Thus all programs must allow the operator to operate them. The program's operator instructions are a part of all possible operator controls.

All WIN instructions begin with a backslash, \ followed by a single letter of the alphabet that categorized the instruction. One or more letters of the alphabet may be required. The following is a list of instructions implemented in my original version of WIN:

\A – enter assembly language
\C – copy
\D – define variable
\E – end/exit
\G – go to
\I – insert word(s) in text.
\IF – conditional IF then DO
\IDLE
\K – keyboard and display direct
\L – name a location within program
\M – math
\N – Internet, NET operations, special IO
\O – open/close file
\P – print
\R – read record from file
\S – START, STOP program
\T – timer operations
\U – Use subroutine
\W – write record to file
Inserting assembly language instructions in program:

\A   Begin assembly language. Assembly language execution continues until a \ indicating WIN language instruction is encountered.

\C   Copy instructions. Copy – make two things identical to each other. Copy A to B - A is the original, B is the duplicate.
\Cn – copy n bytes of A into B.
\CRTV – copy record to variables.
      \CRTV record, V1, V2,, Vn
\CVTR – copy variables to record.
      \CRTV record, V1, V2,, Vn

\D   Data definition instructions:
\DE – make one name a synonym for another name
      Prefer RUN to START then: \DE RUN, START
\DV – define variable.
      \DV name: \E defines a variable named, name with the length in bytes from the colon to \E
Note: constants, actual numbers in decimal don't need defining. Just use them.

\DF define a file.

    \DF file name

\DR define a record within a file

    \DR file name, V1, V2,, Vn

    All variables, V1, V2 ect. must be defined as well.

\DL define a location within the program

    \DL XYZ

    After a location is defined it can be "gone to."

\DEC – subtract 1 from the contents of a variable.

    \DEC Counter

    Counter must have been defined.

\E – end.

\G – jump to a place in the program.

    \G location

    Location must be defined using \DL defining the name of the location to jump to. Program execution continues at the specified location.

\I – insert.

    \I name: - insert a name in a text stream. Useful in printing personalized form letters. Any string of text may be inserted anywhere.

\IDLE   Stop program and leave all as is.

\IF – conditional execution of an instruction.

    \IF A.condition.B instruction\E if the condition is met execute instruction. If the condition is not met skip instruction.

    IF conditions:

    .EQ. - A is equal to B

    .NE. - A is not equal to B

    .LT. - A is less than B

    .LE. - A is less than or equal to B

    .GT. - A is greater than B

    .GE. - A is greater than or equal to B

    Examples:

    \IF A.EQ.B \G locX\E

    If A is identical to B then the instruction \G, (go to) will be executed and the program will pick up execution at location, locX. If A is not identical to B then the \G instruction is skipped and execution continues at the next instruction in line. Any instruction may be used in conjunction with \IF.

\INC – add 1 to the contents of a variable.

\INC Counter

Counter must be defined. One is added to counter's contents. Note: adding one to the letter A makes it the letter B while subtracting one from B makes it A. Of course subtracting 1 from 10 makes it 9 and adding 1 to 9 makes it 10.

\KO – keyboard/display IO operation

\KO @l,c text

Text will be displayed with first letter at present location of the cursor. @l,c says set the cursor to line number l and character on that line, c. Including a cursor locating, @ is optional. If no @ is included then the present location of the cursor is used. The cursor locators, l and c can be constants, ordinary numbers or they can be variables containing constants. @3,10 is the same place as @X,Y where elsewhere we have defined X and Y, i.e. \DV X: 3\E and \DV Y: 10\E. We can also use mixed constants and variables, @3,Y or @X,10

\KI – get input from operator

\KI @l,c XYZ

Get input from operator and echo keystrokes beginning at line l and column c and put keys in variable, XYZ. The @l,c is optional. If it is not included echoing will begin at the present location of the cursor. Echoing simply means sending to the screen the keys hit by the operator so he/she can see what he/she is typing.

Example: \KI @6,14 name:

This reads, get keys from operator and echo keystrokes on screen beginning at line 6, column 14 and put them in variable, name.

\KO – output a text message to the operator's screen.

\KO @l,c text

The @l,c positioning the cursor is optional. If it is not included the text will begin at the present cursor location. The text will be displayed beginning at line, l and column, c or the present position of the cursor. The text can be absolute or it can come from a variable.

\KO @2,12 "All within the quotes"

Printing to screen begins at line 2 column 12.

\KO "All within the quotes"

Printing to screen begins at wherever the cursor happens to be.

\KO @2,12 text

The message to print is in variable text and printing to screen begins at line 2 column 12.

\KO text

The message to print is in variable text and printing to screen begins at wherever the cursor happens to be.

Example:

\KO @6,26 apple:

Elsewhere we have \DV apple: hello world \E both defining the variable and the text to print as well.

Never forget: If you can "make" the computer display "hello world" you have become a computer scientist and you have accomplished the impossible at the same time. Since computers do nothing "making" one do anything is bordering on the miraculous to say the least.

\L – identify a location within the program.

\L add tax:

Somewhere in the program you have identified a location you named, add tax. Perhaps you're totaling up a ticket at the counter and all that's left to do is add the tax. You might have been working from a list of purchases and have identified the last item.

\IF Item#.EQ.Nitems: \G add tax: \G next item:

Either there's more items to add to the total or not. IF it's the end of the list, next item number equals all items then go to add tax. If not the go to add tax is skipped and the go to next item is executed. But of course Item# and Nitems must have been defined with \DV's and are used to count items tallied and how many items altogether. Of course locations add tax and next item must also be defined with \L's.

\IF is how computers make decisions which again is remarkable since computers do nothing. \IF is how programmers make decisions. Programmers tally tickets at the checkout stand, add tax and make change. They do it USING computers and computer peripherals such as keyboards, displays etc. as an extension of themselves.

\IF Item#.EQ.Nitems: \G add tax: \G next item:

Should have been written while saying to one's self, "I will now see if that was the last item on the list. If it is I'll go add the tax. If it's not I'll go add in the next item." I can't go anywhere that doesn't exist thus I must identify places to go and I do that with \L instructions.

\M – mathematical operation, add, subtract, multiply, divide.

There's two ways to do math, and actually three ways if we include assembly language instructions. We'll leave assembly language out for the time being. There's math done the way regular people do using calculators and there's math done the other way, you know like how computer scientists do it. I prefer the calculator method.

Calculator coding:

\M Number .o. Number .o. Number...=Results

Example:

\MC A: + B: / C: = D:

That reads, clear accumulator, enter A, add B, divide by C and put the answer into D. This is how one does arithmetic using an ordinary calculator.

Computer Scientist coding of math:

\MF D: = (A: + B:)/C:

Divide quantity A + B by C and put the results in D.

Integer, whole number arithmetic:

\MI A:/B: = C:

I says integer, whole number with no decimal places. A is divided by B and the whole number results are stored in C. In this case the remainder is discarded.

\MR A:/B: = C:

Again it's whole numbers with no decimal point. A is divided by B and the remainder is stored in C with the whole number answer being discarded.

\N – Internet commands

    \NC – call, dial the number

    \NH – say hello, start conversation

    \NS – speak, send message to connected

    \NL – listen, get message from NET

All computer programs are conversations between two human beings, an operator and a programmer. The operator can be another programmer. In the case of the Internet and other situations it's a conversation between two operators with two middle-persons programmers.

\O – open file.

    \O device, file name, error

The device identifies one of all possible file based peripherals. The file name is as stated, the name of the file one wishes to open. The error is a location within the program to "go to" if there was a problem.

    \OC device, file name, error

The device identifies one of all possible file based peripherals. The file name is as stated, the name of the file one wishes to open. If the file does not exist the C after the \O for open says create it if it doesn't already exist. The error is a location within the program to "go to" if there was a problem.

\P - print

    \P device, text

The print function outputs the text to the selected device that can be a disk file, the display screen or one of the system's printers or some other device.

    \P \screen, "hello world"

Says print hello world on the screen.

    \P \screen, x:

Says print the contents of variable, x on the operator's screen.

    \P \printer, "What hath God wrought iron?"

The backslash before screen and printer are only valid if the system has a screen and/or a printer. Operator selected print device is handled through the operator console with actual physical destination of output handled by the system. Printing can go to files or devices.

\P \printer, variable:

Says print the contents of variable using the printer.

\P device, variable1/text, variable2/text, varaible3/text,, variableN/text

Says print using the specified device the contents of variables and or text until the end of the list of variables and/or texts.

\PS variable:

Says scan picture into the specified variable. Want to make cartoons? Make sketches, scan them one at a time into the computer with:

\PS picture: \STOP
\DV picture:

When this program is executed the scanner will activate, the document on its bed will be scanned into variable, picture and the program will stop with the screen showing the above program with the picture just scanned in the variable, picture. You are free to use the word processing tools to "work" on the picture etc. And you thought you had to buy a program from Microsoft, download it, go back to college and with luck learn how to operate it. Note: there's nothing sacred about the word picture. Any name will work equally well. Oh! Almost forgot, you will need a scanner.

\R – read record from file

\Rr file name, error

Read record number r of file, file name and if there is a problem got to location error.

\R5 names and addresses:, record:, oops:

Says read record number 5 of file named names and addresses into a variable named record and if there is a problem then go to location oops. A variable is usually used instead of a constant for the record number. Example: \RRn reads, "Read record, record number is in variable Rn."

\S – START and STOP programs.

\START location:

Start program at location, location.

\T – timer operations.

\TD VN:

Reads delay VN microseconds. VN is either a whole Number or a variable. \TD 100 says delay 100 microseconds. \TD X: use the contents of variable X to determine the time to delay.

\TS T1,P1,T2,P2,,Tn,Pn

Reads, start program Pi at time Ti. This is extremely helpful for creating orchestrated music as well as machine tool programming. Timing is in microseconds. Microsecond – one millionth of a second.

\TS guitar,100,base,10… The next note from the Specified instrument happens at the interval. Uses are limited only by the equipment and the imagination of the programmer. \U – Use subroutine.

\U search:(A1, A2,, An)

Reads, USE subroutine named search. Use arguments A1 through An. Example: I want to search a file for a particular person given the person's name.

\U search:(names and addresses:, name:, record number:, not found:)

Reads: search file, names and addresses for contents of name and if found return the record number of the record containing name. If no record with name in it is found jump to location, not found.

Remember the fact that all computer based operations are conversations between an operator and a programmer. No other subroutine makes a better example than the search subroutine. Use: A desk clerk has a potential guest on the phone. "What's your last name" she inquires. The potential guest replies, "Smith." The clerk has a form on the screen with the prompt, Name: The clerk types Smith, the programmer within the computer searches prior guest file for the name Smith, finds several and presents them to the clerk in lines across the screen:

Smith John 1234 Any Street, Little Town, MO
Smith John 4321 Old Street, Small Town, AZ
Smith John 2143 New Street, Some Town, MD

The clerk inquires of the person on the phone, "And your address is?" The potential guest replies, "4321 Old Street,

Small Town, Arizona." The clerk sees the person on the phone has stayed there before and clicks on the name. The programmer now knows what file from previous guest file the clerk wants, pulls it and presents it to the clerk in a form on the screen.

And you thought there was some kind of magic going on when you witnessed the above. It's not the computer doing all that magic. It's a human being that could do the same thing using index cards. The program must do the same things a person with a filing system would do to perform the same task. Writing a program to help desk clerks take reservations is an hour or less job using the WIN language. It can be done by anyone with average intelligence and knowledge of how taking reservations is done. The key is universal computer literacy. Then the desk clerk can write his/her own program rather than using one done by a computer scientist who didn't understand the problem.

\W – write record to file

\Wr file name, error

Write record number r of file, file name and if there is a problem got to location error.

\W5 names and addresses:, record:, oops:

Says write record number 5 of file named names and addresses, record is in a variable named record and if there is a problem then go to location oops. A variable is usually used instead of a constant for the record number. Example: \WRn reads, "write record, record number is in variable Rn."

Example program for setting up a names and addresses file. All names of variables used are optional, at the pleasure of the programmer.

\DF names and addresses:

The above reads "Define File" followed by the file's name, "names and addresses."

Files as used in computing is close to ordinary filing. The file as such is the file cabinet. An office might have several file cabinets. In regular offices the cabinet must be identified to the clerk given the task of searching for a record, (folder). Since we can have any number of files each must be named. Like ordinary filing the file cabinet has folders, one each for ever individual known as "records" in computing. Computer records are identical to ordinary records IF and only IF ordinary records are forms with fixed information. There are no margins in computing where things can be written. This does not preclude variable length things like comments.

\DR names and addresses: name, addl1, addl2, city, state, zip\E

The above reads, "Define Record" followed by the name of the file and then the list of the names of variables within a record. Variables listed must be defined. But first a buffer to hold the entire record must be defined.

\DV names and addresses record:
                              \E

\DV name: \E
\DV addl1:   \E
\DV addl2:   \E
\DV city: \E
\DV state: \E
\DV zip: \E

The above line by line reads, "Define variable." The maximum length of a variable is the number of spaces between the colon ending the variable's name and the \E ending the definition.

The base code is \D that says define. The next letter says what kind of variable is being defined. F for File, R for Record and V for ordinary variable. You do know that a variable is anything that varies? The contents of the Variables in a file vary from record to record.

You may have noticed we not only defined the variables in our records, names, addresses, city, state and zip code but we also defined a total record variable with a very long name, "names and addresses record." I suggest shortening that name a little bit. I used the Christian names in order to not confuse you any more than necessary. Individual items within a record are much easier to deal with than "indexing" into a single variable with all datum in it. When creating a new record by way of the keyboard we \KI to the individual items. The following is a program to do that:

First, do some housekeeping, like blank the screen and key-out, \KO, key-out some prompts:

\KO @3,10 "Add person's name and address:"
　　　　\KO @4,10 "　Name:"
　　　　\KO @5,10 " Address:"
　　　　\KO @6,10 "　　Apt #:"
　　　　\KO @7,10 "　　City:"
　　　　\KO @8,10 "　　State:"
　　　　\KO @9,10 " Zip code:"

This puts a form on the screen to be filled in. Beginning at line 4, column 10 on the screen the operator would see:

Add person's name and address:
　　　Name:
　　Address:
　　　Apt #:
　　　City:
　　　State:
　Zip code:

Next the operator fills out the form using a set of key-in instructions.

　　　　\KI @ 4,19 name:
　　　　\KI @ 5,19 addl1:
　　　　\KI @ 6,19 addl2:
　　　　\KI @ 7,19 city:
　　　　\KI @ 8,19 state:
　　　　\KI @ 9,19 zip:

The program gets to this point after the operator has keyed in a person's name and address. The next step is to copy that into the record buffer and then write it to the file. To facilitate that we have the copy variables to record instruction.

　　　　\CVTR record,V1,V2,, Vn

This reads, copy to record the contents of the variables listed. In our example case the instruction would be:

　　　　\CVTR names and addresses record, name, addl1, addl2, city, state, zip

The contents of "names and addresses" variable will be made identical to contents of the variables, name, addl1, addl2, city, state, and zip. STOP the program and look at the variables and find the information you just typed in them, individually in the variables and collectively in the record variable.

The opposite direction operation is:

\CRTV record, V1, V2,, Vn

CRTV reads "copy record to variables." This is used when getting data records from a file and using individual items elsewhere in the program. For example, searching for an individual's record by name. Read each record starting with the first and compare the name to the name of the person you're looking for. It can be done without copying to individual variables but that's mentally taxing. Indexed addressing for most folks is clumsy. I often use indexing rather than distribution, did it routinely myself, too lazy to write a distribute-record instruction.

After making an entry, copying to the record to variables and STOPping the program one would see:

\DV names and addresses record: Jack Smith 1234 N Elm Apt# 27 Big City MO 22222-1234\E

\DV name: Jack Smith \E

\DV addl1: 1234 N Elm \E

\DV addl2: Apt# 27 \E

\DV city: Big City \E

\DV state:MO\E

\DV zip:22222-1234\E

Programming in WIN with a word processor base is as simple as it gets. First one must memorize enough of the vocabulary as needed to write little ditty test programs. I suggest defining a variable and just one \KI instruction to see how data is gotten from the keyboard to variables within a program. I've noticed C people and others insist on the beginner writing "hello world" or an equally sterile message on the console. You might want to read one of their self-teaching books and compare what "they" tell you to do their way and compare it with:

\KO "hello world"

\IDLE

Then click on the START icon and see the screen blank and hello world appear in the upper left hand corner of the screen. Click on the STOP icon and watch your two line program reappear. That should encourage you. Next add an at, @ to the instruction.

\KO @6,35 "hello world"

Then click on START and watch the screen blank and hello world appear down the screen 6 lines and across the screen to almost the middle.

This is called trying out instructions to see what they do. It's nothing more than a tool box with a few new monkey wrenches for tightening and taking off some strange looking nuts. With a little bit of blooming luck it won't drive you nuts. If I can do it anyone can do it and it's too blooming late for I've already done it tens of thousands of times. Why do I have to do all the heavy lifting? Your turn. Have it your way. Why do I get to have all the fun?

Chapter 18, wrong! You will not…

…download an assembly language program, turn off the interrupt system and take over my computer the way you do it to Windows and Apple users. I don't need no stinking interrupts to get control back from you. Your assembly language programs are run under my control at the instruction level. I'm a watching everything you do especially what you intend to do to me. Yes, that's not the computer doing whatever it's me the programmer who wrote WIN. I'm using the computer to keep an eye on you. I trust but I also verify.

Absolutely no high level language covers all possible programming needs. Shortcomings are overcome by allowing the high level language program to use assembly language either as in-line code or in subroutines. So doing ends the possibility of machine independence or portability as it's commonly known. Assembly language being machine dependent using it destroys the portability of software platforms. WIN overcomes this problem by simulating a powerful mainframe computer. Pseudo computing has no machine limitations and is a truly machine independent programming platform.

Yes, assembly language instructions are mixable with WIN high level language instructions. However, the assembly language used is also machine independent. It's the assembly language of a pseudo computer that must be implemented on every make and model of computer that uses WIN. Assembly language instructions are executed the same way and with the same basic cycle as all other instructions. The most significant difference between writing in compiler language and assembly language is in the grammatical structure of lines of code.

WIN compile language instructions always begin with a backslash, \. To enter assembly language a \A is used. After a \A instructions are in assembly language format. Leaving WIN assembly language and returning to WIN compiler language happens automatically when a WIN compile language instruction is encountered.

Here's how it works. We're composing, writing in WIN compiler language. Then we need to do a few assembly language instructions. We write, \A and from that point until a \ is encountered we're in assembly language mode.
\A ← says enter assembly language mode.
Instruction format switches to assembly language format. Once in assembly language format we stay there until a backslash, \ indicating compile language is encountered. Any, \ says a WIN instruction. There is no special operation code to take us back to WIN high level language. Any one takes us back to compiler language.

We've already learned the grammatical structure of the perfect assembly language. Just a quick review. It goes like this:
Label Operation-code,register Address Comment.

Briefly, labels are names given to locations within the program. A Label is optional, only required if a jump to the location is to be done elsewhere in the program or we're naming data locations. Operations-codes are the basic vocabulary. Some instructions do not use registers. Instructions requiring registers are followed by a comma and the register's name. The last part of instructions are addresses but only for instruction types that require addresses. Lastly, comments, notes the programmer writes to self are allowed. The different fields are usually lined up one instruction after the other for readability. At least one space or tab key is used to separate fields. If there is no label then the line begins with either a space or a tab. You haven't already forgotten that things in ( ) reads, "contents of?"
\A enter assembly language

Here	L,R1	X	copy (X) to (R1)
	AI,R1	27	add 27 to (R1)
	A,R1	(R2)	Add (memory at (R2)) to (R1)
	INC, R1		add 1 to (R1)

R1 and R2 must be defined with \DV instructions. There is no DATA pseudo operation. Registers are ordinary variables of any length with the single exception that numbers used in arithmetic operations are limited to 32 bytes long.

Above we have the four possible instruction types relative to addressing and labeling. The first line has a label, "Here." Elsewhere we can have a jump to, jump instruction, JT, JE, JNE etc. to Here or a WIN instruction \G Here: instruction causing execution to pick up at location Here.

The question you should be asking is why I would ever want to do assembly language programming when I have WIN high level language. Again, no matter the high level language there are some things that can't be done with any degree of ease in high level language. Here's an easy to understand example:

I want to code my message to grandma so Aunt Hilda can't read it. It's about Aunt Hilda's birthday party. I don't need to get real fancy about it. I'll simply rotate the entire message one bit to the right changing every letter to some other thing. In grandma's computer I have installed a decoder amounting to rotating her messages from me one bit to the left before presenting them to her on her computer's screen.

For sake of simplicity I'm going to use ABCD for the message. The message is in a variable, M:

\DV M:ABCD\E

On the screen it's ABCD. In the computer's memory the message looks like this:

01000001 01000010 01000011 01000100

The above is ABCD in binary with spaces between letters for readability. You didn't already forget everything in the computer is in switch settings and all switches must be either switch-off = 0 or switch-on = 1. High level language doesn't change that. In fact you really don't care, have no compelling need to know unless you want to code your messages. My purpose here is to show you how easy it is to fold, spindle and mutilate information that is coded in binary, Morse code from the layman's point of view.

Those wanting to create codes and the like don't actually need to know binary. It's helpful but not necessary. Computer literacy begins with knowing the machine language for at least one computer. Those who want their messages kept private have an incentive to become computer literate and do it themselves. Hillary Clinton never ask me or the FBI would be going crazy trying to read her emails while getting nowhere.

In my example I put spaces between the bytes representing ABCD so we can read them a little easier. ASCII A is 01000001, B is 01000010, C is 01000011, and D is 01000100. All email messages are coded in the equal of old time Morse code, a series of dots and dashes represented by zeroes and ones. That includes pictures and those .exe files containing viruses.

Here's a rotate whole message right program with comments so you can see how easy it is to do in assembly language:

\DV R1: \E   ← defines an 8 bit = 1 byte/character register.
\DV M:ABCD\E ← my short message, ABCD.
\A ← says enter assembly language
        L,R1   M+3   last letter of message, D
* M is the base address that points to the letter A in
* variable M. The address of the letter D is the
* address of A plus 3 bytes more.
* After the instruction has been executed R1 will
* contain the letter D which is 01000100 binary
        RRC,R1 1   Rotate right 1, LSB to carry
*Rotate (R1) 1 bit to the right, Least Significant Bit
* to carry, all other bits moved one position right.
        L,R1   M   first letter to R1, A
*We've set up the LSB of last letter to rotate it into
* the MSB of the first letter by shifting it into the carry bit.
        RRC,R1 1   carry to MSB, LSB to carry
* Rotate right, all bits move 1 position to the right with
* the carry bit going into the Most Significant Bit and
* the Least Significant Bit going into the carry bit.
        ST,R1 RM   first letter of rotated message
*Replace first letter with rotated first letter
        L,R1   M+1   second letter, B to R1
*Do same for next letter, B
        RRC,R1 1   carry to MSB, LAB to carry
        ST,R1 RM+1 second letter of rotated message
        L,R1   M+2   third letter, C to R1

*Do same for next letter, C

<pre>
      RRC,R1 1   carry to MSB, LAB to carry
      ST,R1 RM+2   third letter of rotated message
      L,R1 M+3   last letter, D to R1
</pre>
*Do same for next letter, D

<pre>
      RRC,R1 1   carry to MSB, LAB to carry
      ST,R1 RM+3   last letter of rotated message
</pre>
*Entire message is rotated 1 bit to the right.

* any \ ← says exit assembly language

In the above I've used "in line" code. In the real world I'd use indexing. I did it this way so you can see exactly what's going on. Step 1 make the carry bit the same as the least significant bit of the last character, i.e. 01000100 has LSB of 0 so carry has 0. Then one at a time I rotate the carry bit into the most significant bit of the next letter and the least significant bit of that letter to the carry bit. This way I rotate the entire message one bit to the right. The message was:

01000001 01000010 01000011 01000100

The rotated right 1 place message is:

00100000 10100001 00100001 10100010

Before the message was ABCD. Now it's whatever characters 00100000, 10100001, 00100001 and 10100010 be. You can look them up in the ASCII table if you like.

The above is the message sent. Grandma's computer needs to rotate the message as received left one bit before displaying the message. The rotated data above is bit patterns representing some characters within the ASCII codes. Which ones we don't care. All letters of the alphabet, punctuation marks etc. are one and all 8 bit sets of 0's and 1's. Thus all messages are a series of bits commonly known as a bit stream. Bits flow in a stream one bit at a time from the sender to the receiver. Think old time telegraph messages sent and received one dot or dash at a time. To confuse the message we save the first dot or dash and send it at the end.

Now I will show you the programming power of defined computer registers. Above we used single byte registers to rotate the message right one place. Instead of individual assembly language instructions we could have written:

\A RAR,M   1   rotate the entire message

In this case M is the register being rotated. WIN allows registers to be any variables of any length. M could be 10,000 characters/letters long and the above instruction will rotate the entire message one bit to the right.

Grandma's computer must have a program to rotate the message 1 bit left before presenting it to her else she can't read it. The whole idea is to disguise the message.
*Program to decode message rotated 1 bit right
\A RAL,M   1

Rotating right 1 bit and rotating left 1 bit is the same as no rotation at all.

Here's one of my favorite ways to, "Give the KGB a hobby." Let's suppose we pick 10 things, rotate, invert, modulate, scramble, code from table etc. that we can do in any order. And, we settle on doing 10 sets of those 10 things. That gives us 10,000,000,000 possible combinations and the snooper a hobby a one character message could take him several lifetimes to figure out if ever. The key is taking messages as bit streams rather than character streams. Assembly language is best suited for that task. Pseudo computers with any length registers and assembly language instructions makes coding text a breeze for the coding program and decoding that text a lifetime hobby for snoopers.

A byte of data can be broken down into bits using regular high level language arithmetic. One must have more than a basic understanding of binary numbers and math in general. Binary numbers are written in switches. Each bit is either zero or one. A binary number divided by 2 is the same as a binary number right shifted one bit. Using calculator format for doing arithmetic we calculate the least significant bit in byte X by:

\MC X/2 = B
*To get the least significant bit of X into C:

\MC X – 2B = C
*This works in decimal. Let's do an example and
* write a short program to verify:
*First I define 3 variables, X, B and C and I put a test

217

*number, 137 decimal in X.

    \DV X:137\E
    \DV B: \E
    \DV C: \E

*Next I put a math instruction.

    \MI X/2 = B

*M says math. MI says whole number.
*whole number says throw away any
*remainder. Verify what happened by putting:

    \STOP

*Run the program and look at A and B that will be:

    \DV X:137\E
    \DV B: 68\E
    \DV C: \E
    \MI X/2 = B
    \STOP

137 divided by 2 is 68 with remainder 1. The remainder is the least significant bit of the number. Integer arithmetic discards remainders. Add the instruction:

    \MI X – 2B = C

Before the STOP, run the program and you'll see:

    \DV X:137\E
    \DV B: 68\E
    \DV C: 1\E
    \MI X/2 = B
    \MI X – 2B = C
    \STOP

You will notice variable C now has a 1 in it. This is "shuffling" bits the hard way. Right shifting is the easy way to do it and that requires assembly language. An easier way to do the same thing as above is doing /MR, Remainder arithmetic. The above could have been written:

    \DV X:137\E
    \DV B: \E
    \DV C: \E
    \MR X/2 = C
    \STOP

Running the program we see:

```
\DV X:137\E
\DV B:    \E
\DV C:    1\E
\MR X/2 = C
\STOP
```

137 divided by 2 is 68 remainder 1. \MR says remainder only to the target variable which here is C.

Writing in the WIN language allows one to write and run short programs and verify what different instructions do. The screen begins blank like a blank piece of paper. One writes short test programs, runs them and ends them with a /STOP instruction. Since everything, the contents of all variables are visible one can see the results of executing the instruction(s). Felt hats are made of individual hairs properly arranged relative to all other hairs in the hat. Computer programs are made of individual instructions properly arranged relative to all other instructions in the program.

I do believe I read somewhere, "All that is so for writing computer programs is also so for all kinds of writing." In computer class we learn how to write well-behaved computer programs. In English class we learn to write well-behaved themes and term papers. Come to think about it I was the one who said that, scratch the well-behaved part. I included "well-behaved" to give credit where credit is due. Have you ever seen written material misbehave? I'm still looking but my heart isn't in it.

Some will find bit shuffling easier in assembly, some will do in it high level language but most will never do it at all. Shifting is the easy way to do it. Right shifting – bit 0 moves to carry, bit 1 moves to bit 0, bit 2 moves to bit 1, bit 3 moves to bit 2, bit 4 moves to bit 3, bit 5 moves to bit 4, bit 6 moves to bit 5, bit 7 moves to bit 6, and bit 7 is cleared to zero. Example:

10101010 shifted right 1 → 01010101 carry 0

Left shifting is the opposite of right. Decoding a right shifted message is as simple as left shifting it.

Rotating only differs from shifting in what happens to the 0th and 7th bits. Right shift the 7th bit becomes zero. Right rotate the carry is moved to the 7th bit. The opposite for left shift versus left rotate except it's the rightmost bit the 0th bit which becomes zero when shifting left and it gets the carry when rotating left.

Those who really want to give hackers a hobby will CSM, Cut, Shuffle and Merge their messages at the bit level. Before starting, the message has random characters added to in making it an even number of bytes long. Adding random data to messages causes the same message to encode differently with successive encodings. For easy example a single letter message like say the letter A will not encode into the same thing when 127 random letters are added to the message only repeating once every 2 to the 128th power encodings. With every encoding the encoded message changes to one of 2 to the 128th power times before repeating.

Here's how CSM, cut, shuffle and merge is done on a message with added random characters making it an even number of bytes long.

The cut – we have a table of numbers ranging in value from ¼ the length of the massage in bytes through ½ the length of the message in bytes. Example: we have a 120 character long message after adding random characters. The cut is between 120/4 and 120/2 or 30 through 60. Think of it as cutting a deck of cards somewhere above the middle of the deck. We create a table with numbers ranging in value from 30 to 60. The number comes from that table and changes with ever new CSM. It is included in the coded message disbursed in bits so the decoder will know the cut number. The cut is made and the bottom cards are moved to the top.

The shuffle – We have a table of random numbers ranging in value from 0, (zero) through 255. Note: 8 bit bytes are numbers ranging in value from 0 through 255. Using the bytes of the message as indexes each is exchanged with the random value at its location within the table, i.e. 0 is exchanged with the contents of the 0th location within the table, 1 with the second and so on. The letter A being 01000001, 65 decimal will be exchanged with the contents of the 66th location in the table, (we start numbering at zero). I believe this is known in the spy trades as enigma coding.

The merge – The message is cut in half and every other new byte is taken from the bottom half and the top half, i.e. the new message is byte half way in message, byte 0, byte half way in message + 1, byte 1, etc. for the entire message. In the end we've translated into code and relocated every character within the message.

CSM, cut shuffle and merge is my choice for shuffling playing cards and other gaming devices such as KENO balls. In both cases it's a simple matter to continual CSM while waiting for the player to initiate the next play or the end of a hand for card games. The continual CSM of the next deck while the present game or hand is being played randomizes the actual shuffle by the time taken by the players to act. Just a guess but a modern microprocessor running at gigahertz speeds would likely be able to shuffle cards or KENO balls tens of thousands of times between plays.

Would you like to create your own games, compose music and try it out on a computerized orchestra, and encode your messages to grandma? No problem, simply become computer literate, step up to the plate and show us what you got. Universal computer literacy should be the goal as much as literacy is in general. Regular literacy begins with memorizing the ABC's and the sounds they make. Computer literacy begins with memorizing the basic computer cycle followed by memorizing the machine language instructions of some computer. To know one is to know them all after a 15 minute look at the new computer's instruction set.

The next step is coming to an understanding of how to "put the computer on like a jacket" and make it an extension of one's self. The babies will find this to be second nature. Adults even the well-educated will must to give up the prejudices coming from the handful of corporations reaping the billion dollar prizes for keeping the computer cloaked in mystery.

Computers are no more complicated than ordinary light switches. The computer is a tool and nothing more. Do you have a few nuts you'd like to tighten and a few you'd like to remove and discard altogether? Maybe you'd like to create your own music and/or create your own games. Give your brain a chance. Become computer literate.

Some things can be done in high level language and there are some things that cannot without more knowledge than is necessary combined with a bit of jumping through hoops to do them. I demonstrated a little of that earlier. For that reason we include assembly language insertions in our WIN programs. Pro football legend Vince Lombardi famously said, "WINNING isn't everything it's the only thing." I fully agree don't you?

There are a few new rules in WIN assembly language. Registers are defined by the programmer for one of those rules. Registers may be as many in number as desired and any length from 1 byte to however many is needed to do the job. They may not be more than 32 places when defining numbers used in arithmetic operations, add, subtract, multiply and divide. Otherwise there are no restrictions. Smart programmers will realize they can define registers the length of tables of data and copy whole tables from one to another with an L and an ST instruction instead of using \C, (copy).

We examined the assembly language of my DC-3 minicomputer earlier. To it we can add any length shifts, multiply and divide and we can add floating point arithmetic operations as well. Otherwise all is the same.

RR,r	n	rotate right register r n bits.
RRC,r	n	rotate right register r with carry n bits.
SR,r	n	shift right register r n bits.
SRC,r	n	shift right register r with carry n bits.
RL,r	n	rotate left register r n bits.
RLC,r	n	rotate left register r with carry n bits.
SL,r	n	shift left register r n bits.
SLC,r	n	shift left register r with carry n bits.
M,r	addr	multiply (r) by (addr)
D,r	addr	divide (r) by (addr)
FA,r	addr	floating point add (addr) to (r)

FS,r	addr	floating point subtract (addr) from (r)
FM,r	addr	floating point multiply (r) by (addr)
FD,r	addr	floating point divide (r) by (addr)

If you don't know what floating point arithmetic is that means you will never need it. You never needing it means I don't need to explain it to you. Those who need it already know what it's all about. As a matter of curiosity, floating point numbers are more than 31 digits long thus they are too long to fit in a 32 place register, sign + 31 digits and commas. The first place in numbers is the sign of the number, i.e. a space or + for positive numbers and a minus sign, - for negative numbers. 31 digits with commas to make long ones readable are enough to hold the national debt?

The nice part about a pseudo language is the ability to make additions. Such things as trig functions and log functions can be added as single instructions. Remember, those who get carried away will likely be carried away so watch your step adding new and especially confusing instructions to WIN. Now take C for example of getting carried away inventing ways of making the computer do things. C is a computer language that needs to be given a decent funeral. You don't want to get all gummed up in syntax sugar while struggling to create well-behaved programs. Sorry, meant to say, well-behaved sketches. Take a fool's advice. Never use permanent markers when making sketches.

If you had a WIN system learning would be simple. How simple? Well, write what I call ditty programs, run them and see what happens. Is the notion of loading and storing registers kind of foggy? Do this:

```
\DV R:      \E
\A
LI,R      1234
STOP
```

Click on RUN and watch 1234 appear between the colon after the R in the \DV R: instruction. But of course you'll need to memorize the vocabulary first. Well, at least the LI instruction.

LI says, "Load Immediate data" into register. We could try regular direct addressing with:

223

\DV R: 1234\E
\DV X: Adam\E
\A
L,R   X
STOP

Click on RUN and watch Adam be written over the 1234 in R. After running the screen will have:

\DV R: Adam\E
\DV X: Adam\E
\A
L,R   X
STOP

This should take all the guesswork out of what's going on when programs are "RUN." There is no substitute for hands-on learning. WIN is the simplest high level language for hands-on learning. Everything is people readable. All registers and data are there. Nothing is "behind the curtain" requiring imagination.

In C++ variables are categorized, integer, text etc. with instructions like:

Int A;

Almost forgot the semicolon. Where is A? What's in it? By the way what's an Int? Only C++ knows for sure where variables are and what they look like. Compare this with defining variables in WIN.

\DV Z: contents of Z\E

The babies should learn the basic computer cycle using a basic computer with a control panel. There is no substitute for total knowledge of what the computer is and how it works. The older generation with all the propaganda from computer corporations branded on their brains will need a lot of retraining. Old bad ideas die hard.

Necessity is the mother of invention so I've heard. Is there an English major who would like to become computer literate here? How about a theatrical arts student who would like to make cartoons? Is anyone musically inclined? The computer is the monkey wrench of machines adjustable to fit all nuts. Almost forgot, is there a physics student who would like to do a little orbital mechanics calculating? I did a little of that myself. I'm a veteran of Project Apollo. Maybe you have a new formula for digital integration? No problem if you're computer literate and have a WIN system. You can program a numerical integration subroutine in WIN in less than two minutes provided you can type with two fingers.

But of course the big bucks are in time wasting programs, games they're called. You see how easy it is to scan a picture into the computer. A simple, \PS variable, does the job in one easy step. The old, highlight – copy, cut and paste is there just for the editing and even the moving of characters around on the screen. If you got talent you'll figure out how to make characters move under program control rather than having to draw and scan every individual frame. Did you get it yet? You have every reason to become computer literate. Being computer illiterate and still using the computer is like a mechanic who doesn't know wrenches work tightening and removing nuts. Not on my car!

WIN is a training tool like no other in the history of computers. There is no substitute for hands-on all visible learning. Programs can be written and RUN in seconds to try-out instructions and actually see what they do. Those instructions are the tools you need to tighten and remove the loose and unwanted nuts in your life.

I don't see why I need an Internet access middle man. Why can't I be my own Internet site? OK so I need a phone line. I can buy a router and plug it into the phone line can't I. Why can't people send email directly to me? Why do I need Google, Yahoo or any other middle man? One war at a time. We know the big computer corporations were there when Internet protocol was being decided and they carved out a big slice of the huge dollars pie for themselves. First become computer literate and then you're qualified to bypass them or at a minimum start a secure messaging service and compete with them.

One last thing. Isn't it stupid of large data base operators to not encode those data bases so snoopers cannot read them without knowing the code? The notion of letting downloaded programs run "unattended" is stupid enough all by itself. Letting them access data bases without knowing the encoding only adds fuel to the fire. Of course those systems were created by computer experts. We don't want to be one of them experts. We only want to know what we're doing. I began my career in computing solving a problem in my discipline, engineering data analysis. When someone ask me to write them a program I always said, "I'll have to learn how that's done" not meaning how to program but how what they wanted computerized was done by hand.

Accountants and only accountants are qualified to write accounting programs. Programmers must learn accounting before they can write accounting programs that do the accountant's job properly. Maybe it would be easier to teach accounts to program? When all the babies become computer literate all accountants will, WIN, bigtime.

Chapter 19, fool that I am…

…I will attempt to teach you how to program without the benefit of a computer. Learning about machinery of all kinds usually involves what's commonly known as hands-on experiences. There is no substitute for hands-on experience. Simply said I will attempt to substitute for that for which there is no substitute. After all we're talking about a mental thing, learning how to do something.

The meanings of words is key to knowing the details in any field of endeavor. I learned early on the dictionary is useless when it comes to the meanings of math words. Words such as integration, partial derivative and differential are there but their definitions are far from what the words mean within a mathematical context.

You probably think you know the meaning of the word resolve. It's not a difficult word is it? The dictionary says, "Settle or find a solution to, (a problem, dispute or contentious matter)." In computing we "resolve" addresses. Addresses here are not a problem and they are not disputed or contentious. At this point they may be a problem for you if you don't know how to program.

The word address does have the same meaning here as that found in the dictionary. An address is where something resides, can be found. In computing addresses are resolved. That's a problem. It's not a disputable problem but it does require math. Not a whole lot of math but a little and usually only addition. I can't think of a computer that resolves addresses using any mathematical operation other than addition.

One of the greater difficulties arises when the meanings of one word not in the dictionary relies on the meanings of other words also not in the dictionary. Resolving address is one of these situations. It relies on the meaning of the word "instruction." Before we can resolve addresses we must first know the meaning of the word "instruction."

Complications set in when there are several words that are used interchangeably with all meaning the same thing.

Instruction is one of those words. Instructions are referred to as commands, requests, words, lines of code and operations to mention a few.

Cook books assume the cook knows where different ingredients are located. It says, "2 eggs." Computer instructions also say what ingredients to use but must also say where to find them. Instead of saying "2 eggs" in programming we must include the "address" of the eggs.

The words are resolve, address and instruction. All rely on each other for their meanings within the context a computer program. In our above "2 eggs" example the cook can only find the eggs after resolving the address of the eggs. The eggs are in the refrigerator that is in the kitchen. The same is true for the CPU. Eggs equal data.

All instructions involving data must include the address of the data. We can't load, store, do arithmetic, and compare without the address of the data just like the postman cannot deliver mail without an address. We can't add without knowing the location of the number to add.

All program flow control instructions, call, jump and conditionally jump instructions must include the address of the new location where processing will continue. Imagine being instructed by the boss to go or call without saying where to go to or who to call.

Addresses are where data is found and where to go in the case of call and jump instructions. Many situations require complex addressing. Addresses can be simple meaning a part of the instruction or they can be complex meaning the address portion of the instruction is itself an instruction. Complex addresses instruct the CPU telling it where the address is to be found. A memory location is a simple address. The contents of a memory location or a register is a complex address. In complex addressing the address portion of the instruction points to where the CPU will find the address. Before the complex address can be used it must be resolved to simple.

Programs are sets of instructions written on/in memory. Instructions are sets of switch settings with a rigorous format that varies from one processor to another. We've taken a glimpse at the instruction format of the DC-3 processor earlier. The DC-3 is typical of all CPU's. All have different instruction formats. Most all have the same complex addressing types.

Instructions have two parts, an operation code and an address. Addresses have two parts, an address code and, for lack of a better way of saying it a sub-address. The address code tells the CPU the addressing mode. The CPU examines the address code and resolves the address to simple as the third step in the FIRE – Fetch, Increment IP, Resolve address and Execute the instruction.

Resolve - reduce the complex to the simple. Some addresses begin simple and need no resolution.

Examples of simple addresses:

L,7   X   ← X is the address, simple

INC,2   ← no address at all, data 1 implied

\C3   A:,B: ← A and B are simple addresses

Examples of complex addresses:

L,7   X,5   ← X + (5) is the address, complex

*register 5 is used as an index register above and below.

L,7   (5)   ← (5) is the address, complex

*in WIN complex address are written:

\C3   A:(I),B:(J) ← A + (I) and B + (J) are the addresses

This is usually how indexing is done in compile language. A + (I) is written A(I) and reads, the address is the address of A plus the contents of variable I. Resolution is adding the contents of I to the address of variable A. A is simple. A + (I) is complex. The CPU must have a simple address before it can access the data. Thus the third step of the basic execution cycle has 2 parts: part 1 resolve the address and part 2 execute the operation.

There's ways of making remembering things easier. I like FIRE as the way to remember the basic computer cycle. FIRE - Fetch, Increment, Resolve, and Execute. Fetch the next instruction. Increment the instruction address. Resolve the data address. Execute the operation.

You didn't forget things in parentheses, ( ) means, reads "contents of" and not the thing itself. Mail is (mail box).

Let's make sure we understand that.

\C A:(I),B:(J) ← A + (I) and B + (J) are the addresses

WIN adds the contents of variable I to the location of A and the contents of variable J to the location of B to resolve the addresses of the data to be copied.

Let's suppose we write:

\DV A:God bless America\E
\DV B:Please   \E
\DV I: 4\E
\DV J: 7\E
\C A:(I),B:(J)
\STOP

We click on RUN, the screen will blink and like magic we'll have:

\DV A:God bless America\E
\DV B:Please bless America   \E
\DV I: 4\E
\DV J: 7\E
\C A:(I),B:(J)
\STOP

WIN resolved the addresses by first locating A and I and adding the contents of I to the location of A. I has the number 4 thus the resolved address is the location of A + 4. The location of a variable is the address of its first byte. Start counting using zero for the first byte of A. A by itself is A + zero. A +4 is the 5th byte of A which is b. WIN does the same thing with B and J to "resolve" the destination address.

You may have noticed the C, copy instruction may have a blank count field. Ordinarily we copy a definite number of bytes that are specified by, \Cn where n is a whole number. If there is no specified number then the copy begins with the first two addresses, source and destination and continues until a \E is encountered in either source or destination. That's a special copy, copy-all.

We're discussing words, resolve, address and instruction and their relations to each other. Address are resolved when instructions are executed. Addresses may be simple or they may be complex. In the basic computer cycle the execution portion involves the resolution of addresses prior to actually doing what the instruction says.

Now we can examine syntax, an often heard word but rarely understood by non-computer types. Just for fun I looked the meaning of syntax up in the Merriam Webster dictionary. It has several meanings of course. This one, "a connected or orderly system: harmonious arrangement of parts or elements." I like the word harmonious don't you? Harmony is the key to not getting yelled at by inanimate computer object. Actually it's the programmer who wrote the assembler doing the yelling and it's really not yelling at all but rather pointing out oversights. Harmony is also the key to getting one's mail delivered to the right address.

How addressing is done varies from one assembler to another and from one compiler to another. We're talking about programs that translate instructions into binary codes for the computer. We have both an assembler and a compiler in WIN. Assembly language instructions may be mixed with compiler language instructions. Of course we've talked about syntax before and referred to it as grammatical structure. Syntax most closely means grammatical structure in computing.

There are two things, grammatical structure and the spelling of words. Syntax is a conglomerate of the two. We've examined the general grammatical structure of instructions and have used it in several example programs already. In WIN compile language it's:

\operator details addresses.

The back slash says instruction. The operator say what particular instruction. The details are things like counts in moves and cursor positioning in key-in and key-out instructions. Every instruction has its own set of details. We're discussing the last part of instructions, one or more addresses that are resolved by WIN before executing the particular instruction.

Syntax is how we write instructions with addresses being the most complicated part. There are several addressing possibilities.

Direct – a variable or program location by name. Examples: X where there is a \DV X:...\E or a \L label:

Direct with offset – a variable name with + or – a whole number. Example: X+4 resolves to the address of X with 4 added to it. X+4 resolves to the address of the 5th byte/character of variable X. X is the 1st byte. X+1 the 2nd byte ect.

Direct with index – a variable name and another variable name in parentheses. Example: X(Y) resolves to the address of the first byte of X plus the contents of variable Y.

Indirect – Variable name contained within parentheses. Example: (X) resolves to the address that is the contents of variable X. Loading the address of a variable in another variable requires: \A LI,X variable-name. If I want to address an array one element at a time I can enter assembler with \A and load immediate, LI into my pointer variable/register the address of the first byte of the array variable.

Let's look at some actual code to get a feel for how we write instructions. The word is syntax that is often heard has as many definitions as there are assemblers and compilers. We are confined to WIN here but keep in mind there are many. Some even have syntax sugar. Once you've learned one you can easily learn another unless it happens to be C or one of its family members. Try reading a book on the C compiler and you'll quickly see what I mean.

Resolving addresses is the topic. Computing is often described as data manipulation. Nowhere is this truer than the things our non-computer types will most likely want to do. Make animated movies and create the next generation of music to mention a couple. Others may want to have a go at artificial intelligence. That's provided one hasn't given up on finding some intelligence somewhere on this earth. In that case it's creating intelligence, forget the artificial part.

It's all about data manipulation to realize a goal. An easy way to see what I mean is knowing how Pac Man is made to move around the screen and how he eats things. The picture on the screen results from an array of data. Pac Man is a sub set of that array with a present location that will change with his next move. It's all about the location of bytes of data within an array of bytes of data. Of course it's a little more complicated than that but not much.

The actual picture on the display is laid out in lines from top to bottom. The image of any character will occupy more than one line and be some distance from the upper left hand corner of the screen. Thus a penny's worth of geometry is necessary just to visualize. I'll do my best to explain what is needed to address a character on the screen with a crude picture made with ABC's and periods.

```
0.................................................................
1.................................................................
2.................................................................
3.................xxx.............................................
4.................xxx.............................................
5.................xxx.............................................
6.................................................................
7.................................................................
8.................................................................
9.................................................................
```

Above we have a 10 line display with a character like Pac Man identified with x's. I've numbered the lines for clarity. There are no line numbers in the actual display. The problem is to address the x's, our cartoon character's image and move them to a new location, one line up to make it easy on ourselves. The new screen after we're finished:

```
0.................................................................
1.................................................................
2.................xxx.............................................
3.................xxx.............................................
4.................xxx.............................................
5.................................................................
6.................................................................
7.................................................................
8.................................................................
9.................................................................
```

Line 3 X's have been moved to line 2. Line 4 X's to line 3. And, line 5's X's to line 4. Periods, the background replaced the X's in line 5. To the one looking at the screen the character would appear to be moving up the screen.

It's all about addressing. If you wanted to mail one of the X's a letter how would you address it? All we have to do the addressing, locate the character are numbers. There's two numbers associated with every dot making the character, its line number from the top and the number of dots from the left hand side of the screen. It's two numbers, line number and dot number.

The whole screen is in the computer's main memory. It begins at an address and is a string of bytes down the memory. The first byte is the upper left hand corner of the picture with the rest one after the other to the lower right hand byte.

.

.

.

X

X

X

.

.

Etc.

We won't actually draw out the entire memory in this book because of its size. What we can do is see how data making up display pictures are arranged:

Line 0

.

.

Line 1

.

.

Last line

.

Last byte.

The address of the first byte of the first line of the picture is the base address of the screen's memory. The address of the first byte of the second line is the base address of the screen's memory plus the length of a line, all lines being the same length in bytes. Thus the address of the first byte of any line is the base address of the screen's first byte of memory plus the line number times the length of a line.

The address of the first byte of line 7 is:

The base address of the first byte of the screen's memory plus 7 times the length of a line. If the length of a line is 80 bytes for example the address is, the address of the first byte of the screen's memory + 7 X 80 which resolves to the first byte of the screen's memory + 560.

In any given computer system with a screen and its memory shared with the CPU's memory the address will be a hard number. The location within memory of shared memory devices is determined at the time the computer system was manufactured. The WIN operating system allows users to access that address via a fixed memory address that contains it.

\DV displayad: \E
\A L,displayad address

The address equals the hard number containing the address of the display. The above will copy the address of the first byte of the display to variable, displayad. Any name may be given the display address, the shorter the less likely it will be misspelled later. We'll use displayad and take our chances we might misspell it.

Generally speaking all the video game characters are displayed in rectangles. That includes those with moving objects like swords. Both the character and the object move at the same time. That means there must be a picture with every possible position of both character and object. All motion is done by writing over the character's previous location with the background. That removes the character altogether. Then the character is written over the background at the new position. These operations are done on rectangular shaped sections of the total picture.

We need 4 numbers as well as the dimensions of the picture to identify the data associated with a particular rectangular section of the picture. We need the starting line number and the distance from the left margin. We need the width in dots and height in lines of the rectangle containing the image.

The address of the first dot in the upper left hand corner of the character's rectangle can only be addressed using complex addressing.

Its address is: Line number times the length of lines plus the distance from the left margin. Example, suppose the upper left hand corner is on line 4, 12 dots from the left and lines are 80 bytes wide. Line number, 4 times the length of lines which is 80 plus the distance from the left margin, 12. This resolves to: 4 X 80 + 12 = 332

The problem is to copy a rectangular shaped image into the picture memory. The image is a string of bytes located somewhere in memory in a defined variable. Let's use the name image. We have:

\DV image:...a string of bytes making the image we want to put somewhere in our picture...\E

...we also have the address of the first byte of the display in a variable, displayad:

\DV displayad: \E

...and we have the length of a display line:

\DV displayll: \E

...and we know the line number of where we want the new image to go:

\DV Imageline: \E

...and we know the distance from the left margin:

\DV Dleftmargin: \E

...and we know the length of the character's lines:

\DV ChlineL: \E

...and we know the number of lines in the character:

\DV Nchlines: \E

...we'll need some temporary variables so we don't destroy the display's specifications. They're pointers:

\DV Spoint: \E ← Source pointer
\DV Dpoint: \E ← Destination pointer
\DV Lline: \E ← Length of character line

236

\DV NClines: \E ← Number of lines to copy

Our source is the image in memory. We need to copy its address to a temporary location in order to preserve it.

\C image:, Spoint:

Now we can calculate the address of the destination, where the first byte in display memory is located.

\M displayll: .X. Imageline: + Dleftmargin: = Dpoint:

…and the number of lines to copy:

\C Nchlines:, NClines:

\L next line:

Are we finished copying the image?

\M NClines: - 1 = NClines:

\IF NClines: .LT. 0 \G finished:

Is the number of lines left to copy less than zero? When the number of lines left to copy goes negative we are finished. If it is not negative then:

\C, Lline: (Spoint:), (Dpoint:)

The above copies one of the character's lines to the display. Now we need to update our pointers.

\M Spoint: + Lline: = Spoint:

\M Dpoint + diaplayhll: = Dpoint:

The length of the image's lines are added to the source pointer and the length of the display's lines to the destination pointer. Not only is pointing not rude but it's necessary.

…and go back to the top.

\G next line:

\L finished:

We get here after the entire image has been copied.

I may have mentioned earlier the most difficult part of programming is naming variables. I believe the above will serve well to verify that. Ordinarily I'd use letters of the alphabet but since I'm trying to explain how to do something I have at least attempted to pick names that make a little sense. Only you know how well I did. The toughest part of the problem is naming variables and then remembering those names next year when you need to make changes.

At first glance the above may look complicated. The problem is simple, copy a string of data into a rectangular shaped chunk of a matrix of numbers. It's a matter of addressing two things, a source picture to replace a destination area within the matrix. That means a source pointer and a destination pointer. Of course one needs to realize pictures on display screens are made of numbers.

Motion is achieved by copying numbers from one area to another using rectangular shapes. This is primitive to say the least. Images of people, places and things are rarely if ever rectangular shaped. Even Sponge Bob has a non-rectangular shape once one gets beyond his pants. Representing non-rectangular figures requires a lot more numbers to identify the outline and locate the data within the display's memory. It's the key to making inanimate objects come to life.

At present motion is achieved by writing over the old image and rewriting it in the next location all done using rectangles. To make a figure move under computed control, make faces for example by doing a calculation and only changing the face requires a lot of data addresses. The figure must be represented in irregular shapes and formulas of motion written and implemented. The power of the light switch is only limited by your imagination. You've gotten this far so you must have something in mind you'd like to do.

Desire is the prime mover on all occasions.

Chapter 20, tick-a, tick-a, tick-a...

...timing isn't everything it's the only thing. Well, not exactly. We'll need a little more but timing is necessary in many places. The all-time greatest breakthrough in human thinking came with the realization all happens with respect to time. Time is the universal independent variable of all that varies. The computer allows humans to amplify their thoughts and capture them in time to be repeated over and over again.

Nowhere is timing more necessary to achieving harmonious results than in music. Truly timing is the only thing when it comes to sounds of all kinds. Of course sound is the product of vibrations. Vibrations happen as a function of time. A vibrating guitar string vibrates at some rate. A rate is the number of times per unit of time.

Vibrating is going back and forth in cycles. Oh yes, like the computer that FIRE's like machine guns in cycles, fetch, increment IP, resolve address and do what the instruction says and do it again and again and again in harmonious cycles. If I didn't know better I'd say the computer is a musical instrument just waiting for a musician to play a tune. Those who are computer illiterate including musicians are shut out from playing anything except what the computer corporations allow to be played on the computer.

Where's the computer's strings, its vibrating reeds, its boomers and clangors you ask. They're all there and multitudes more sound makers that have yet to be heard. Every sound possible one wishes to make can be made using a computer with proper sound making device(s). Computers consists of a CPU and memory only. We end up using the word computer to mean computer system. Computers alone are like brains is jars, worthless.

To play a tune using the computer the computer system must have a peripheral that can be used to make sounds. A digital to analog converter driving a speaker does the job well. How well depends on the goodness of the equipment. Two new words, digital and analog. Digital, exact numbers like the odometer in one's auto. Analog, an approximate number like the volume control on the radio in one's auto. All sounds are analog. They can be and are being created using digital. Digital must be converted to analog. All sound making devices operate in analog.

All sounds are the product of vibrations. When you hear a sound you know something is vibrating. Guitar strings go up and down but not exactly up and down meandering around a bit giving them more than a single sound. Reeds in reed instruments vibrate to make the sound. Sounds coming from computers are made by vibrating something.

If we want to make music worth hearing we'll need a little quality in our vibrating devices. And we must be able to control them from within the computer. A digital to analog converter driving a speaker will do the job well provided it's of sufficient quality.

At present the possibility of inventing a new electrically operable vibrating device to make music and voices as well is in the domain of computer scientists. The world of music making and the world in general are stuck in a computer science rut the getting out of being left to a handful of greedy corporations that control the computer world. That's a problem easily fixable by a little education.

I don't know this for sure but I strongly suspect all possible sounds can be generated using three speakers arranged in a triangle facing the center of the triangle. Any color can be made using red, yellow and blue. Intuitively any sound can be made using three broad band speakers arranged in a triangle. I'd try that first if I was musically inclined. I am!

I used the computer to play a tune way back in 1963 while employed by North American Aviation, Project Apollo. My job title was senior programmer. I was one of a number of programmers. We had a small at the time computer made by Control Data Corporation. It had a speaker attached to the least significant bit of its accumulator register. It had no clock so timing had to be done using time delay loops, i.e. load register with number:

```
     LDA          10000
LOC  DECA
```

```
JNZ          LOC
```
Load 10,000 into the A register. At location, LOC subtract one from the contents of the A register. JNZ, jump not zero to LOC. This adds a delay of 20,000 instruction times. By trial and error we developed delay loops that allowed us to toggle the speaker bit and cause it to make screechy sounds.

I didn't act alone. With help we managed to play, "Whatever Lola Wants Lola Gets." After as little as five minutes we were threatened with being lynched by our fellow workers if we didn't stop that horrible noise.

With a single bit driving the speaker it could only make a single level sound based upon switching from 0 to 1 and back again. The speaker being a low quality one didn't help. The best comparison to what we had is a hillbilly band with a handsaw player making twangy sounds by bending the saw's blade, plunking it and varying the bending. Use your imagination it's several times more pleasant than having to listen to it.

Our goal is to make a programmable musical instrument people will enjoy hearing. To do that we need to learn a little about how speakers make sounds. Of course all sounds are the product of vibrations. Speakers are no exception to that rule. They have diaphragms that move back and forth along an axis. Their motion is relative to the amount of electric current passing through a coil of wire creating an unbalanced magnetic field. At zero current the field will be zero and the motion in turn either stays at zero if at rest or returns to zero if not zero at the time current is removed.

At maximum current the diaphragm will be extend to its maximum. All currents in between zero and max will extend it a relative amount. To cause the speaker to make a sound using a digital to analog converter set the converter to one value and then after a slight time delay set it to different one. That causes the diaphragm to move some distance. With an 8 bit digital to analog converter I can position the speaker 256 different places and I can change from one position to another as fast as the computer can run AND the speaker can react. First discovery, the computer runs so fast the speaker cannot possibly keep up. Enter time into the music making equation.

If we're going to make music with a degree of sophistication the computer system must have a clock. Delay loops will work but they are faulty to a fault. The computer has a clock, an oscillator used to orchestrate its operation. A 16 bit counter driven by the CPU's clock at an IO address is sufficient to time music generators. Different sounds are made by changing the digital to analog converter driving a speaker relative to time. It takes as few as 6 settings per vibration to do the job.

We're talking about a new world, places no one has ever gone before. I cannot tell you what to do because I don't know what settings at what timings make what sounds. I can tell you how to experiment and find out what causes whatever sound, and how to capture that and keep it for later use.

Now we need to talk about dimensions. Sounds are three dimensional. The spoken word radiates out from the speaker in all directions. Thus three sets of numbers for positioning three speakers are required to make every possible sound. Every possible two dimensional sound with the third dimension as a matter of chance can be made using a two dimensional tables of numbers. It's easier to understand than using all three dimensions.

Each entry in the table is:

Speaker position, time to hold that position

A variable containing this table named sound would look like:

\DV sound:N1,T1,N2,T2,, Ni, Ti\E

Where N is a number 0 through 255 and T is the time to hold the setting in millionths of seconds. Vibrations at the rate of 300 per second have a wave length of 3330 microseconds. It takes at least 6 different speaker settings for one complete vibration. Thus the time delay from one setting to the next is 3330/6 or 666 micro seconds. When we get to the higher frequencies the delay time shrinks to nearly zero. The highest frequency possible is the speed of the computer. Maybe we should do our timing in nanoseconds?

Let's do a sample program in WIN and see if we can get a handle on making beautiful sounds using a computer with an 8 bit digital to analog converter driving a speaker.
*Program to create a sound.
\DV note:128,666,255,666,255,666,128,666,
000,666,000,666,128,666\E
Sound waves go both positive and negative. A guitar string goes up and down. An 8 bit digital to analog converter goes from zero to 255. Thus to create sound waves that go both up and down we must use a bias of 128, half way between 0 and 255 as the center line. Waves go up and down through 128. Numbers lower than 128 are equal to negative numbers.
*Defining variables.
\DV spointer: \E
*spointer points to next speaker setting
\DV dpointer: \E
*dpointer points to next time delay
\DV count: \E
*the number of settings, time-delays in the table
\DV speaker: \E
\DV timer: \E
\L Start: ← next complete wave begins here
        \CC spointer
*CC – copy clear, set speaker setting pointer to first, 0th setting.
        \A LI, dpointer
*Set delay pointer to first delay, 4th location in note.
        LI, count   8
*set a counter to the number of settings, time-delays.
\L next setting: next speaker setting and delay starts here
        \C3 note:(spointer), speaker
*Copy next speaker setting to variable speaker
        \IOO DTA, speaker
*output data in variable speaker to a digital to analog
* converter the address of which is in variable, DTA.
*The actual address, DTA is determined by the
* equipment manufacturer and varies from
* one manufacturer to the other.
        \C3 note:(dpointer), timer

*delay time from note table to variable timer
        \TD timer
*delay the number of microseconds in variable timer
        \M spointer + 8 = spointer
        \M dpointer + 8 = dpointer
*update pointers to point to next entries in note
        \M count - 1 = count
*subtract one from the count, number of settings, delays
        \IF count .NE. 0 \G next setting:
*The above reads, If count is not zero go to next setting.
*When count goes to zero the "go to" is not executed.
        \G start

This program runs in a loop repeating the same note until the operator clicks on the STOP icon. Then the program appears on the screen. Change "note" and do it again. Try different time delays between speaker settings instead of the same one for all. Expand note to more settings. The only way to find out which sounds are made by what settings using whatever time delays is to experiment. Once one finds a beautiful sound save those settings in a file to be used later.

An 8 bit digital to analog converter allows for 256 different speaker diaphragm positions from nothing to maximum. For every bit added to the converter, say 8 bits to 9 bits the number of different settings doubles. A 16 bit digital to analog converter has 65,536 different speaker diaphragm positions from nothing to maximum. It's only a guess but I'd guess the sound of 1,000 Stradivarius violins is possible with a 16 bit digital to analog converter and three speakers of modest quality. Music majors need hobbies too you know.

It's often said, "There's no business like show business." Let us add, "There's no show business worth the producer's salt without music." It's more often said, "Computers never take coffee breaks, fail to show up for work or go on strike demanding higher wages." To that we can add, "Computers never fiddle out of tune." Waiting for computer scientists to "make" the computer fiddle is like waiting for the second coming of the Messiah. I'll wager I can teach musicians to fiddle using computers as their instruments with less difficulty than musicians can teach computer scientists to fiddle writing sketches in C++. Make that well-behaved sketches.

The computer opens the door for the creation of a new generation of musical instruments. We can rightly call that a revolution in musical instrumentation. Of course the human voice is itself a musical instrument that can be synthesized using the computer with proper sound making equipment.

Who's to say the speaker is the proper device to make music using the computer. Not me. I have faith that those skilled in sound along with a little computer literacy will invent new electrically operable vibrating devices. Sound is vibrations and nothing more. The number of different vibrations possible with a 16 bit digital to analog converter is 65,536 squared. That's any setting to any other setting. Of course the number of combinations of any two of the above is 65,536 raised to the 4th power. And when you get finished trying all of those out I'll let you try them in sets of 3. Until you become computer literate you'll be limited to doing what the billion dollar corporations that hold the computer hostage are capable of and willing to let you in on. You're not one of the unfortunates who bought a genuine IBM-machine and it don't do nothing are you? What a pity.

Chapter 21, the answer is…

…universal computer literacy. With the present attitude about the computer and in particular the reliance on a handful of corporations to decide what people will and will not be allowed to do using computers whole universes of possible new things are shut out. The answer is universal computer literacy. The place to begin is here and the time for you to begin is now.

Computer programs are documents. They are written by people. Does the word written ring any bells for you? Where do the little children learn how to write? It's a matter of writing that brings the writer to life. We can think of a program as actually being the program's author. Programming isn't just writing stories its living them. Every time a program is executed the programmer comes to life. To think is to live. Programs are programmer thoughts that are rethought over and over again every time the program is executed.

Execution is like a phonograph record with a flip side. On one side execution is a special case of causing the death of living person. On the other side execution is the special case of bringing a dead person back to life. Programs are their programmer's thoughts thus they are their programmers who are dead until executed.

Did I hear you say only God can bring the dead back to life? Now you know computers through program execution bring dead people back to life. That says computers are the equal of God. What can be done using computers has no limit is another way of saying the same thing.

FIRE – Fetch, Increment instruction pointer, Resolve address and Execute the instruction is all there is to it. Ordinary bullets kill. Computer bullets bring to life.

Now you know computers are made of nothing but switches no more complicated than ordinary light switch. How many light switches does it take in a set of light switches before you to say, "I just can't understand it all?" Computers are sets of two position switches with one of those switches being continuously switched on and off. That special switch is called an oscillator and referred to as the system's clock.

The oscillator switch is the only one with any degree of complication. Most are made with nothing more than a sliver of a rock. Well now they're not made out of just any old rock. Think of it as low quality glass, kind of opaque – can't read through it.

Now you know computers have but two simple parts, two separate sets of switches, central processing units and memories. That's two sets of switches connected to each other with wires. Make that cyber wires. Never mind.

In the beginning the electrically controllable parts of computer switches were made of coils of wire wrapped around iron rods. The wires connecting them together looked like spider webs or perhaps bird nests. Now those switches have been reduced to specks of rust on glass and the wires connecting them to each other is so tiny and short they can only be seen through microscopes.

MOS – metal oxides on silicone. CMOS – combined metal oxides on silicone. In reverse order. Silicone – the primary ingredient in glassware. Metal oxide – rust. You'll need a microscope to look at it but you won't need much in the way or technical training to know what you're looking at.

The professor, "good morning class. Today we begin a journey into the highest of high tech worlds the digital computer. When we're finished we'll know things so sophisticated ordinary people will have no idea what we're talking about. The three main topics we'll be studying hard are light switches, glass and rust. All three are well beyond human comprehension. That's why it takes 4 full years and 160 units to know enough to pass a test by making the computer say, hello world. Let's get started."

What incentive do the big corporations that control the world of computer have to properly educate the public? The answer is they have every incentive to keep the computer shrouded in ignorance. And they are encouraged to allow, even help parasites with names like virus and malware to suck the life's blood out of the computer. Every time they allow one more parasite in they add a nail to the computer's coffin.

Why do we let this happen? The answer is simple, we're computer illiterate. Make that past tense, we were computer illiterate, I hope but fear not yet? If we were computer literate we'd buy ourselves a real computer that can be programmed by any computer literate and write the SOB's out of our world. And it would last a lifetime running at the same speed from day one until they carry both us and it out on a stretcher.

Since you've read this far I know you know a lot more than you used to know about computers. You know they're nothing but a bunch of switches. And most of all you know they don't do anything. You know computers are tools and used as tools and not independent thinking machines or any of the other nonsense ignorant people say about computers. I'll wager you're already wondering about things like cyber attacks. Now you should see how incredibly stupid it is to use software that allows itself to be modified and then not doing as little as informing the owner it happened. Above all why isn't it possible to start from zero with the original unmodified system software? Why does the software allow itself to be permanently modified? You don't suppose the idea comes by way of a plan to force you to buy new software? "Oh, your old software broke. Here, have a new one. It only costs…"

Saying software broke is like saying a book broke. It's like saying words fall out of a books until so many are gone they're no longer readable. What do viruses, spy-ware and the like do to books called computer programs? They write over the original words and add unwanted words. That's all that can be done. Computer programs are documents like cook books. How would cook books be contaminated? But of course a little bitters and poison can be added to the stew's recipe.

Once upon a time the system's software was in read only memory and couldn't possibly be modified or have unknown programs attached to it. How about that? There really were "good old days" at least there were "good old days" in computing. Then came Apple and Microsoft and the computer fell into a black hole.

It may well take an act of congress to rescue the most important invention since the wheel from the clutches of a handful of greedy corporations. As long as those corporations give generously to political campaigns and the gullible public falls for the political propaganda the computer will remain a prisoner of greed.

You've probably heard the expression, "Fight fire with fire." The one who brings the real computer to market will become the next billion air. What is a real computer? But of course it must be programmable. Apple this' and PC that's are not programmable by you thus they are misidentified. Maybe the first step is a law suit to stop the false advertising. The things being sold as computers are in reality appliances with computer controllers. The dishwashing machine in your kitchen has a computer controller in it. You don't call it a computer. Why call any appliance that does not satisfy the very first requirement of a computer, programmability a computer? You can't program the dishwasher only operate it. You can't program the PC only operate it. Either your dishwasher is a computer or your PC isn't a computer.

There's nothing wrong with appliances. There's something terribly wrong with calling them computers when they're not programmable. The computer market is wide open. The prize for filling it is billions and billions of dollars. Make that the real computer market that is yet to be tapped. Real computers can be programmed.

This journey into tomorrow begins the same place all such journeys begin, in the classroom. All classroom journeys begin with a thing called literacy taught by the literate. The same set of literates now teaching literacy are the ones to bring computer literacy to a computer ignorant world, a world so computer ignorant the average person thinks Apple sells computers. If it isn't programmable by you it isn't a computer stupid. Want to make movies? Want to make music? Want the awesome power of the computer at your fingertips to make something you and I can't even think of at the moment? Then do your share to bring computer literacy to a computer illiterate world.

Chapter 22, is artificial intelligence…

…even possible? Now you know. Computers are nothing more than collections of switches flipped on and off to the drum beat of a special switch called system's clock. You also know that all computer programs, no exceptions are conversations between two people, a programmer and a user/operator. Yes indeed, the programmer and operator can be the same person in which case the programmer has a conversation with him/herself. I understand. You've just learned this and you're still a little shaky about it all.

Before we get started talking about artificial intelligence let's make a note of something very important. Computers are mental monkey wrenches. Computer programs are made of thoughts. Monkey wrenches amplify one's ability to do physical work. Mental monkey wrenches amplify one's ability to do mental work, think. Add the monkey wrench to the computer and operate it with thoughts.

Computing is not only what you think but rather how fast you think as well? Embody your thoughts in a computer program and think them millions of time faster than you can without the computer. That includes making decisions, operating machinery and doing arithmetic. How fast can you add 2 + 2 in your head or using pencil and paper? You can do it by programming in less than one millionth of a second. You can add very long numbers just as fast. And, you can make logical decisions just as rapidly. It's always you and never the machine making the decision.

This alone tells us there is no such thing as artificial intelligence. Artificial intelligence falls in the category of things like cyber. Its only purpose in life is to confuse the unwary. The intelligence of the computer is the intelligence of a single switch times the number of switches. Artificial intelligence is really nothing more than switch intelligence. Are switches intelligent? Are you intelligent enough to know when someone is "putting you on" "pulling your leg?"

We know the only intelligence possible in a computer is that of the programmer(s) who wrote the program that happens to be running at the time. Thus the only computer based intelligence possible is that of computer programmers. They are people. Only artificial people are capable of possessing artificial intelligence. Artificial people are the stuff of science fiction.

Artificial people are biological machines with computer brains that look and act like people. They are indistinguishable from real people. The computer literate should realize there's one or more people called programmer(s) inside the artificial person's brain doing all the thinking regardless of how intelligent or otherwise it may appear to be.

Yes indeed it is entirely possible to fool the ignorant. R2D2 the cute little trash can with light bulb eyeballs robot of "Star Wars" fame is a person or persons housed in a mechanical body with every word and deed preprogrammed. When R2D2 speaks it is a programmer doing the talking not an artificial creature. What R2D2 says is preprogrammed and thus limited to what the programmer(s) thought about saying at program writing time.

Let's pare the problem down a little. Artificial intelligence is impossible regardless. It's always the intelligence of a person. That does not rule out intelligent machines. Rather the computer rules them in. The computer illiterate attributes the intelligence to the computer. The computer literate knows the intelligence is that of the people who wrote the programs and programs are the real source of computer based intelligence.

There are now computer driven automobiles. Self-driving automobiles have computers instead of people doing all the things people do when they do the driving. That's what the talking heads on television say. Is it so? Do computers drive automobiles? If I've accomplished even a small piece of what I set out to do you immediately rejected "computer driven." You know computers do nothing. Driving is something therefore computers are not capable of driving.

I don't expect you to either know or understand. I do expect you to realize the incredibly subtle ignorance inherent in the statement, "computer driven automobiles." Who or what is doing the driving a machine or a man using a machine?

Let's say it this way, "To drive is human." People who drive other people's automobiles are called chauffeurs. Inside computers that drive automobiles are chauffeurs with the title, computer programmer. To write a program that drives an auto like a chauffeur is to write a chauffeur simulator program.

Simulators simulate. Simulators do the same things the real McCoy does. Mocking birds simulate the sounds made by other birds. Mocking birds make real sounds. Programmers and not computers drive automobiles. Programs that drive automobiles simulate chauffer's. Chauffer's are people. Only people drive automobiles. People can do the driving themselves or they can use chauffer's. The chauffeurs driving self-driven automobiles are computer programmers using computers to operate the automobile's controls. Such programs simulate chauffeurs doing all the things chauffeurs do.

Earlier we discussed a simulator program that simulates computer hardware. That's what programming platforms do. They are programs running on one computer that imitate another computer. Simulators simulating computers are computer mocking birds. WIN is a pseudo computer, a computer mocking bird. A pseudo computer is a theoretical computer. Win simulates a theoretical computer that is a real mental computer.

Pseudo means functionally identical to and most importantly pseudo means indistinguishable from the real thing. A program written to run on a WIN pseudo computer looks like, is indistinguishable from one written to run on an ordinary real computer. A robot that looks like and acts like a human being is a pseudo human being. Chauffeurs are humans. Therefore a chauffeur simulator simulates a human and can be no more intelligent than a human.

Artificial intelligence is the embodying of the brain of a human in a machine. It's only as artificial as the brain of the person embodied is artificial. The computer can be no more intelligent than the programmer whose program it's executing at any moment in time. How intelligent is a program that allows itself to be altered by a program from an unknown source? You know the source is Moscow so it's not unknown? I see, knowing where it comes from makes it OK.

Artificial intelligence can at best be just another way to fool people. It's never the machine. It's always the machine operator. Computers are machines operated from within. Thus the operator is out of sight. This gives the appearance the machine is autonomous doing things all by itself. Programmers are like puppet operators giving puppets the appearance of living critters.

Appearances are deceiving. People with agendas can be deceiving and often are deceiving. No other tool of deception comes close to the computer. Deception thrives on ignorance. How about the Microsoft and Apple? Are they for real or are you being deceived? Has your identity been stolen again lately? Intelligent, real intelligent?

If I've achieved my goal here you didn't need to be told saying, "computer controlled" is an expression of ignorance. Now you know. **Computers do absolutely nothing** therefore they cannot control anything**.** That which does nothing at all is not capable of controlling anything. That's not a matter of belief or faith of some kind. It's a matter of knowledge. When you hear someone say computer controlled anything you know that person is computer ignorant. It's a programmer(s) doing the controlling using a computer not a computer doing it.

There is no such thing as an autonomous machine of any kind unless you think animals including human beings are machines. Animals are biological machines with electronic brains. Animals are preprogrammed computer systems that are capable of learning. Animals have biological peripherals. Preprograming is called instinct. Learning is adding to instinct.

Human beings are capable of learning. Human beings can get inside machines called computers and learn. Thus the appearance of a learning computer is entirely possible. It's not the computer doing the learning it's the human being inside it. Since human beings can learn then it is entirely possible for one to create a learning computer by putting him/herself inside the computer in the form of a program that learns. This is routinely being done already and has been done since the first ever computer. All programs that input data and remember that data are learning programs. That includes all useful programs.

Animals are computer systems. They input data, what they see, hear, smell, taste and feel. They remember some of those inputs by way of their senses to their computer brains. Writing programs that make the computer imitate animal brains is entirely possible. Making programs that can learn beyond their programmer's ability is not only possible but is being routinely done. All data bases are learners. They learn the data input to them. No person is capable of remembering all the names and addresses in large data bases.

Making programs capable of independent thought is not possible. All thoughts of any kind coming from the computer or elsewhere are the thoughts of the thinker who created the thinking device by the charter of the device. This does not rule out the appearance a device of some kind is independently thinking. Again, appearances can be deciving.

Computer based action games appear to make decisions based upon inputs. In reality those decisions are being made by their programmers. Adding probability to the formula does not add intelligence.

I have several things I can do in most situations. What I do is relative to some outside stimulus that has a probability factor. Example, most of the time when he is tapped on the shoulder he turns around slowly. Every so often he turns around quickly swinging his hand to back-hand the one who tapped his shoulder. Probability is not an intelligence amplifier.

People are preprogrammed just like cats and dogs are preprogrammed with built in characteristics. There is zero doubt in my mind that animal brains, humans included look an awfully lot like computers. There's a central processing unit and there's memory. And, there's two kinds of memory, ROM that is written once naturally and RAM that is written when learning. Actions like heart beat and breathing are programmed in ROM. Reflex actions are the product of preprogrammed memory. Another name for reflexive actions is instinctive actions.

We store what we learn in RAM. Since we forget our brain-RAM must be like if not identical to DRAM. Neurons are tiny little capacitors that are charged or not charged when learning. How much they are charged determines how well the information is remembered. That's why repetition improves learning. Over time neurons lose their charge causing the knowledge to be forgotten.

In my studies of ancient peoples I found writings that said the insane were victims of electrical malfunction suggesting memories are made of neurons that are capacitors. If our brains store data using capacitors then electrical imbalance would cause one to forget or alter bits within the memory creating confusions of thought, insanity.

Scholars reading the same ancient writings I read saying the problem was the work of electrical forces saw gods where I saw electricity. I don't just believe it I know the ancient Egyptians had no gods or even a picture-word that meant god. Try telling that to certified experts on ancient Egyptian culture. They have gods coming their ears. Gods are a smoke screen concealing the real facts. The belief in man's ability to create an independent thinking machine is a similar smoke screen.

I hate to leave you dangling. If those strange looking ancient Egyptian critters aren't gods then what are they? Think about it. They must belong a common class of everyday things. Begin by realizing they're not gods. What other kind of critters could they be if not gods? Are they man-made, artificial? Are the things they do also done by other beings of record? Surely they're not imaginary beings. What are they?

Any artificial human or animal must have both instinct and the ability to learn. Perhaps the most important thing is the ability to selectively forget. It is well within the reach of man to make a machine that remembers everything. That machine will have the intelligence of its maker and nothing more.

I have a pet theory, "lies are more difficult to learn than truths." The human mind rejects lies automatically. This is why some scientific theories are so difficult to remember. Those theories are false. I believe every human is born with all the knowledge possible in the subconscious mind. Learning is bringing knowledge from the subconscious mind to the conscious mind. If it isn't in the subconscious already it can't possibly be learned. You already knew all about computers you didn't realize it until now.

Don't confuse lies with aspirations. People believe what they want to believe even if it isn't so. Politicians peddle dreams using the propaganda tool. They appeal to what they think people want and not what is either possible or wise. Propaganda is telling the truth in such a way it deceives. The spoken word that deceives is a lie. Propaganda transmutes truths into lies. Religion, beliefs in gods transmutes lies into truths. Do the right thing I always say.

Creating artificial animals that look and act like real ones is well within reach. The not often ask question is who is qualified to pursue it. With the computer shrouded in ignorance, in a world that reeks with computer illiteracy the job of inventing and implementing artificial animals falls into the domain of computer science. If the computer science conjured C language is any indication of what it will look like you don't want to C the animal they create. Move over centipede the competition for the animal with the most legs yet without a leg to stand on is heating up.

After almost 6 decades of "doing" computer I know the fewer the number of programmers there are inside those computers doing the driving the less likely it is the auto will be driven into the ditch. That should encourage you. Yes you can! You can write programs that allow you to control any machine of any kind using a computer. Who's doing the driving? The programmer. That can be you. No one is ruled out. You can memorize a short vocabulary, learn a simple grammatical structure and write instructions in any computer language. You too can become computer literate and program computers. And, you don't need to know the first thing about electricity unless you're curious about how electronic switches actually turn on and off. Knock yourself out learning transistor switches only to find out they're being replaced. A switch is a switch is a switch.

Computer literacy is all about programming. Computer programming is all about computer literacy. Literacy is all about reading and writing, throw in a little arithmetic just for the flavoring. I heard this somewhere, "The three R's of education are reading, writing and arithmetic." Any computer fresh from the computer factory begins knowing nothing at all. Programming, educating the computer is duplicating one's own knowledge in it.

Artificial people brains are the product of simulating the human brain. In order to program a computer to imitate a people one must know about one's self. How much do you know about you?

Is it possible to turn a computer into an artificial person brain indistinguishable from the brain of a real person? But of course, a brain in a jar with no attachments and a computer with no peripherals are equals at the observation level. Both are electronic brains with no means of communication with the outside world. By the way, who or what is inside human brains to communicate with anyone or anything? I think therefore I am, I hope.

Making a robot that looks like a human is a much more difficult task than making the robot with a brain that imitates a human brain. I wouldn't know where to begin to make a machine that looked like a human and also had the mechanical capabilities of a person. All that's necessary for me to make a human brain is put myself inside the computer in the form of a program that does all the things I do. Making the human body is worlds more difficult. To duplicate the human body I must make eyes and ears to see and listen, arms, legs and muscles to operate them. The brain is the easy part. Come to think about it the brain has already been duplicated in inorganic form. Putting it into a living artificial human body is another problem altogether.

Making an inorganic mechanical man is a different problem altogether. A man imitating machine, a robot that can go to the refrigerator and get you a beer is a nothing to do compared to making a flesh and blood organic artificial man.

We have all the technology needed to make a robot. It's being done already many places. Robots are the drivers of self-driving cars. Eyes are nothing more than television cameras. That's old worn out technology. Everybody knows how to television. Ears are microphones and even older technology than television. No problem with sight and hearing. Taste, touch and smell are a little trickier to implement but far from impossible. The presently doable problem comes with the operation of the human brain.

The computer programmed like the human brain is programmed must do all the things the human brain does. We know that's continuously inputting from the 5 senses, remembering part of what is sensed and continually deciding what those inputs mean while operating the muscles to take appropriate actions.

People are programmed like fishes in schools. Schools are run by people called educators. Educators are electronic people-brain programmers. Who is best qualified to program the computer to simulate the human brain, computer scientists or teachers?

At this time with computer education being a separate department cloaked in mystery the possibility of anyone duplicating the human brain via a computer program is highly unlikely. Robots are material for science fiction writers. Turning science fiction into science fact isn't just a horse of a different color but a horse at a different race track altogether.

If we can question anything about artificial intelligence it's the name itself. We know the intelligence in all computer based controls of any kind is the intelligence of a human being with the job title, programmer. When an artificial people is created it will have the brain of a person. That person will by definition be a programmer.

The very first thing the computer literate can say is artificial intelligence is impossible to create using the computer. All computer based intelligence is actually human intelligence coming from a person or persons. Computers do nothing. They appear to do things. No matter what is programmed computers are actually people. Thus computers are already intelligent but no more intelligent than the people who programmed them.

If it was up to me to decide I'd turn the job of creating an artificial people brain over to the Language and Literature department. The last thing we want to create is an illiterate artificial person. Now take the troubles of e-val sciontists Frankenstein for an easy to understand example of what happens when brainless people are created. We got more than enough brainless people running the government already. Keep looking, there just has to be a measurable amount of military intelligence out there somewhere.

Chapter 23, let's take a crack…

…at outlining the WIN pseudo computer. When we're done all that's left to do is wiggle your fingers on the keyboard and live forever. Think in WIN pseudo computer language and your thoughts become immortal allowing you to keep on thinking after your body is dead.

Pseudo computers are programs that simulate computers. They operate just like real computers. There's a big plus. Multi-programming is included, a part of the machine itself thus no operating system as such is used. Say goodbye to Microsoft and Apple.

The minimum computer system where WIN can be used has a display screen, a keyboard. An I-phone with Apple software removed will work just fine. WIN has a built in operating system that is operated primarily by clicking on icons on the display thus a mouse is highly desirable. Fingers on a touch screen works equally well.

Before we write a single line of code we need to outline the flow of the program. This is the equal of outlining a paper before writing it.

Let's look at an overall map of the system.

WIN resides in the lowest part smallest address numbers of memory.

Memory

0000 WIN

    .

Next First user program written in WIN
      Compiled program's codes.

    .

Next Next user program written in WIN
      Compiled program's codes

    .

Next Last user program written in WIN
      Compiled program's codes
All other memory is unused.

All programs have initialization sections that can be empty. WIN goes through an initialization process involving but a very few steps. The first few instructions initialize the system. The next instructions execute the pseudo computer's instructions simulating the WIN pseudo CPU. After the WIN CPU simulator is the continuously running operator control program. All programs running are started by the operator and reside in memory after the operator control program. At power on time the operator control program is the only program running unless there's an auto start for an application program.

WIN includes the operator control program. The overall system runs in foreground-background mode meaning there are always at least two programs running. Running in the foreground is the operator control program. WIN pseudo computer CPU runs in the background. Foreground – is visible, seen by the operator. Background – out of sight, as though it wasn't there. Computers like human brains are not seen with only their housings visible. WIN is a computer.

Both WIN and the operator control programs are written in the assembly language of the host computer. All other programs are written in WIN language. Moving WIN from one make of computer to any other requires rewriting it in the language of the new computer. All programs written in WIN language run on all computers with WIN. Programs written in WIN language are portable from one computer with WIN to any other computer with WIN.

Resident in the computer at all times is the WIN CPU program and the operator control program. Computers with WIN can be powered on with a WIN program as the starting program. At power on time the bootstrap loader loads WIN from bulk storage device and transfers control to WIN. This is a near instantaneous process. Optionally a user program can be loaded and executed automatically after WIN gets control. Again this is a near instantaneous process. Power on and immediately the system is ready. Dedicated systems will come up running so to speak by way of a power on option in WIN. It's real easy to do. WIN has a base program it executes that is either a blank or a "load and run program instruction."

In either case the screen will have operator control icons that are used to Start, Stop, and Compose new programs and so on as well as the ability to select the outputs to the display of any running program. Most programs have outputs to the display. When two or more programs are running only the outputs of one at a time can be shown else there's conflicts. New programs can be written while others program(s) are running.

Strangely enough the operator control program does the bulk of the work. WIN CPU imitator program is rather small by comparison. The operator control program includes a word processor for composing, a loader for reading programs from bulk storage as well as all operator controls.

The poet noted "good feces make good neighbors." Keeping WIN CPU separated from, putting a fence between it and the operator control program makes good computing. WIN is the interesting part of the system.

At power on WIN:
>Blanks the screen.
>Loads a starter WIN program
>Sets the number of programs running to 1.
>Sets the program running que pointer to first program

Main CPU cycle begins here:
>Call the operator control program
>Operator control programs returns here

Execution of a major WIN cycle begins here:
>Set the present-program pointer to first program
>Set the program que counter to zero

Present program serviced here:
>Using que pointer execute 1 present-program instruction
>Update que pointer and que counter
>Question: Is there another program in the que?
>If there is then go to **Present program service here**:
>Otherwise go to **Main CPU cycle begins here:**

The above is the big picture of what's going on when WIN is running. The operator control program is called once every major cycle. Most all of the time the operator control program will be waiting for an operator input. In this case it tests for input ready, finds it isn't and returns. When an operator control is ready the operator control program does what the operator requested and then returns. This is how programs are composed, started and stopped as well as other operator functions while other programs are running. Every major cycle the operator control program gets a turn during which it does what the operator requests and then returns to the main cycle control program that called it.

Let's look at the major cycle in the big picture:

Top   Operator control program is called and returns.
       One instruction is executed, 1st program.
       One instruction is executed, 2nd program.
       One instruction is executed, 3rd program.
       .

       .

       One instruction is executed, last program.
       End of major cycle, go to Top and do it again.

A minor cycle is the execution of a single FIRE cycle. WIN simulates a theoretical computer. Programs are written freehand using \OP to indicate instructions and what they do. They are written in people readable ASII. When a program is run it's loaded into the next available memory locations. A compiler reads the program and translates instructions and their associated data and addresses into binary that is stored immediately after the program. Both source code and compile code of all running programs are resident in memory. Instructions codes are the addresses of pseudo execution routines within WIN. For example, /KO generates the address of the KO routine within the set of WIN's instruction execution routines.

Every different instruction type has a routine to execute it. The compiled instruction has the address of the particular code's routine as its first word. To get to the routine and execute the instruction a jump to that address is done. When the instruction has been executed a jump to **Present program serviced here:** is done.

Example: \C3 A,B compiles to:
First word - the address of the copy routine.

263

The second word is 3, the number of bytes to copy.
The third word has the address of A.
The fourth and last word has the address of B.

When the instruction is executed 3 bytes of A are duplicated in B. Then the copy instruction execution routine jumps to **Present program serviced here**. All instructions execute the same way always jumping to **Present program serviced here** when finished.

Actual execution is done using the compiled program. Compile means translate statements into numbers. The addresses of different execution routines are numbers. Counts and address of variables are numbers. The running programs que has the address of the present program's instruction pointer register pointing to its present instruction. It merely loads the instruction pointed to by the program's instruction pointer into a register that is the address of the routine to execute the instruction. \instruction generates the address of the routine to do what the instruction says do.

All the FIRE steps are done by WIN thus WIN is truly a computer. The instruction pointer is in the running programs Que. It is used to **fetch** the present instruction. If data addresses or a program location is required and they are not simple addresses then the reconcile address is done for each address and/or location. Some instructions have multiple addresses.

In a nutshell, FIRE:

Fetch the present instruction and jump to the address pointed to by the present instruction.

Increment instruction pointer, add as many as necessary to the instruction pointer so it points to the next instruction.

Reconcile all addresses.

Execute the instruction.

End of minor cycle - executing one instruction of the present program.

Major cycle – execute one session with operator control program and execute one instruction each for every program in the programs running Que.

Minor cycle – execute present instruction of present program. Same as FIRE cycle with more than 1 added to instruction pointer and more addresses and addressing modes.

WIN does this giving all running programs a turn one after the other. It's the operator's turn, 1st program's turn, 2nd program's turn,, last program's turn and do it all over again just as fast as you possibly can. Using a modern computer executing 5 million instructions per second a major WIN cycle will take less than a millisecond, (.001 seconds) average. All programs appear to be running at the same time. We know they're actually taking turns.

If my prose haven't failed me too awfully much you now see how incredibly simple it is to make a rock solid completely understandable pseudo computer with people readable programs written in ASCII and run in multi user mode. WIN uses no interrupts at all. I'm willing to wager tender body parts WIN, a pseudo computer will outrun anything in use today. Interrupts require much greater overhead time than actual WIN FIRE cycles.

Push the power on switch and WIN is running. Start a program and it comes on immediately. Windows, Apple's operating system and all other interrupt based systems spend most of their energy getting nothing done while flailing about servicing interrupts pushing and popping stacks. Every interrupt requires at least 32 memory accesses to save and retrieve registers that does nothing compute wise.

Interrupts require all registers and flags to be saved. 16 registers means a minimum of 16 memory accesses that are 16 instruction times. That has to be done twice, once in and once out. There's a call to the interrupt service routine. It saves all the registers and flags. Then it must retrieve its registers and flags saved the last time it was interrupted. Finally the called program gets a few instructions. Then it gets interrupted and all the time wasting register and flag saving and retrieving has to be done all over again to let the next program get a turn. One little oversight on the programmers part and over the cliff the goes the whole system. Has that ever happened to you? Now you know how "they" do it to you. Why "they" do it is a graduate course in computer science. Don't ask why interrupts are necessary else the reasons will cause you to lose your lunch.

There's an overwhelming reason to use WIN. WIN being a pseudo computer rules out the possibility of any program "hogging" the computer. The only program running in the host computer's language is WIN itself. Programs downloaded over the internet must be WIN programs with no possibility of taking over the system. WIN slams the door closed to viruses, spy ware, systems corruption and all the other nonsense that are featured in Windows.

Using a Motorola 68000 type microprocessor with gigantic direct memory addressing makes the job of allocating memory like a cool summer breeze. The system occupies the top of the memory, memory's lowest numbered addresses beginning at address zero in most cases. The first user program is loaded immediately after the system. All programs are in people readable source code that is compiled. The quick running compiled code goes immediately after the source code.

Any subsequent program loads after the previous program's compiled code. It's WIN program, 1st user program's source code. 1st user program's compile code, 2nd user program's source code, 2nd user programs compile code and on and on for every program. When a program is "closed" both its source code and its compile code are removed. The system moves all programs after it up so there is no unused gap from one running program to the next. In this case moved is the correct way of saying it. The old locations are written over meaning the information there before has actually been moved to somewhere else. Of course that's done by duplicating switch settings. You already knew that didn't you.

I've implemented WIN on three different computers. The first time I did it to solve the multiple registers running at the same time problem in retailing applications, 1972 on the DC-3 computer. The next time I implemented WIN on the 8085 microprocessor, 1981. The third and last time I put WIN on the

PC, 1990. I worked alone. It took me less than a week from nothing to running WIN applications. Complete WIN packages were done and completely debugged in less than 90 days by me acting alone using software development tools I made myself. I haven't used anyone else's assembler or other systems software since 1968 always writing my own. One reason to do that is to become familiar with a new computer.

I'm telling you this because I want to encourage you. You may well find a BAL or another "standard" assembler and become discouraged. I learned early on it took more time for me to figure out all their, if this' then that's and maybe's controls than it took to simply write my own. Struggle through it once, replace it with yours and after you're done throw the trash in the trash can where it belongs.

Now you know how I feel about it. The world is smothered in computer ignorance. My goal is your computer education. This might sound a little corny but the fate of the world may well depend on you. Tamper proof, cyber attack proof systems is the name of the game. There could be a big financial reward in it for you. All I can promise you for sure is sweat, tears and toil. Your success may be rewarded with nothing more than that wonderful feeling one gets when a job is well done. At present the gateway to tomorrow is closed. It will stay closed until you decide to blow it open. WIN, anyone?

The End